Asset Attack Vectors

Building Effective Vulnerability Management Strategies to Protect Organizations

Morey J. Haber
Brad Hibbert

Apress®

Asset Attack Vectors: Building Effective Vulnerability Management Strategies to Protect Organizations

Morey J. Haber
Heathrow, Florida, USA

Brad Hibbert
Carp, Ontario, Canada

ISBN-13 (pbk): 978-1-4842-3626-0
https://doi.org/10.1007/978-1-4842-3627-7

ISBN-13 (electronic): 978-1-4842-3627-7

Library of Congress Control Number: 2018946558

Managing Director, Apress Media LLC: Welmoed Spahr
Acquisitions Editor: Susan McDermott
Development Editor: Laura Berendson
Coordinating Editor: Rita Fernando

Cover designed by eStudioCalamar

Cover image designed by Freepik (www.freepik.com)

Distributed to the book trade worldwide by Springer Science+Business Media New York, 233 Spring Street, 6th Floor, New York, NY 10013. Phone 1-800-SPRINGER, fax (201) 348-4505, e-mail orders-ny@springer-sbm.com, or visit www.springeronline.com. Apress Media, LLC is a California LLC and the sole member (owner) is Springer Science + Business Media Finance Inc (SSBM Finance Inc). SSBM Finance Inc is a **Delaware** corporation.

For information on translations, please e-mail rights@apress.com, or visit http://www.apress.com/rights-permissions.

Apress titles may be purchased in bulk for academic, corporate, or promotional use. eBook versions and licenses are also available for most titles. For more information, reference our Print and eBook Bulk Sales web page at http://www.apress.com/bulk-sales.

Any source code or other supplementary material referenced by the author in this book is available to readers on GitHub via the book's product page, located at www.apress.com/9781484236260. For more detailed information, please visit http://www.apress.com/source-code.

Printed on acid-free paper

To our wonderful wives who support us through thick and thin with endless patience and love.

Table of Contents

About the Authors

With more than 20 years of IT industry experience and co-author of *Privileged Attack Vectors* (Apress, 2018), **Morey J. Haber** joined BeyondTrust in 2012 as a part of the eEye Digital Security acquisition. As the Chief Technology Officer, he currently oversees BeyondTrust technology for both vulnerability and privileged access management solutions. In 2004, Morey joined eEye as the Director of Security Engineering and was responsible for strategic business discussions and vulnerability management architectures in Fortune 500 clients. Prior to eEye, he was a Development Manager for Computer Associates, Inc. (CA), responsible for new product beta cycles and named customer accounts. Morey began his career as a Reliability and Maintainability Engineer for a government contractor building flight and training simulators. He earned a Bachelor of Science in Electrical Engineering from the State University of New York at Stony Brook.

As Chief Operations Officer (COO) and Chief Strategy Officer (CSO) and co-author of *Privileged Attack Vectors* (Apress, 2018), **Brad Hibbert** provides the leadership for the organization's solutions strategy, product management, development, services, and support. He brings over 25 years of executive experience in the software industry aligning business and technical teams for success. He joined BeyondTrust via the company's acquisition of eEye Digital Security, where Brad led strategy and products. Under Brad's leadership, eEye launched several market firsts, including vulnerability management solutions for cloud, mobile, and virtualization technologies. Prior to eEye, Brad served as Vice President of Strategy and Products at NetPro before its acquisition in 2008 by Quest Software. Over the years Brad has attained many industry certifications to support his management, consulting, and development activities. Brad has his Bachelor of Commerce, Specialization in Management Information Systems; and MBA from the University of Ottawa.

About the Technical Reviewer

 **Derek A. Smith** is an expert at cyber security, cyber forensics, health care IT, SCADA security, physical security, investigations, organizational leadership, and training. He is currently an IT program manager with the federal government; a cyber security Associate Professor at the University of Maryland, University College, and the Virginia University of Science and Technology; and runs a small cyber security training company. Derek has completed three cyber security books and contributed a chapter for a fourth. He currently speaks at cyber security events throughout America and performs webinars for several companies as one of their cyber experts. Formerly, Derek worked for a number of IT companies, Computer Sciences Corporation and Booz Allen Hamilton among them. Derek spent 18 years as a special agent for various government agencies and the military. He has also taught business and IT courses at several universities for over 25 years. Derek has served in the U.S. Navy, Air Force, and Army for a total of 24 years. He completed an MBA, MS in IT Information Assurance, Master's in IT Project Management, MS in Digital Forensics, a BS in Education, and several associate degrees. He completed all but the dissertation for a doctorate in organizational leadership.

Acknowledgments

Special Thanks to:

Alex DaCosta, Director Product Management, BeyondTrust

Chris Burd, Senior Director of Marketing, BeyondTrust

Peter Schumacher, Director of Marketing, BeyondTrust

Scott Lang, Director of Marketing, BeyondTrust

David Allen, Vice President of Development, BeyondTrust

Angela Duggan, Experience Architect, BeyondTrust

Chris Silva, Chief Architect, BeyondTrust

Grace Hibbert, Student, Queen Mary University of London

John Titor, Time Traveler

Preface

Building effective defenses for your assets is a dark art. Mark my words; it is so much more than any regulation, standard, or policy. After 20 years in the information technology and security industry, it is easy to say implement a vulnerability management program. It is easy to say patch your operating systems and applications. Compliancy standards from PCI, HIPAA, ASD, and others all say do it. They tell you how you should measure risk and when you must comply with getting systems patched. In reality, it is difficult as hell to do. No one technology works, and no one vendor has a solution to cover the enterprise and all of the platforms and applications installed. It's a difficult task when you consider you need to build an effective strategy to protect assets, applications, and data. Vulnerability management is more than just running a scan, too. It is a fundamental concept in building your strategy and the regulations tell you, you must do it, but not how you can actually get it done. What problems, pitfalls, and political pushback you may encounter stymies most teams. Yes, there are team members that will actually resist doing the right thing from vulnerability assessment scanning to deploying patches. We have seen it many times, all over the world. It is a cyber security issue and it is not naivety either. It is a simple fear of what you might discover, what it will take to fix it, what will break if you do, and the resistance to change. All human traits.

Protecting your assets is fundamental security hygiene. In a modern enterprise, everything connected to the network from router, to printer, and camera is a target. This is above and beyond traditional servers, desktops, and applications. If it communicates on a LAN, WAN, or even PAN, it can be targeted. If it's wired or wireless, a threat actor does not care either; it can be leveraged. Knowing if it's brand new versus end of life and no longer receiving patches helps evaluate the risk surface, but not even knowing what's on your network makes it near impossible to prioritize and take effective action. This is completely outside of modern threats that are still your responsibility in the cloud and on mobile devices including BYOD.

While I have painted a picture of doom and gloom, the reality is that you are still responsible for protecting these resources. Being on the front page of the newspaper is not an option. The regulations, contracts, and security best practices clearly highlight the need to do it.

This book is dedicated to this dark art. How do you actually create an asset protection strategy through vulnerability management (and a lesser degree patch management) and accomplish these goals? We will explore years of experience, mistakes, threat analysis, risk measurement, and the regulations themselves to build an effective vulnerability management program that actually works. In addition, we will cover guidance on how to create a vulnerability management policy that has real-world service-level agreements that a business can actually implement. The primary goal is to rise above the threats and make something actually work, and work well, that team members can live with. Vulnerability management needs to be more than a check box for compliance. It should be a foundation block for cyber security within your organization. Together, we can figure out how to get there and how to improve even what you are doing today. After all, without self-improvement in cyber security, we will be doomed to another breach. Threat actors will always target the lowest hanging fruit. An unpatched resource is an easy target. Our goal is to make it as difficult as possible for an intruder to hack into our environment. If somebody has to be on the front page of the newspaper due to a breach, we would rather it be someone else's name and business, not ours.

—Morey J. Haber

Introduction

The foundation of cyber security defense has been clouded by point solutions, false promises, and "bolt on" solutions that extend the value of a given technology based on a need. After all, if we count how many security solutions we have implemented from anti-virus to firewalls, we find dozens of vendors and solutions implemented throughout an organization. The average user or executive is not even aware of most solutions, even though they may interact with them daily from VPN clients to multi-factor authentication.

If we step back and try to group all of these solutions at a macro level, we will find each one falls into one of three logical groups. These form the pillars for our cyber security defenses, regardless of their effectiveness:

- **Identity** – The protection of a user's identity, account, and credentials from inappropriate access

- **Privilege** – The protection of the rights, privileges, and access control for an identity or account

- **Asset** – The protection of a resource used by an identity, directly or as a service

While some solutions may be supersets of all three pillars, their goal is to unify the information from each in the form of correlation or analytics. For example, a Security Information Enterprise Manager (SIEM) is designed to take security data from solutions that reside in each pillar and correlate them together for advanced threat detection and adaptive response. Correlation of common traits across the pillars enables a broader more holistic or lifecycle view of the environment. An identity accessing an asset with privileges provides a simple example of how the pillars support this cyber security foundation of your company. Let's look at a simple correlation.

- Who is this user (Identity)?

- What do they have access to (Privilege)?

- What did they access (Asset)?

- Is that access secured (Privilege)?

- Is that asset secured (Asset)?

This answers the question, "What is inappropriately happening across my environment that I should be concerned about?" A good security program should provide coverage across all three pillars as illustrated in Figure I-1.

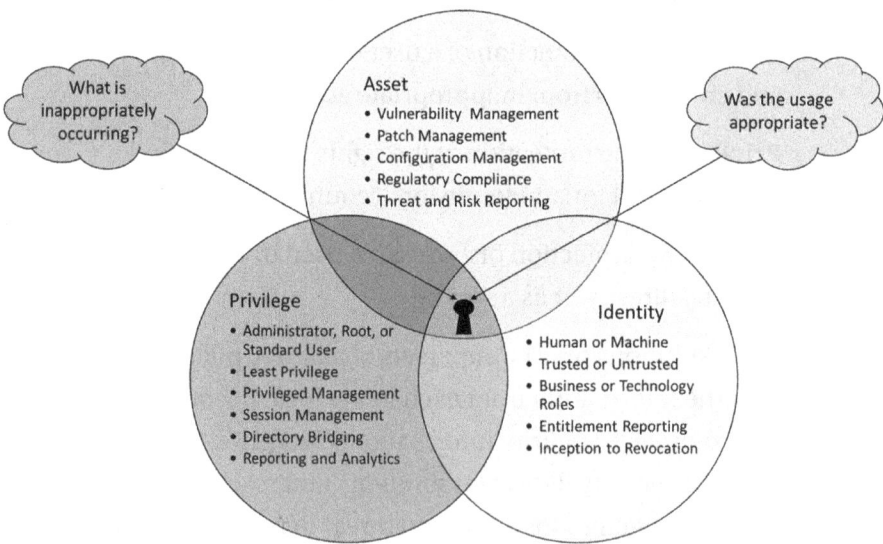

Figure I-1.The three pillars of a cyber security program

Having this level of oversight and control helps answer the questions:

- Are my assets and data secured?

- Are the privileges appropriate?

- Was the access appropriate?

For most vendors and businesses, the integration of these three pillars is very important. If security solutions are isolated, do not share information, or only operate in their own silo (one or two pillars), their protection capabilities are limited in scope. For example, if an advanced threat protection solution or anti-virus technology cannot share asset information, or report on the context of the identity, then it is like riding a unicycle. If pushed too hard, an environment could lose its balance and fall over. If that analogy does not resonate with you, imagine not tracking privileged access to sensitive assets. You would never know if an identity is inappropriately accessing sensitive data. Moreover, you would never know if a compromised account is accessing sensitive data. That is how threat actors are breaching environments every week.

When you look at new security solutions, ask yourself what pillar they occupy and how they can support the other pillars you trust and rely on every day. For example, intrusion prevention, segmentation, security orchestration and response, and even threat analytics, when implemented correctly, derive value from, and provide value to, all three pillars. If a new security investment must operate in a silo, make sure you understand why and what their relevance will be in the future. To this point, what is an example of a security solution that operates only in a silo? Answer – One that does not support integrations, log forwarding, has concepts of assets (even it if it just IP based) or even basic role access. Sounds like an Internet of Things (IoT) device. An IoT door lock that provides physical protection for assets based on a static identity that cannot share access logs or integrate with current identity solutions is a bad choice for any organization. A stand-alone anti-virus solution that has no central reporting on status, signature updates, or faults is another. There is no way of knowing if it is operating correctly, if there is a problem, or even if it is doing an exceptionally good job blocking malware. Why would you essentially pick a consumer-grade anti-virus solution for your enterprise? Unfortunately, this happens all the time, and we end up with the "bolt on" approach to solve the problem.

As we stabilize our cyber security best practice and focus on basic cyber security hygiene, consider the longer-term goals of your business. If you choose a vendor that does not operate in these three pillars, has no integration strategy, or is an odd point solution, be aware of the risks. Everything we choose as a security solution should fall into these pillars; if they do not, then ask a lot of questions. For example, why would you choose a camera system without centralized management capabilities? It falls into the asset protection pillar, can monitor physical access by an identity, but without centralized capabilities and management, it is a stand-alone pole not supporting your foundation. It needs to support all three pillars to be an effective security solution and ultimately provide good information for correlation, analytics, and adaptive response. Some may argue there could be four or even five pillars for a sound cyber security defense including education, partners, etc. We prefer to think of all tools and solutions in these three categories. Why? A three-legged stool never wobbles!

From a Vulnerability Management perspective, it's no secret that identifying and correcting mitigatable security holes is critical to protecting any business from harmful attacks. However, the process of vulnerability assessment and remediation often gets overlooked as a critical component for business continuity. While it is supposed to be an ongoing process, inadequate resourcing or laziness in maintaining a proper vulnerability assessment workflow results in incompetent prioritization and remediation practices; and only when disaster strikes are organizations forced to inspect their process and its flaws in detail. Even then, some businesses fail to learn the lesson of proactive vulnerability management and remediation. In addition, many organizations look at vulnerability management in isolation or as strictly a cost center. Our advice is to take a step back and look at the wealth of asset and risk information captured in a vulnerability scan and prove how it can improve security, availability, and business continuity. Examine how this data can not only help prioritize patches and mobilize IT resources, but also how the information can be used to strengthen other security investments across the organization including asset management, patch management, application control, analytics and threat detection – to name a few.

The following are some common misconceptions about vulnerability assessment and its role in properly secure computing environments with this three-pillared approach. To start, the difference between vulnerability assessments and vulnerability management is simple but noteworthy. Assessments are the act of running a threat risk profile while management refers to the entire life cycle. Unfortunately, the security community tends to blend the concepts together, and it can lead to nontechnical teams believing they are safe with other technology or incomplete management life cycles. These are called "Vulnerability Management Myths."

My Firewall Protects Me

Reality: Despite all the attention that firewalls, anti-virus applications, and Intrusion Detection System (IDS) receive, security vulnerabilities still plague organizations. The implementation of these tools often leads administrators into believing that their networks are safe from intruders. Unfortunately, this is not the case. In today's complex threat environment of malware, spyware, disgruntled employees, and aggressive international hackers, developing and enforcing a strict and regular network security policy that incorporates ongoing vulnerability assessment is critical to maintaining a business continuity. Firewalls and IDS are independent layers of security. Firewalls merely examine network packets to determine whether or not to forward them on to their end destination. Firewalls screen data based on domain names or IP addresses and can screen for some low-level attacks. They are not designed to protect networks from vulnerabilities, exploits, and improper system configurations if assets are exposed, nor can they protect from malicious internal activity or rogue assets inside the firewall. To make my point, firewalls (especially perimeter firewalls) are of little value once an attacker is inside your network and within a zone. They will only help if traffic egresses through them like command and control of malware. If they are operating autonomously, they are essentially useless.

Similarly, an IPS inspects all inbound and outbound network activity and identifies suspicious patterns. IPS can be either passive or reactive in design, but either way, they rely on signatures and/or behavior of known attacks to prevent intrusion. Most sophisticated attacks can easily trick IDS and penetrate networks. Likewise, an IPS may not protect against vulnerabilities that may be exploited by remotely executed code. A vulnerability assessment system will look at the network and pinpoint the weaknesses that need to be patched – before they ever get breached. With over 80 new vulnerabilities announced each week, a company's network is only as secure as its latest vulnerability assessment and patches deployed. An ongoing vulnerability process, in combination with proper remediation, will help ensure that the network is fortified to withstand the latest attacks.

Why Target My Company?

Reality: If you look at vulnerability and exploit history, you will see that not all attacks are targeted. Code Red, Blaster, Sasser, Bagel, Big Yellow, WannaCry, Petya, etc., attacked enterprises and systems at random, based on specific vulnerabilities. It is not just large enterprises that need to be concerned about targeted attacks. Any organization can become the target of a disgruntled employee, customer, or contractor. So, it is important to move beyond the "it can't happen to me" feeling of security and look at the hard facts.

My Vertical Is Safe

Reality: The Computer Security Institute (CSI) reported that 90% of survey respondents detected computer security breaches within the last 12 months. Eighty percent of these companies acknowledge significant, measurable financial loss as a result of these breaches. For the fifth year in a row, more respondents (74%) cited their Internet connection as a more frequent point of attack. One-third cited their internal systems.

Sometimes the attacks are quite targeted, whereas other times the random nature of worms, ransomware, and viruses can be equally harmful. For example, Code Red indiscriminately infected over 250,000 Web servers in its first 9 hours and caused over $2.6 billion in reported damage over 15 years ago. Nothing has changed. We have similar statistics for the Miria Botnet and WannaCry, Petya, etc.

Additionally, "targeted" attacks occur in a variety of ways and are not necessarily the result of uninterested parties. Intrusions can originate from inside or outside of a network as a result of weaknesses being exploited. Contractors, disgruntled employees, vendors, etc., all can take advantage of network vulnerabilities to violate security policy. Though alarming, there is an ironic bright side. CERT/CC (the federally funded research and development center operated by Carnegie Mellon University) reports that nearly 99% of all intrusions resulted from exploitation of known vulnerabilities or configuration errors. Essentially, malicious intrusions are avoidable if companies adopt a strong security policy and adhere to regular ongoing vulnerability assessments and proactive remediation strategies.

Patch Management as Protection

Reality: Vulnerability assessment takes a wide range of network issues into consideration and identifies weaknesses that need correction, including misconfigurations and policy noncompliance vulnerabilities that a patch management system alone cannot address. It provides a comprehensive picture of all systems, services, and devices that can breach a network, as well as a complete, prioritized list of vulnerabilities that need to be addressed. Remediation is the follow-up stage after vulnerabilities have been accurately identified and associated risk prioritized. The two work hand in hand and form a complementary process. This illustrates the difference between a vulnerability assessment and the entire process of vulnerability management.

While there are automated remediation systems (commonly called patch management) that can provide some low-level identification of outdated files; vulnerability assessment is far more comprehensive. Vulnerability assessment solutions test systems and network services such as NetBIOS, HTTP, FTP, DNS, POP3, SMTP, LDAP, RDP, Registry, Services, Users and Accounts, password vulnerabilities, publishing extensions, detection and audit wireless networks, and much more to build a risk profile.

Additionally, a vulnerability assessment solution can quickly perform custom audits for more than just vulnerabilities. For example, users seeking to identify rogue services or banned applications can quickly run a scan of the entire network and identify offending assets. These otherwise unknown systems can be unsecured portals into a network and thwart all of an enterprise's security efforts. When these implementations are partially sanctioned by other departments, they transition from rogue assets to ShadowIT. Those are implementations not under current information technology or security ownership and potentially not even under their jurisdiction. The end result is to drive remediation (patch management) efforts, and that can only be done on known and managed systems. Network discoveries will help determine which ones these are, and also support assessments that can check legacy (or custom) software for issues that still may be present even when there have been initiatives to remove them in the first place. Quite simply, a comprehensive assessment and risk identification is step one in the vulnerability management workflow. Remediation is the second step. Using only remediation as a shortcut in the overall security process leaves a network vulnerable to attack. We will look at this workflow in depth as we progress through the chapters in this book.

Homegrown Is Best

Reality: While theoretically, it is possible for an information technology team to handle assessment and remediation manually, it is not very realistic to expect the audits to be thorough or timely. Even if a dedicated internal team worked around the clock, it would not be enough manpower to meet the challenge. A vulnerability perfect storm – a rapidly growing number of vulnerabilities meeting a dramatically shrinking time to remediate – is overwhelming security management efforts.

CERT/CC reports that computer security vulnerabilities have grown exponentially – with annual unique vulnerability averages going from 500 (1995–99) to over a thousand (2000–01), to over 4000 (2002–03) in no time. But it is not just the number of attacks that are daunting; it is also the speed at which they are coming – dozens per week and growing.

Enterprises trying to utilize a homegrown system quickly learn that understanding vulnerabilities and devising software to identify them accurately is a major undertaking. All too soon they realize that the only way to effectively combat the growing number of weaknesses inherent in network operating systems, applications, vendor appliances, IoT devices, cloud platforms, mobile devices, and more is to utilize a comprehensive scanning engine that is supported by proactive, dedicated vulnerability research.

Homegrown systems and immature scanning engines that have not been thoroughly proven in the field often create an unwarranted sense of security with false-negative reports. Typically, these tend to be signature-based scanners built on limited or outdated research and lacking the auto-update functionality to ensure that the latest vulnerabilities are identified and addressed in a timely fashion. Since they are unable to detect a vast amount of the newer vulnerabilities, they produce inaccurate, false-negative vulnerability reports. We commonly see this in parallel security solutions for NAC and VPN that have added some form of rudimentary vulnerability assessment capabilities. They are just not good enough.

To reduce the potential for false-negative reports, it is imperative that the vulnerability assessment solution:

- be based on a proven, regularly updated scanning engine

- be supported by a company dedicated to vulnerability research

- can overcome false negatives by utilizing advanced technology to detect weaknesses beyond those covered in the signature file

Enterprise Scalability

Reality: Trying to use freeware or a limited deployment of network security assessment scanners in an enterprise can cause a bandwidth overload and result in farms of decentralized data per scan engine. Enterprise-level solutions can deliver tremendous time savings and dramatically improve network security by consolidating the results and scan jobs. When selecting a vulnerability assessment solution for an enterprise, it needs to be able to handle the workload and be technically designed for such a purpose. Vendors like BeyondTrust, Rapid 7, Tenable, and Qualys use the industry-standard best practices with a robust set of enterprise-specific management tools to centrally capture and manage the assessment, prioritization, workflow, and remediation of vulnerabilities. This can be done without compromising bandwidth or network resources. These problems can cause performance issues that are unique to your business and must be accounted for in a successful design and implementation.

It Is Too Expensive?

Reality: The cost of not implementing a vulnerability management solution is far more expensive. Just as with insurance, building alarms, and data backup systems, vulnerability management solutions should be considered a standard element in ensuring business continuity, basic cyber security hygiene, and mitigating potential business risks.

In terms of alternative security methods, the return on investment for an enterprise-ready vulnerability management solution is significant. Hiring a team of dedicated security specialists, for example, to continually research and monitor network vulnerabilities and prevent attacks is not financially feasible. The time required to identify and "x" vulnerabilities across the enterprise without the assistance of a vulnerability assessment solution is just not feasible in a modern environment. It's not uncommon for internal systems to overlook a vulnerability that is later exploited and causes significant damage to the network, productivity loss, or data theft. That could put you on the front page of the newspaper too. That concern alone can be the most compelling reason to invest in the protection afforded by proactive vulnerability management technology.

Laggards

Reality: The true benefit of vulnerability management is that it is a powerful proactive process for securing an enterprise network. With vulnerability management solutions, potential security holes are fixed before they become problematic, allowing companies to fend off attacks before they occur. The simple truth of the matter is that virtually all attacks come from already-known vulnerabilities. CERT/ CC (the federally funded research and development center operated by Carnegie Mellon University) reports that nearly 99% of all intrusions resulted from exploitation of known vulnerabilities or configuration errors. With that in mind, it is important to evaluate a vulnerability management vendor's research team and commitment to providing database updates. If you or your solution is a laggard, then you might become a part of CERT's statistics.

Customized and Legacy Systems

Reality: It's true that the majority of intruders focus on the vulnerabilities in mainstream applications to gain entry into a network. More advanced attackers, however, will focus on lesser-known applications (i.e., custom applications and outdated programs still being used within an organization) as a way to gain entry. For environments running custom applications, it is important to select a scanner that can accommodate custom scans and is not reliant only on a single signature for known attacks. Not all scanners can accommodate this, and not all solutions contain checks for legacy environments going back over 20 years.

The Money Pit

Reality: The time it could take for an information technology team to repair and an enterprise to recover from a vulnerability exploitation will have a far greater impact on its business than the short amount of time it will take to get the enterprise up to speed on a vulnerability management solution.

Modern vulnerability assessment scanners are built for ease of installation and operation and feature intuitive user interface and wizards to speed the learning curve. After all, no solution can be effective if no one uses it. Well-designed solutions do not require advanced security knowledge to install and can be implemented in days for even a small organization.

The more advanced scanners automatically handle the detailed network evaluation and clearly identify issues and solutions to resolve exposed vulnerabilities using advanced analytics. Some vulnerability management solutions even have automatic remediation capabilities built in or integrate with technology partners, allowing misconfigurations, patches, and improper settings to be resolved with a single mouse-click. This ensures the cost structure of a solution does not become a money pit by implementing the entire life cycle in one solution.

Complacency Factor

We have become complacent about cyber security threats and breaches. We are aware of the threats; we hear it in the news almost every day; and too many experts have advice on how to secure our mobile devices, credit cards, social media accounts, and the Internet of Things. We have created new words to describe these threats like Skimming and Cyber Bullying. Citizens have become numb to their meanings, recommendations, and obtuse reality unless we become a victim of the attacks ourselves. We have truly become complacent. Not only in our personal lives, but also in business. It is impossible to run a marathon at full pace, yet cyber security issues are continuing to escalate, and the acceleration has backfired within efforts implemented by organizations and governments. Instead of executives and lawmakers becoming even more strategic, security professionals becoming more acute, and users becoming more self-aware, we find ourselves accepting the daily barrage of security information as commonplace and in some cases, acceptable. The truth of the matter is that we have a problem to overcome. We have become desensitized to the facts, and it is one of the biggest threats to enterprise security.

If you live in an old house, ask yourself a very simple question. How many layers of paint are on the walls? How many times has this bedroom or kitchen been redone? Cyber security is very similar. Without a demolition down to the foundation, we often layer solutions (wallpaper for example) on top of existing material to form a new look, better visibility, and better appearance. We truly do not fix the rotten wood, remove end-of-life components (old plumbing), and replace bricks and mortar until absolutely needed. Enterprise security complacency is not about the flaws in our new products; we are all aware of the latest flaws in Microsoft, Apple, Oracle, and Google solutions. We are tired and worn down about the constant flaws in the material and solutions holding our businesses and governments together. Whether these have actual security flaws that need to be patched (been there – done that before) or end-of-life technology that just has to go due to sustainment issues. Teams are bored with patching operating systems, applications, infrastructure, and websites that have been around for even a few years. How many times can you ask a team to patch Windows Server 2008 R2 before the task is mundane, boring, repetitive, and the owners become complacent? Unfortunately, it happens all the time. Operations and security professionals need to be challenged, their minds exercised, and taken out of the path of routine, so tasks and awareness are stimulating and not repetitive insanity. That is how we got to this problem in the first place. Too many of the same issues over and over again, too many layers of paint to cover the fundamental problems.

In cyber security, there is virtually no room for a mediocre job. Security has to be done correctly from the start and enterprises must avoid complacency. Following a few basic recommendations (from yet another security professional) can help you avoid this growing pandemic and keep your teams off the front page of the newspaper. That is why we wrote this book.

The Bottom Line

Today's network environments are dynamic, requiring a multitude of defense measures to effectively prevent attacks and efficiently mitigate vulnerabilities across the entire enterprise. Organizations must not only be aware of threats, but also the impact of those threats on their infrastructure. Security administrators require a solution that can put them in a position to rapidly and effectively respond so that risks can be measured versus being unknown.

CHAPTER 1

The Attack Chain

As highlighted in many articles, breach reports, and studies, most cyber-attacks originate from outside the organization. The Verizon Data Breach Investigations Report (DBIR) for 2018 calculates this at 73%. While the specific tactics may vary, the stages of an external attack follow a predictable flow. This is illustrated in Figure 1-1.

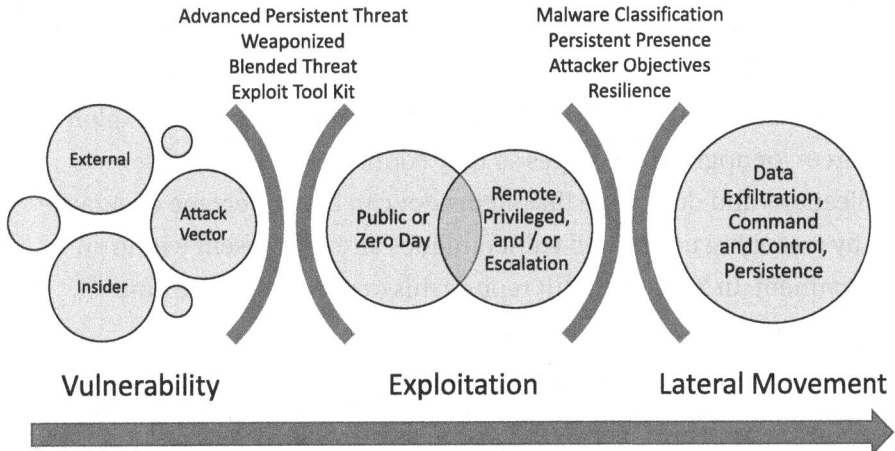

Figure 1-1. *Cyber security attack chain*

First, threat actors attack the perimeter.

Threat actors are less likely in a modern environment to penetrate the perimeter directly, but more than likely they execute a successful drive-by download or launch a phishing attack to compromise a user's system and establish a foothold inside the network. They do this all the while flying

© Morey J. Haber, Brad Hibbert 2018
M.J. Haber and B. Hibbert, *Asset Attack Vectors*,
https://doi.org/10.1007/978-1-4842-3627-7_1

"under the radar" of many traditional security defenses. (This assumes they did not penetrate the environment due to a misconfiguration of a resource on-premise or in the cloud.)

Next, hackers establish a connection.

Unless it's ransomware or self-contained malware, the attacker quickly establishes a connection to a command and control (C&C) server to download toolkits, additional payloads, and to receive additional instructions.

Social attacks were utilized in 43% of all breaches in the 2017 Verizon Data Investigations Report dataset. Almost all phishing attacks that led to a breach were followed by some form of malware, and 28% of phishing breaches were targeted. Phishing is the most common social tactic in the Verizon DBIR dataset (93% of social incidents).

Now inside the network, the attacker goes to work.

Attackers begin to learn about the network, the layout, and the assets. They begin to move laterally to other systems and look for opportunities to collect additional credentials, find other vulnerable systems, exploit resources, or upgrade privileges so they continue to compromise applications and data. Note that an insider can either become an attacker just by exploiting unpatched vulnerabilities already present within an environment. In 2018 the DBIR reports this occurs 28% of the time.

Mission Complete.

Last, the attacker collects, packages, and eventually exfiltrates the data.

One product will certainly not provide the protection you need against all stages of an attack. And while some new and innovative solutions will help protect against, or detect, the initial infection, they are not guaranteed to stop 100% of malicious activity. In fact, it's not a matter of if, but a matter of when you will be successfully breached. You still need to do the basics – firewalls, endpoint AV, and threat detection and so on. But you also need to identify and patch vulnerabilities throughout the environment. Properly managing these risks can help at all stages of the attack. From reducing the attack surface to protecting against lateral movement, to detecting breach progress, to actively responding and mitigating the impact of that breach, this book will examine how vulnerabilities, exploits, and remediation strategies can block progress for a threat actor through the cyber-attack chain.

CHAPTER 2

The Vulnerability Landscape

A vulnerability is the quality or state of being exposed to the possibility of an attack, degradation, or harm, either physically, electronically, or emotionally. While the first two translate easily into cyber security, emotion vulnerabilities can manifest themselves in hacktivism, nation-state attacks, and even cyber bullying. Understanding the vulnerability landscape is important in order to design a proper defense and in many cases, our physical and electronic worlds can be blurred when considering the potential threats.

Vulnerabilities

A vulnerability itself does not allow for an attack vector to succeed. In fact, a vulnerability in and of itself just means that a risk exists. Vulnerabilities are nothing more than a mistake. They are a mistake in the code, design, implementation, or configuration that allows malicious activity to potentially occur via an exploit. Thus, without an exploit, a vulnerability is just a potential problem and used in a risk assessment to gauge what could happen. Depending on the vulnerability, available exploit, and resources assessed with the flaw, the actual risk could be limited or a pending disaster. While this is a simplification of a real risk assessment,

M.J. Haber and B. Hibbert, *Asset Attack Vectors*,
https://doi.org/10.1007/978-1-4842-3627-7_2

5

it provides the foundation for privileges as an attack vector. Not all vulnerabilities and exploits are equal, and depending on the privileges of the user or application executing in conjunction with the vulnerability, the escalation and effectiveness of the attack vector can change. For example, a word processor vulnerability executed by a standard user versus an administrator can have two completely different sets of risks once exploited. One could be limited to just the user's privileges as a standard user, and the other could have full administrative access to the host. And, if the user is using a domain administrator account or other elevated privileges, the exploit could have permissions to the entire environment. This is something a threat actor targets as a low-hanging fruit. Who is running outside of security best practices and how can I leverage them to infiltrate the environment?

With this in mind, vulnerabilities come in all "shapes and sizes." They can target the operating system, applications, web applications, infrastructure, and so on. They can also target the protocols, transports, and communications in between resources from wired networks, Wi-Fi, to tone-based radio frequencies. Not all vulnerabilities have exploits, however. Some are proof of concepts, some are unreliable, and some are easily weaponized and even included in commercial penetration testing tools or free open source. Some are sold on the dark web for cybercrimes and others used exclusively by nation-states until they are patched or made public (intentionally or not). The point is that vulnerabilities can be in anything at any time. It is how they are leveraged that makes them important, and if the vulnerability itself lends to an exploit that can actually change privileges (privileged escalation from user's permissions to another), the risk is very real for a privileged attack vector. To date, less than 10% of all Microsoft vulnerabilities patched allow for privilege escalation. A real threat considering hundreds of patches are released every year for their solutions alone.

In order to convey the risks and identification of vulnerabilities, the security industry has multiple security standards to discuss the risk, threat, and relevance of a vulnerability. The most common standards are the following:

- Common Vulnerabilities and Exposure (CVE) – a standard for information security vulnerability names and descriptions.

- Common Vulnerability Scoring System (CVSS) – a mathematical system for scoring the risk of information technology vulnerabilities.

- The Extensible Configuration Checklist Description Format (XCCDF) – a specification language for writing security checklists, benchmarks, and related kinds of documents.

- Open Vulnerability Assessment Language (OVAL) – an information security community effort to standardize how to assess and report upon the machine state of computer systems.

- Information Assurance Vulnerability Alert (IAVA) – an announcement of a vulnerability in the form of alerts, bulletins, and technical advisories identified by DoD-CERT, a division of the United States Cyber Command; and they are a mandated baseline for remediation within the government and Department of Defense (DoD).

- Common Configuration Enumeration (CCE) – provides unique identifiers to system configuration issues in order to facilitate fast and accurate correlation of configuration data across multiple information sources and tools.

- Common Weakness Enumeration (CWE) – provides a common language of discourse for discussing, finding, and dealing with the causes of software security vulnerabilities as they are found in the code.

- Common Platform Enumeration (CPE) – a structured naming scheme for information technology systems, software, and packages.

- Common Configuration Scoring System (CCSS) –a set of measures of the severity of software security configuration issues. CCSS is a derivation of CVSS.

- Open Checklist Interactive Language (OCIL) – defines a framework for expressing a set of questions to be presented to a user and corresponding procedures to interpret responses to these questions that cannot be electronically automated or queried for a resource or environment. Essentially, they are questions that require human intervention to answer but are expressed in a standardized markup language.

- Asset Reporting Format (ARF) – a data model to express the transport format of information about assets and the relationships between assets and reports. The standardized data model facilitates the reporting, correlating, and fusing of asset information throughout solutions and governing or dependent organizations.

- Security Content Automation Protocol (SCAP) – a synthesis of interoperable specifications based on existing standards. For example, ratified version 1.2 of SCAP is comprised of XCCDF, OVAL, OCIL, ARF, CCE, CPE, CVE, CVSS, and CCSS at specific individual versions. This allows each standard to evolve separately but freezes versions in order to communicate them as a collection.

- Open Web Application Security Project (OWASP) – an online community that provides a not-for-profit approach to developing secure web applications by providing methodologies, tools, technology, and an assessment approach for vendors, organizations, and end users.

The results from all this information allow security professionals and management teams to discuss and prioritize the risks from vulnerabilities. In the end, they must be to prevent exploitation and any of the possible attack vectors that could come from their abuse. Without a common language and structure to discuss them between vendors, companies, and government, assessments would be nearly meaningless between organizations based on their implementation of security best practices. A critical risk for one company may not exist for another simply based on their environment. Standards like CVSS allow for that to be communicated correctly to all stakeholders.

Configurations

Configuration flaws are just another form of vulnerabilities. They are, nonetheless, flaws that do not require remediation – just mitigation. Standards like CCE help identify and communicate these types of flaws using a common industry standard language. The difference between remediation and mitigation is key for this discussion. Remediation implies the deployment of a software or firmware patch to correct the vulnerability. This is commonly referred to as Patch Management. Mitigation is simply a change at some level in the existing deployment that deflects (mitigates) the risk from being exploited. It can be simple change within a file, group policy, or updating certificates. In the end, they are vulnerabilities based on poor configurations and can be exploited as an attack vector just as easily by a threat actor. The most common configuration problems that are exploited involve accounts that have poor default security best practices. This could be blank or default passwords upon initial configuration for administrator or root accounts, or insecure communication paths that are not locked down after an initial install due to a lack of expertise or undocumented backdoor.

Regardless, configuration flaws just require a change to fix. And, if the flaw is severe enough, a threat actor can have root privileges without running any exploit code.

Exploits

Exploits require a vulnerability. Without a documentable flaw, an exploit cannot exist. It can take some time for security professionals to reverse engineer an exploit to figure out what vulnerability was leveraged. This is typically a very technical forensics exercise. As mentioned in the "Vulnerabilities" section, exploits can also take on many different "shapes and sizes" too. They can be used to leak information, install malware, provide surveillance, but ultimately, the goal is to create a sustainable and undetected beachhead within a resource or create immediate chaos and destruction. Exploits themselves can be very destructive in their execution methodology, but the most successful ones do exactly the opposite. An exploit that can gain privileges, execute code, allow for lateral movement, exfiltrate data, and go undetected is very dependent on the vulnerability but also depends on the privileges the exploit has when it executes. This is why vulnerability management, risk assessments, and patch management are so important. Exploits can only execute in the confines of the resource they compromise. If no vulnerability exists due to remediation, they cannot execute. If the privileges of the user or application with the vulnerability are low (standard user), and no privileged escalation exploitation is possible, then the attack is limited in its capabilities. However, don't be fooled; exploitation, even at standard user privileges, can cause devastation in the form of ransomware or other vicious attacks. Fortunately, the vast majority can be mitigated (contained) just by lowering privileges and minimizing the surface area for a privileged attack. Exploits succeed the best with the highest privileges; root or administrator, or a flaw for the exploit itself to elevate privileges. Therefore, stopping exploits can occur through remediation (patch management), mitigation (if one is available), and through lowering privileges. Lowering privileges does not fix the vulnerability, just the likelihood of a successful attack and in itself is not an acceptable security fix. It is just a mitigation strategy.

False Positives

Vulnerability management vendors use a variety of terms to describe their actual checks, policies, and scan settings. They are not common between solutions and terms like audit, policies, options, unsafe check, and groups mean different things within different tools. While the differences are minor, all vendors use some common terminology outside of standards. A very important one is called a "False Positive." A false positive is the positive identification of a vulnerability on a resource when in fact the risk is not real, or the threat has been remediated or mitigated. Vulnerability management vendors struggle to keep the percentage of false positives they have to a minimum, but there are a variety of things that can cause a false positive:

- Poorly written vulnerability checks that do not cover all aspects of the vulnerability, its characteristics, and operational metrics.

- Backporting of security patches that do not allow for easy identification of a vulnerability.

11

- Vulnerability checks that return obtuse or incomplete results that leave ambiguity in the checks findings.

- Version and patch supersedence that do not honor product versions or newer patches that have been applied that remediate the vulnerability.

In general, false positives are a very undesirable result of a vulnerability assessment. Minimizing them is critical because it can divert resources to investigate a problem that does not really exist. For persistent false positives, many vulnerability management vendors offer a feature called "Exclusions." This suppresses the finding as a known vulnerability that is of minimal concern due to other reasons or a false positive that cannot be corrected by the manufacturer.

False positives are an important part of our discussions since we need to assume that when a vulnerability is identified, it is accurate; but in reality, every environment will experience their fair share of false positives throughout their life cycles. And from a vendor perspective, when creating vulnerability checks, vendors would prefer to overreport a finding and a potential false positive versus providing a sense of improper security with a false negative.

False Negatives

The antonym of a false positive is a false negative, but not for the reasons you may think. A "False Negative" is when a vulnerability is present, but the vulnerability assessment fails to identify it. There are many reasons for a false negative:

- A vendor does not provide a check for the vulnerability.

- A vendor does not support checks for a specific vulnerability within a given operating system, application, or platform.

- The vendor's check is incomplete and does not check all the necessary requirements.

- Credentials or authentication required to validate the check are incorrect or not present.

- The lag time for a vendor to release a reliable check is not timely enough for your assessments.

False negatives are the worst-case scenario for an organization. A vulnerability is missed in reporting and from assessments, and if the threat is significant enough, the risk cannot be prioritized and remediated.

While in recent years, the number of false negatives between solution vendors has decreased significantly, it is still a real-world problem that appears from time to time. To manage this problem, some environments do not rely on one solution alone to identify vulnerabilities. Any vulnerability identified in one solution, and not the other, can then be classified as a false positive, or false negative if the conditions for the assessment are equal.

Malware

Malware, commonly referred to as viruses, spyware, adware, ransomware, etc., is any class of undesirable or unauthorized software designed to have malicious intent on a resource. The intent can range from surveillance, data leakage, disruption, command and control, to extortion. If you pick your favorite crime that can be translated to an information technology resource, malware can provide a vehicle to instrument cybercriminal activity for a threat actor. Malware, like any other program, can execute at any permission from the standard user to administrator (root). Depending on its creation, intent, and privileges, the damage it can do can be anything from an annoyance to a game over event. Malware can be installed on a resource via a vulnerability and exploit combination or through legitimate installers, weaknesses in the supply chain, or even social engineering such as phishing. Regardless of the delivery mechanism, the motive is to get unauthorized code executing on a resource. Once running, it becomes a battle of detection by anti-malware vendors and threat actors to keep executing, avoid detection, and remove the threat. This includes malware adapting itself to avoid detection as well as disabling defenses in order to continue proliferation. Malware itself, based on intent, can perform functions like pass-the-hash and keystroke logging. This allows for the stealing of passwords to perform attacks based on privileges by the malware itself or other attack vectors deployed by the threat actor. Malware is just a transport vehicle to continue the propagation of a sustained attack and ultimately needs permissions to obtain the target information sought after by the attacker. It is such a broad category of malicious software that when discussing vulnerabilities and exploits, we focus on how to remediate a vulnerability so that malware cannot be used as the payload for an exploit.

Social Engineering

Considering the modern threats in the cyber world from ransomware to recording our voices on a phone call, the outcome can become much more severe than anything the most negative people can imagine. At the risk of becoming paranoid about every email we receive and phone call we answer, we need to understand how social engineering works, exploits and vulnerabilities in people too, and how to identify it in the first place without losing our sanity. This learned behavior is no different from figuring out whether your sibling has lied about a message from your parents or not. Sometimes you just need to verify the message before taking action and understand the risks from the outcome. From a social engineering perspective (vulnerabilities in people), threat actors attempt to capitalize on a few key human traits to meet their goals:

- Trusting – the belief that the correspondence, of any type, is from a trustworthy source.

- Gullible – the belief that the contents, as crazy or simple as they may be, are in fact real.

- Sincere – the intent of the contents is in your best interest to respond or open.

- Suspicious – the contents of the correspondence do not raise any concern by having misspellings and poor grammar, or by sounding like a robot corresponding on the phone.

- Curious – the attack technique has not been identified (as part of previous training), or the person remembers the attack vector but does not react accordingly.

If we consider each of these characteristics, we can appropriately train team members not to fall for social engineering. The difficulty is overcoming human traits and not deviating from the education. To that end, please consider the following training parameters and potential self-awareness techniques to stop social engineering:

- Team members should only trust requests for sensitive information from known and trusted team members. An email address alone in the "From:" line is not sufficient to verify the request, nor is an email reply. Their account could be compromised. The best option is to learn from two-factor authentication techniques and pick up the phone. Call the party requesting the sensitive information and verify the request. If the request seems absurdly insane like requesting W-2 information or a wire transfer, verify this is acceptable according to internal policies or other stakeholders such as finance or human resources (it could be an insider attack). Simple verification of the request from an alleged trusted individual, like a superior, can go a long way to stopping social engineering. In addition, all of this should occur before opening any attachments or clicking on any links. If the email is malicious, the payload and exploit may have executed before you have any verification.

- If the request is coming from an unknown source but is moderately trusted—such as a bank or business you interact with—simple techniques can stop you from being gullible. First, check all the links in the email and make sure they actually point back to the proper domain. Just hovering over the link on most computers and mail programs will reveal the contents. If the request is over the phone, never give out personal information. Remember, they called you. For example, the IRS will never contact you by phone; they only use USPS for official correspondence. Don't let yourself fall for the "sky is falling" metaphor. Figure 2-1 shows a transcription for this type of call captured on voice mail. More often than not, threat actors will use a synthesized voice to hide accents or make the call sound more official too.

Hi Morey,

New York NY has left you a Voice Message

Voice Message attached.
From: New York NY, +1 3███████████2
Received: February 17, 2018 at 8:43 AM

"This call is officially a final notice by the IRS Internal Revenue Service. The reason behind this call is to notify you that IRS is filing a lawsuit against you so before your case gets downloaded into the court house. Call back on our department number 3███████████2. I repeat 3███████████2 goodbye."

Figure 2-1. *Fake IRS social engineering phone call*

- Teaching how to identify genuine correspondence or not is rather difficult. Social engineering can take on many forms from accounts payable, love letters, resumes, to fake human resources correspondence. Just stating "if it seems too good to be true" or "nothing is ever free" only handles a very small subset of social engineering attempts. In addition, if peers receive the same correspondence, it only eliminates spear phishing attempts as the probable attack vector. The best option is to consider if you should be receiving the request in the first place. Is this something you normally do, or is it out of the ordinary to receive it? If it is, default back to trust. Verify the intent before proceeding.

- Suspicious correspondence is the easiest way to detect and deflect social engineering attempts. This requires a little detective-style investigation into the correspondence by looking for spelling mistakes, poor grammar, bad formatting, or robotic voices on the phone, and if the request is from a source that you have no interaction with. This could be an offer of a free cruise, or from a bank at which you have no accounts. If there is any reason to be suspicious, it is best to err on the side of caution: do not open any contents or verbally reply, and delete the correspondence. If it is real, the responsible party will call back in due course.

- Curiosity is the worst offender from a social engineering perspective. What could happen, what will happen, and nothing should happen to me since I am fully protected by my computer and company's information technology security resources. That's a false assumption. Modern attacks can circumvent the best systems and application control solutions— even leveraging native OS commands to conduct their attacks. The best defense for a person's curiosity is purely self-restraint. Do not reply to "Can you hear me?" from a strange phone call; do not open attachments if any of the above criteria have been fulfilled, and do not believe nothing can happen to me (even for people using Mac OS). The fact is it can, and your curiosity should not be the cause. Being naïve will make you a victim.

Social engineering is a real problem, and there is no technology that is 100% effective. People themselves are vulnerable, and exploits occur due to our nature. Spam filters can strip out malicious emails, and anti-virus solutions can find known or behavior-based malware, but nothing can stop the human problem of social engineering and insider threats. The best defense for social engineering is education and an understanding of how these attacks leverage our own traits to be successful. If we can understand our own flaws and react accordingly, we can minimize the threat actor's ability to compromise resources and gain access due to our own shortcomings.

Phishing

We have all heard these clichés: "Curiosity Killed the Cat," "Nothing Bad Will Happen," "Did You Know They Removed Gullible from the Dictionary?," and "It Can't Happen to Me." But as we have learned, phishing scams pray on these types of attitudes to invoke user behavior and perpetuate an attack via missing security patches and vulnerable systems. To that end, let's consider these four clichéd bad user attitudes one at a time and then explore how vulnerability management can resolve them.

Curiosity Killed the Cat

Let's say you receive a phishing email and it eludes your junk email box. Figure 2-2 is a perfect example of one commonly received. The payload is in the Word document and is typically ransomware (W97.Downloader in this case).

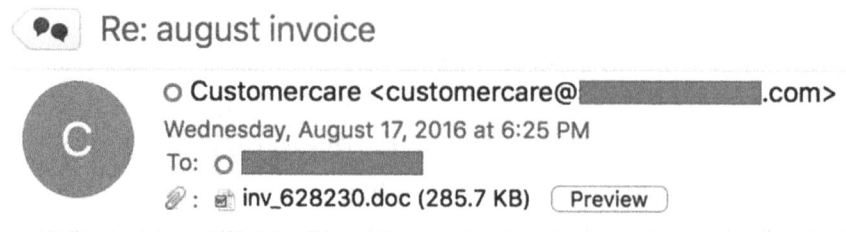

Figure 2-2. *Sample phishing email*

Hopefully, any experienced computer user would recognize this and just delete the email. However, for the typical nontechnical user, especially someone in, say, the accounting department, they may not be expecting this type of email and just open the attachment to see what it is and if it is a bill that should be paid. Honest curiosity based on the job alone could completely infect their entire environment. This would be a targeted behavioral response based on the end user's profession.

Nothing Bad Will Happen

In all fairness, I think every security professional has done this at least once, even for testing purposes. You have a system (probably a virtual machine) built up, fully protected with every security tool you have or stripped down to bare basics, and you execute malware (known or unknown payload) to see what happens. Unfortunately, to our surprise, our best defenses crumble, the system is compromised, and you end up pulling the network cable or hitting Power Off for the VM because things got out of control too quickly.

Phishing emails are no different. Consider the first time someone tested the file mentioned above with an Anti-Virus solution. Better yet, here are the current findings from Virus Total: Only 26% identified it as malware and if your protected VM contained the 74% of the other solutions, you might have been a victim of "nothing bad could happen if my security tools are fully up to date," even today. Figure 2-3 shows a VirusTotal scan from the email's attachment.

SHA256:	efd23d613e04d9450a89f43a0cfbbe0f716801998700c2e3f30d89b7194aff81
File name:	inv_0288772.doc
Detection ratio:	14 / 54
Analysis date:	2016-08-17 21:44:37 UTC (1 hour, 41 minutes ago)

Figure 2-3. *VirusTotal scan of phishing email attachment*

Phishing emails to security and technology professionals rarely succeed. However, the work we do in the lab is not always containable and the outcome potentially devastating if not properly controlled. If an overzealous actor within the organization executes the file and you are exposed to the vulnerability, they may think nothing bad could happen, but in reality, the results can be very different as well.

Did You Know They Removed Gullible from the Dictionary?

This one is short and sweet. Remember when Apple launched a campaign that Macs do not get viruses? It's scary that this actually was a real advertising campaign. But here is reality: 1989 saw the first Mac Malware and things have evolved for MacOS (OS X) just like for Windows (although not in the same quantity due to Apple market share). While the payload came from sharing files in Transmission, the torrent for sharing could have easily come in an email or web page. For anyone that says Macs do not get Malware or are not susceptible to phishing attacks, he or she really thinks that a word like "gullible" can be removed from the dictionary.

It Can't Happen to Me

This phishing attack plays to every ego in the room from executives to hired expert contractors. Phishing emails do not discriminate, and when they employ techniques to target specific individuals (i.e., spear phishing), the results can be financially disastrous. Recent attacks against executives and their team members to conduct fraudulent wire transfers have cost millions and their jobs. If any team member thinks they cannot be a victim of phishing due to the seniority or perceived importance, they are grossly mistaken.

How to Determine if Your Email Is a Phishing Attack

The best way to prevent the potentially damaging effects of phishing attacks is enforcing basic education and solidifying your vulnerability management practice just like putting on your seatbelt when driving a car. Here are five steps to take to verify whether the email you received is a phishing attack:

1. Verify that the email address is really an internal address and from a trusted source.

2. If your name is not in the To: or CC: line or many of your colleagues are listed (dozens or even hundreds), question the source.

3. If there are simple typos or grammatical mistakes, or the subject line seems odd, it could potentially be a fake.

4. Verify the links are for real domains and not questionable like .ru.

5. Never open attachments even if you believe you are
    fully patched and the anti-malware solution is up
    to date. There are plenty of attack vectors that can
    bypass these security solutions like office-based
    macro malware.

Basic technology can stop an attack even if the end user makes a mistake since many of the phishing attacks leverage known vulnerability. Here are five best practices to mitigate the risks of phishing attacks:

1. Make sure all security patches are up to date on a regular
    basis for all systems, especially for common attack
    vectors like Microsoft Office, Adobe Flash, and Java.

2. Ensure the end user is running with proper
    privileges and not logged in as an administrator
    answering emails. This just makes it easier for
    malware to own the system and bypass defenses.

3. Ensure defense software like the anti-virus is up to
    date including engine and signatures.

4. Disable automatic macro execution in Office and
    only run macros that are digitally signed (the sample
    file discussed above).

5. Deploy and maintain SPAM filters, next generation
    firewalls, etc., to stop malicious emails before
    they end up in an end user's inbox and establish
    command and control of the hijacked system.

If administrators can implement these concepts, users be trained to identify a potential attack, and security and operations stay vigilant with the entire life cycle, phishing attacks leveraging vulnerabilities can drastically be minimized even with industry changes and regulations like GDPR that effect the reliability of security solutions detecting a phishing attack.

Ransomware

Let me get this out right off the bat: There is no one solution that is 100% effective in mitigating the risk of ransomware. Some technologies are claiming to have tested hundreds of samples, and that their tool can stop 100% of the samples. I'm sorry, but that is a falsehood. Why? If any single vendor had a solution that solved the problem completely, ransomware would not be such a problem.

Application control solutions, endpoint protection products, and patch management solutions have various degrees of success in mitigating ransomware, but none are 100% effective. Why? Modern ransomware can leverage social engineering, exploit vulnerabilities, and sometimes targets obscure devices like smart TVs. We have seen a spike in ransomware that uses Microsoft Office macros to propagate the threats and even versions that use JScript embedded in a document to conduct malicious activity. These are all different types of vulnerabilities.

The delivery of the payload is equally as impressive to identify. It can come from an exploitable vulnerability, an errant executable (the easiest to stop), PowerShell script, or embedded as a macro or script in a file or website. What makes this a little more disturbing is that many attacks combine methods and use a command control server to hold encryption certificates versus locally based per infection that can be cured with a decryption solution. The exploit and privileges ransomware executes will help dictate how successful the malicious infiltration will be.

This is why ransomware is so difficult to stop and no one technology is 100% effective.

There are some actions you can perform with vulnerability management, configuration hardening, and patch management to minimize the threat. Unfortunately, nothing will ever replace training users to not select Run Macros when opening an unknown file. When they do, the most important thing is to have pristine backups to potentially recover from the worst-case scenarios. However, here are a few rules that are easy to implement that will block the vast majority of mistakes users can make, stop droppers from executing, and block vulnerable applications from being leveraged against your assets:

- Block Untrusted Executables – Application Control solutions allow for application control and the ability for rules to elevate applications based on rules or policies. This will stop any non-authorized application from executing regardless of the source if it is not properly digitally signed or tries to execute a malicious child process as a dropper.

- Stopping Droppers – Unfortunately, trusted applications can launch other applications to perform their intended functions. This includes browsers, mail programs, and even PDF readers. The consistent part of this problem is that these executables almost always launch from temporary file directories. Using endpoint protection solutions to manage file integrity, administrators can track, alert, and block rogue dropper executables that appear in these directories or do not meet minimum reputation requirements.

- Vulnerable Applications – Continuous monitoring solutions typically have a reputation service engine or other technology to measure the risk of an application before its launch. This component allows for real-time assessment of the health of an application for malware, vulnerabilities, permissions, and privacy. To that end, policies can be established to deny (or notify of) the launch of risky applications that could be leveraged in a ransomware attack. This helps ensure service-level agreements are being met for cyber security hygiene and no system is left out that could pose an unacceptable risk.

This lesson from ransomware revolves around vulnerabilities. The risk of a successful ransomware attack can be minimized by shrinking the gaps in allowing vulnerable applications to execute and the human traits that may cause them to execute. While no approach is 100% effective, the vulnerability management life cycle can certainly help address some of it.

Insider Threats

For most security professionals, we are tired of hearing about Insider Threats. They are not new; it is an old-school attack that has been made public due to the nature, quantity, and sensitivity of the data being stolen electronically. Years ago, these attacks occurred on a regular basis but did not have the same labels or stigma they have today. I am not saying they were acceptable back then either. We just need to be realistic about what an Insider Threat is and acknowledge that it has been going on in various forms for hundreds of years.

By definition, an Insider Threat is an internal person behaving as a threat actor. Regardless of the techniques, they are using, they are not behaving in the best interest of the company, potentially breaking the law, and exfiltrating information they do not have permission to possess. An old-school example of this type of threat is client lists. It's an Insider Threat that's still relevant today, by the way. A salesperson, executive, etc., that is planning to leave an organization may have photocopied or printed client lists and orders before leaving the organization to have a competitive edge when they start with a new employer. The volume of paper potentially would have to be substantial to make an impact but leaving with confidential information on printed paper is still an insider threat. Obviously, they were not leaving with file cabinets of material, but today with electronic media, and the Internet, that volume of data could easily be egressed without anyone noticing. And, as a reminder, that file cabinet of sensitive information can easily fit on a USB thumb drive in a person's pocket. Therefore, we now have a label for this type of threat and insider threats are becoming more relevant. It still makes security professionals sick to their stomachs because the crime is old, but the methods and volume are now something to consider and require a new strategy to protect against.

Insider threat occurs for a variety of reasons. This includes aspects of a human persona looking to hurt or gain an advantage against an organization. Regardless of their intent, it's the digital aspect of an Insider Threat that warrants the most attention. Human beings will do the most unusual things in the direst of situations, but if they are not permitted to, many of the risks of Insider Threats can be mitigated. Consider the following for your business:

- How secure are the systems that contain sensitive information?

- Could an insider leverage a simple vulnerability or misconfiguration to gain access?

- Is access secured to specific networks and users?

- What is the SLA for remediating identified risks?

So, in fairness, answering those questions honestly could be opening a Pandora's box. Nonetheless, you should answer them if you care about Insider Threats. Here is why:

- Resources that contain sensitive information or Personally Identifiable Information (PII) should be flagged as crown jewels. Identifying and remediating risks on them is good cyber security hygiene and required by many regulatory compliance initiatives.

- The exposure time of any vulnerability dictates the likelihood it will be breached. Waiting until once a quarter to patch critical vulnerabilities on sensitive systems or even assets on the Internet is just too slow. The long they are at risk, the larger the threat.

- Sensitive access to systems should not only be restricted by user and privileges but also by networks and segments. This limits vulnerability exposure to only trusted resources versus potentially the entire Internet or even guest networks.

- Measuring service-level agreements from the time of public disclosure to vulnerability identification, all the way through remediation will help keep the vulnerability management life cycle working well. Any gaps or overages will allow you to address any deficiencies in addressing threats quickly.

With these recommendations in mind, if an insider is accessing a sensitive system to steal information, session monitoring can document their access and how they extracted the information and when you can determine if they gained access via a privileged access management flaw or vulnerability. Figure 2-4 illustrates how an exploit can be used as a beachhead and for lateral movement.

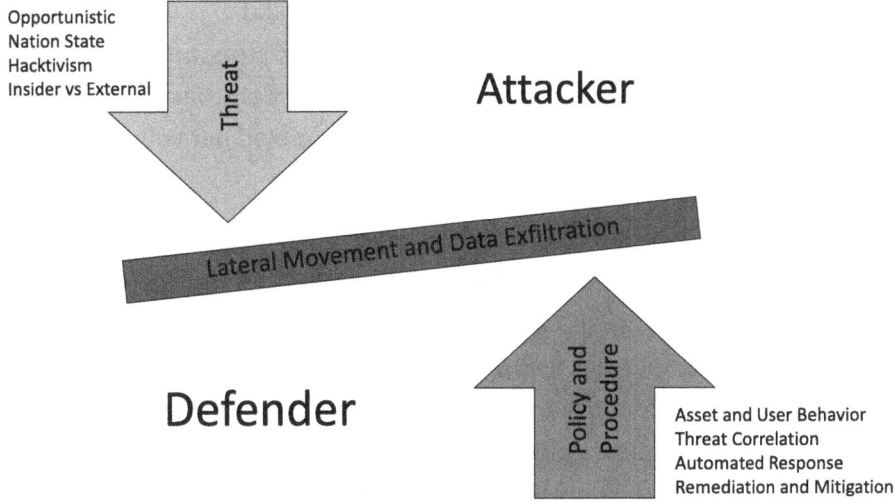

Figure 2-4. *Lateral movement after successful exploitation of a resource*

If you think that if you follow all of these steps to protect against Insider Threa that you will be safe, you are wrong. A threat actor could install malicious data capturing software, leverage a system missing security patches for lateral movement, and access resources using backdoors to conduct similar types of data-gathering activities. Insider Threats are about stealing information and disrupting the business, but depending on the sophistication of the threat actor, they can use tools that are traditionally associated with an external threat. Therefore, we need to realize Insider Threats come from essentially two sides: excessive privileges and poor security hygiene (vulnerability management). To that end, all organizations should also regularly perform these privileged access tasks to keep their systems protected:

- All users should never use administrative accounts for day-to-day usage like email. This includes administrators themselves, in case their accounts are compromised too. All users should have standard user privileges.

- All access to sensitive data should be for valid employees only. Former employees, contractors, and even auditors should not have access on a daily basis. These accounts should be removed or deleted per your organization's policy.

- Employees come and go. If the passwords are not changed when employees leave and new hires are onboarded, the risk to sensitive data increases since former employees technically still have known passwords to the company's sensitive information. This is a similar problem to shared passwords since more than one person knows how to access potentially sensitive systems, and some of these people are no longer even employees.

- Monitoring privileged activity is critical. This includes logs, session monitoring, screen recording, keystroke logging, and even application monitoring.

While these seem very basic, the reality is that most businesses do not do a good job at even the most basic security. If they do, the risk of Insider Threats can be minimized by limiting administrative access and keeping information technology resources up to date with the latest defensives and security patches. Insider Threats are not going to go away. They have been around for hundreds of years, but the medium and techniques for stealing information have evolved with modern technology. The goal is the same: stop the data leakage and be aware that an Insider has multiple attack vectors to achieve their goals. As security professionals, we need to mitigate the risks at source. A briefcase of paper is still an Insider Threat but not as relevant as a USB stick with your entire database of client information. How they stole the information is either due to a vulnerability and exploit or poor privilege hygiene.

External Threats

Organizations typically consider external threats from threat actors and nation-states as the primary source of risk when building strategies to protect assets. It is uncommon for a threat actor to leverage a vulnerability and exploit as an insider but it has happened from time to time in some of the highest profiled insider breaches. It is important to note that external attacks are conducted to achieve an advantage inside the environment without being detected or to cause disruption in the form of an outage or denial of service attack. This is why perimeter defenses, external vulnerability assessments, and intrusion prevention systems of all types are still relevant. While an entire book can literally be written on the types of external threats, there is a specific focus that organizations should take when trying to measure their risk: a SWOT Analysis (developed by Albert Humphrey in the 1960s).

A SWOT Analysis is a simple exercise to measure strengths, weaknesses, opportunities, and threats. It can be applied to external threats once an understanding of what your external threats actually are and where they may come from. Consider a typical business with a home office, website, and some cloud services such as Office 365 or Salesforce. Any publicly accessible system through the Internet or guest network is in scope for an external threat; even if you subscribe to their services. Every place a person can electronically (Internet) touch your information technology assets, log in publicly to access company data, or you provide Internet access as a guest has an external risk surface. If it is poorly configured, vulnerabilities are present, and if it is not properly managed, a breach will happen at some point in time. It is just a matter of time.

A SWOT Analysis will help you prioritize and manage the threats from external risks. In order to get started, consider Table 2-1 as a worksheet and the questions in each title.

Table 2-1. *SWOT External Risk Worksheet*

Strengths	Weaknesses
• What protection do you have in place that is working well? How is it measured? • What are you trying to protect against? • How do others view protection strengths?	• What threat detection could you improve? How is it measured? • Where are there gaps in your threat detection? • How do others view your weaknesses?
Answers:	Answers:
Opportunities	**Threats**
• What changes can you make to protect against threats better? • What trends in threat prevention can you take advantage of? • How can you take your threat detection strengths and turn them into opportunities?	• What external threats are you worried about and can harm your organization? • What are your peers and competitors doing? • What threats do your weaknesses mean to the organization
Answers:	Answers:

While these can be spun to virtually any scenario, the primary purpose is to help you understand what is working, what is not, and how you could improve. If you take this approach and apply it to all of your external resources, you will end up with multiple sheets and action items to secure each one. For example, how would you answer these questions for your public website versus a new application you plan to host in the cloud? If all team members contribute to the answers, and there are no right or wrong answers, an effective strategy against external threats can be developed. If you consider that external threats are any type of attempt to compromise the integrity, data, and operations of your business through the Internet (or even electronically if you have wireless cameras and personal area networks), a starting place will always be the hardest step in building a strategy. Just consider, unless your environment is fully air gapped, has no Internet access at all, does not support wireless devices of any type, and is only accessible via physical lock and key, you have external resources that can represent a threat to your organization. Next step, what do you do about it? It may require a public or internal vulnerability disclosure depending on the exposure and risk to others.

Vulnerability Disclosure

Vulnerability disclosure is the policy, procedures, and practice of reporting security flaws (vulnerabilities) in computer software, hardware, or firmware. Once identified, vulnerabilities may be disclosed to the originators or the technology or parties responsible maintaining the solutions. This includes public and private vendors as well as open source communities. Typically, vendors or developers will delay publicly announcing the details of the vulnerability until a security patch or mitigation strategy is available. When this information is public before a path to correction is available, the vulnerability is typically referred to as a zero-day vulnerability.

Vulnerability disclosure and the policies governing the disclosure can be a contentious issue between vendors, researchers, and end users. Vendors prefer to wait until a patch is available before public disclosure, even if it takes a relatively long period of time. Many researchers prefer a timeline of disclosure, giving vendors 30, 60, or 90 days to develop and release a patch before publicly disclosing the details of the vulnerability. While this is a higher risk, knowing you can be compromised in a specific manner is theoretically better than assuming a system is secure. End users prefer the entire cycle happen as fast as possible. The identification, patch, and disclosure occur in short order so the exposure time is minimized and a patch applied in a timely manner.

Despite the preferences based on persona, there are multiple types of vulnerability disclosure. Responsible disclosure follows this simple workflow (Table 2-2):

Table 2-2. *Workflow for vulnerability disclosure*

1) Vulnerability Identification	2) Private Disclosure	3) Private Investigation	4) Public Disclosure
Researchers, Security Professionals, or Zero Day Identification	Vendor or Responsible Provider Notification	60 to 120 days or longer	Vendor Announcement, Patch Release, and Notification to NVD*

* The NVD is the United States government repository of standards-based vulnerability management data represented using the Security Content Automation Protocol (SCAP). This data enables automation of vulnerability management, security measurement, and compliance. The NVD includes databases of security checklist references, security-related software flaws, misconfigurations, product names, and impact metrics. It is important to note that not all vendors participate in NVD and CVE notifications and classification.

Since the onset of the modern vulnerabilities and their corresponding exploits, notable vulnerability disclosure has involved researchers and vendors working closely together to understand the threat, techniques for exploitation, and testing of remediation strategies. After all, a poor fix can lead to other vulnerabilities and just make the situation worse. This has been seen in the past including remediation strategies that even break functionality. Based on this collaboration, or lack thereof, there are several options for vulnerability disclosure:

- Self-Disclosure – when vendors of solutions publicly report the vulnerabilities. This is typically when a patch is available versus simply exposing an un-mitigatable risk.

- Third-Party Disclosure – when the public announcement of the vulnerability is not performed by the vendor or responsible owner of the technology. Third-party disclosures are typically made by security researchers but can also come from leaked sources like Wikileaks that have obtained exploit information illegally. The notification may be done responsibly to governing bodies like NVD or CERT or not. When not done responsibly, it is often done out of the belief the vendor is taking too long to remediate the solution.

- Vendor Disclosure – when the security researcher reports the flaws directly to the vendors or responsible parties and does not pursue any other public disclosure.

- Full Disclosure – occurs when full public disclosure of the vulnerability is announced and can occur anytime during the vulnerability disclosure life cycle.

According to the National Telecommunications and Information Administration, organizations and researchers should develop and maintain a Vulnerability Disclosure Policy (VDP). A VDP is a responsible method for people, organizations, and services to manage the process of vulnerability disclosure. A VDP policy should include the following:

- Security Statement – a commitment, often in the form of a service-level agreement, to address security risks in a timely fashion and perform responsible disclosure of any known threats.

- Security Scope – a private statement of which technologies are applicable to the Security Statement. Internal systems are typically not "fair game" for third-party security researchers unless explicitly contracted for a penetration test or other security assessments.

- Legal Issues – if research is conducted illegally within an organization, or without proper consent, what are the legal ramifications for a researcher? This can also be true for compiled code when a researcher attempts to reverse engineer a product in order to reveal security flaws. Vendors have threated to sue security professionals if this occurs and is typically a dangerous slope to conduct research.

- Communication – a VDP should provide a clear vehicle for secure communications without repercussions for security researchers to communicate with an organization. Typically, this communication vehicle is publicly exposed and has rules governing submission and disclosure. These can include:

  - No public disclosure under a remediation (patch) is available

  - A timeline for discussions and when an extension may be required

- A potential bounty for following the guidelines and payment terms

- Rights to name vulnerability based on the flaw or other researcher-based criteria

- Escalation of Findings – an internal procedure should be in place to process any identified vulnerabilities and properly prioritize their remediation.

Unfortunately, not all researchers agree on these procedures, VDP guidelines, or timelines for public disclosure. Exceptions, negligence, vendor denial, and many other human traits lead to extreme deviations for these policies and procedures worldwide. Vulnerability disclosure can be managed responsibly, but unfortunately, vendors cannot always rely on the honest intent of the security researcher (or government).

CHAPTER 3

Threat Intelligence

Whenever an organization performs a risk assessment, they try to consider multiple variables based on the user, asset, criticality, location, and many technical criteria like hardening, exploits, vulnerabilities, risk surface, exposure, and maintenance. A complete risk assessment model is a daunting task to manually complete if you consider all the possible vectors and methodologies to actually quantify the risk.

In general, risk assessments start with a simple model (as shown in Figure 3-1) and each vector gets documented and a risk outcome assigned. When we are dealing with multiple risk vectors, the results can be averaged, summed, weighted, or used with other models to produce a final risk score. To make this process efficient and reliable, automation and the minimization of human interaction is of primary concern. Anytime human judgment is applied to a risk vector, the potential for deviations in the results is higher due to basic human opinions and errors. This implies that risk assessment models benefit the most when reliable and automated data is readily available for interpretation versus just user discretion and assignment.

© Morey J. Haber, Brad Hibbert 2018
M.J. Haber and B. Hibbert, *Asset Attack Vectors*,
https://doi.org/10.1007/978-1-4842-3627-7_3

Risk Matrix	Impact				
Likelihood	Negligible	Minor	Moderate	Significant	Severe
Very Likely	Low Medium	Medium	Medium High	High	High
Likely	Low	Low Medium	Medium	Medium High	High
Possible	Low	Low Medium	Medium	Medium High	Medium High
Unlikely	Low	Low Medium	Low Medium	Medium	Medium High
Very Likely	Low	Low	Low Medium	Medium	Medium

Figure 3-1. *Typical risk matrix*

When documenting risks for cyber security, the industry has several well-known standards we discussed previously from CVE to CVSS. In the latest revisions, these focus on the technical and environmental aspects of cyber security and more reliable overall scoring. Models such as CVSS have been designed to capture two distinct characteristics of the vulnerability. First, they provide a mechanism to communicate the inherent risk associated with the weakness in a "base" score. The model then enables an organization to adjust the risk base using an environmental and temporal modifier. The environmental modifier is used to adjust the risk for a specific organization by examining the vulnerability in terms of frequency and criticality of the assets for which it is found. The temporal modifier is used to adjust for the likelihood of the vulnerability actually being leveraged, which may change over time. Together these two modifiers can be implemented to account for specific environmental factors, exploits, criticality, and threat intelligence as a part of their risk assessment. Unfortunately, while these modifiers can help to determine the "real risk" associated with vulnerabilities to more appropriately prioritize risk and mobilize remediation activities, the reality is that many organizations do not actively and consistently utilize environmental and temporal scoring mechanisms due to complexity and time. It is, after all, a manual process to assign them to assets and vulnerabilities. In addition, limiting the risk analysis to only these elements does not take into consideration several other factors including, but not limited to:

- The existence and availability of the vulnerabilities in noncommercial exploit toolkits

- The successful leveraging of the vulnerabilities to breach companies in the wild

- The association of vulnerabilities to specific control objectives within regulatory mandates

- The likelihood and detection of a breach based on the behavior of the users, mitigating controls, and detection capabilities of the organization

For example, an application may have a vulnerability. It may have a CVSS score and have a security patch from the manufacturer, and the risk score is consistent when communicating the results. This operates as expected. User behavior aspects like application usage, vertical markets targeted for the vulnerability, zero-day exploits, etc., all represent threat intelligence data that must be considered as a part of your risk assessment in order to truly understand the threat.

As an example, consider the recent WannaCry outbreak based on EternalBlue and DoublePulsar. It represented the highest and most extreme risk from a vulnerability and exploit perspective. That was true from day one and is still true today. However, without Threat Intelligence, there is no gauge to understand if the actual threat to the organization is the same today as when it was propagating through corporate networks in 2017. The risk is the same (CVSS vulnerability score), but the actual threat is lower due to the kill switch discovered and implemented on the Internet to stop the wormable aspects of the ransomware. Traditional vulnerability assessment solutions do not take this into consideration and still provide the same score when the threat is actually much higher. The same is true for Meltdown and Spectre based on Intel Microcode. As of the writing of this book, the CVSS score is a 5.6 (out of 0 to 10), but the actual perceived threat is significantly higher. It then begs the question, is it hype, reality, or truly something to watch for the future? A RowHammer attack might actually be perceived as a bigger threat due the nature of its exploitation.

Threat Intelligence is more than just a data feed of user behavior, real-time threats in the wild, active exploits, and temporal data. It gains the highest value when it is merged with relevant information from your organization and your business vertical to provide a profile of the risk and threat: much like the sample risk matrix Impact versus Likelihood. Threat Intelligence helps define the Likelihood in the matrix based on activity in the wild and within other organizations, while traditional technical measurements define the Impact.

Threat intelligence with well-established methods for application, user, and environmental risk provides the foundation for enhancing vulnerability data. If you can calculate the risk of vulnerable applications, application usage (user behavior), and threat intelligence (exploits), all aspects of the risk can be reported in an automated and coherent fashion. This provides a perspective over time, based on real-world problems and the threats your users and assets face as they use information technology to perform their daily business tasks. Figure 3-2 illustrates this mapping from a sample environment. It illustrates Impact to Risk and asset vulnerabilities to known exploits (shown by numbers in parentheses). It is processed based on current temporal parameters to decide the highest risk (and threat) information for assets in your organization and provides a view that encompasses the requirements for threat intelligence.

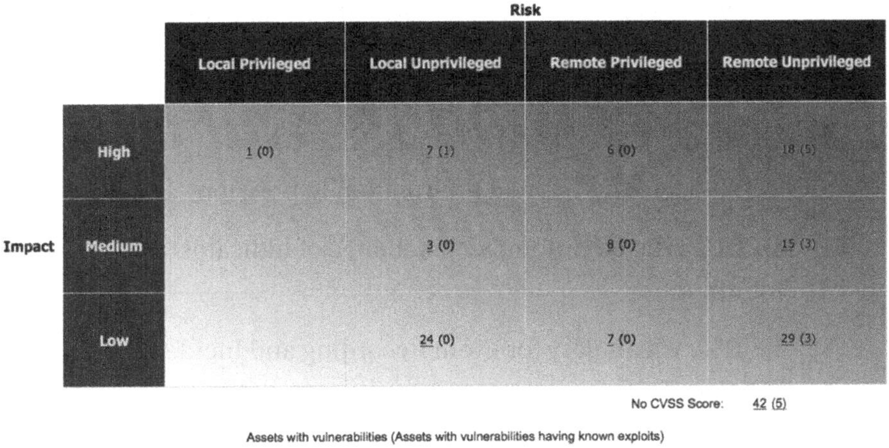

	Risk			
	Local Privileged	**Local Unprivileged**	**Remote Privileged**	**Remote Unprivileged**
High	1 (0)	7 (1)	6 (0)	18 (5)
Medium		3 (0)	8 (0)	15 (3)
Low		24 (0)	7 (0)	29 (3)

No CVSS Score: 42 (5)

Assets with vulnerabilities (Assets with vulnerabilities having known exploits)

Figure 3-2. *Risk Matrix for vulnerability data and exploits*

Vendors often bolt on or integrate with industry standard models and implement proprietary and sometimes patented threat analytics technologies that can be run stand alone or integrated into broader risk reporting and threat analysis solutions. When making security investments, it is important to understand how these solutions will fit into your overall security program. When examining vulnerability and risk information, plan ahead and know where and how this data may be used including a SWOT analysis. Perhaps consider how this information may be shared across solutions and potentially across organizations. While the focus of this book is not threat analytics or threat intelligence, it is important to acknowledge that there have been a lot of advancements in common frameworks, standards, and community projects that may be applicable to your environment and your vulnerability management program:

- CybOX – Cyber Observable eXpression

- CIF – Collective Intelligence Framework

- IODEF – Incident Object Description and Exchange Format

- MILE – Managed Incident Lightweight Exchange

- OpenIOC – Open Indicators of Compromise framework

- OTX – Open Threat Exchange

- STIX – Structured Threat Information Expression

- TAXII – Trusted Automated eXchange of Indicator Information

- VERIS – Vocabulary for Event Recording and Incident Sharing

It is clear that to achieve meaningful threat analytics, organizations need a core set of security tools to provide the foundational elements for analyzing the risk. It is important to understand that vulnerability visibility provides a wealth of information to drive better threat analytics. As well, threat analytics provides a wealth of information to drive a better understanding of risk and improved remediation response. When planning your vulnerability program, examine your entire security stack to understand where and how to integrate these feeds and to extract as much value and knowledge from your investment. The data should never be an island within the organization. Additionally, organizations should consider augmenting their internal data and threat sources with external sources and service providers to fill in gaps and help target "real" risk where possible. That is intelligence.

CHAPTER 4

Credential Asset Risks

How much money would you spend to secure your passwords from being stolen? If you actually could safeguard all your passwords, would you worry as much about a privileged breach as a vulnerability and exploit? I think the majority of executives and security professionals would ante up a reasonable sum to make this a reality, but protecting an asset is more than security patches and configuration. It is about the damage a compromised privileged account could cost an organization from a momentary perspective and a reputation perspective. If you need proof of this, consider the recent breaches at Equifax, Duke Energy (based on a third-party software vendor), and Yahoo. Each one of these affected the company's stock, executive bonuses, acquisition terms, and even the ability to do basic business like accepting payments in due terms.

A compromised privileged password does have a monetary value on the dark web for a threat actor to purchase but also has a price that can be associated with an organization in terms of risk.

What is the value and risk if that password is exposed and the contents it protects exposed to the wild? It can influence a vulnerability score as well. A database of personally identifiable information (PII) is quite valuable, and blueprints or trade secrets have an even higher value if sold to the right buyer (or government). My point is simple: privileged accounts have a value (some a very high value), and the problem is not

© Morey J. Haber, Brad Hibbert 2018
M.J. Haber and B. Hibbert, *Asset Attack Vectors*,
https://doi.org/10.1007/978-1-4842-3627-7_4

always securing them but rather identifying where they exist in the first place. So how do you discover privileged accounts and rate their risk? A vulnerability management solution is capable of doing this, and you just need to know where to look to get this information. It is a natural extension to any existing vulnerability management process if you are not already doing this.

A vulnerability assessment solution is capable of performing user enumeration for operating systems, applications, and databases. Within that data, the results should include accounts and their creation date, last login date, password age, and which groups they belong to—including administrators group or root. The results of these scans are generally ignored by vulnerability assessment teams but invaluable to security teams attempting to gauge the exposure of privileged accounts. If you can discover where privileged accounts exist, you can measure their risk and then monitor for their usage. Any inappropriate access can be highlighted using log management or a SIEM and properly escalated for investigation. This extends the processes and procedures we have been discussing and maximizes the usage of the data that is collected.

All privileged accounts are not equal. Some are worth very little and others a lot more based on risk. A domain administrator account is of higher value than a local administrator account with a unique password (although that may be good enough to leverage for future lateral movement). Treating every privileged account the same is not a good security practice for securing an asset. You could make the same argument for a database admin account versus a restricted account used with ODBC for database reporting. Both are privileged, but owning the database versus just extracting data is not the same. Yes, both could be a devastating attack vector responsible for a breach, but owning the database is the highest privilege you can get. Therefore, this could potentially allow a threat actor to maintain a persistent stealth presence (if cynical and crafty enough) until the organization identifies the breach.

So, we are now at academics. What should you do to take credentials and privileges to the next level as a part of your vulnerability management program:

- Identify crown jewels (sensitive data and systems) within the environment. This will help form the backbone for quantifying risk. If you do not have this currently mapped out, it is an exercise worth pursuing.

- Discover all of your privileged accounts using a vulnerability assessment solution, free solutions (there are plenty), or via a dedicated privileged solution.

- Map the discovered accounts to crown jewel assets. This can be done by hostname, subnets, AD queries, zones, or other logical groupings based on business functions. This could be assigned as Criticality in your vulnerability management solution.

- Measure the risk of the asset. This can be done using basic critical/high/medium/low, but it should also consider the crown jewels present and any other risk vectors like vulnerabilities. Each of these metrics will help weight the asset score. If you are looking for a standardized starting place, consider CVSS and Environmental metrics.

- Finally, overlay the discovered accounts. The risk of the asset will help determine how likely a privileged account can be compromised (via vulnerabilities) and help prioritize asset remediation outside of the account mapping.

In the real world, a database with sensitive information may have a few critical vulnerabilities from time to time, in between patch cycles, and be considered a critical risk when they are present regardless of the accounts identified. When patch remediation occurs, the asset may still be a high risk if privileged access is not managed and will drop in risk if privileges are session monitored and access controlled. Criticality can come from vulnerabilities or unrestricted, unmanaged, and undelegated access, in addition to attack vectors that have workable exploits. Therefore, privileged accounts, especially ones that are unprotected, have stale passwords, guessable passwords, or even default passwords represent another risk that must be mitigated for your assets.

CHAPTER 5

Vulnerability Assessment

Vulnerability assessment is a process to assess the risk posed by vulnerabilities across the wide range of computers, applications, and devices across an organization. The result of the vulnerability scan provides a sense of the potential attack surface that may be leveraged by hackers to gain illegitimate access to systems, applications, and data. To gather this information, organizations may opt to engage in active vulnerability scanning, passive vulnerability scanning, or use a mix of both techniques. When performing active vulnerability scanning, there are two methodologies used for performing vulnerability assessment regardless of patch assessment or compliance verification. One philosophy revolves around the need to penetrate a system to prove its vulnerability, and the other uses available information to postulate the status of the vulnerability. Long-standing discussions have centered on the merits of either type of scanning, as well as their potential liabilities. In summary, since a vulnerability assessment scanner can emulate an attack, each of these methods mirrors an attacker's style of compromising a host.

© Morey J. Haber, Brad Hibbert 2018
M.J. Haber and B. Hibbert, *Asset Attack Vectors*,
https://doi.org/10.1007/978-1-4842-3627-7_5

Active Vulnerability Scanning

Active vulnerability scanning requires that remote scanning software communicate and connect with a network node. At that point, the vulnerability scanner sends data to the network's nodes, examining the responses, and evaluates whether a specific node represents a weak point within the network. A network administrator can also use an active scanner to simulate an attack on the network, uncovering weaknesses a potential hacker would spot, or examine a node following an attack to determine how a hacker breached security. Active scanners can take action to autonomously resolve security issues, such as blocking a potentially dangerous IP address when integrated with other solutions.

Passive Scanners

Passive scanners can identify the active operating systems, applications, and ports throughout a network, monitoring network activity to determine the presence of vulnerabilities. They are typically implemented using port mirroring, inline network taps, or port spanning. While passive scanners can provide information about weaknesses, they can't take action to resolve security problems on there own because they are just monitoring network traffic. Passive scanners can check the current software and patch versions on networked devices by listening to their **unencrypted** traffic on a network and analyzing port and IP address communications. This indicates which devices are using software that presents a potential gateway for hackers and tools can cross-link this information to public databases containing lists of known threats and current patches. A network administrator can set passive scanners to run continuously or to operate at specified intervals. The primary intent is to "listen" passively to network traffic to isolate applications that may have vulnerabilities. In concept, this is similar to an IDS/IPS solution but in lieu of looking for an active threat, deduction is used to determine if their could be a potential risk. And, unlike IDS/IPS solutions, the solution is typically not inline with all network traffic but rather sniffing all network traffic.

Intrusive Vulnerability Scanning

Proponents of intrusive scanning cite the ubiquitous availability of attack scripts for vulnerability exploitation. They hypothesize that by attacking a system in the exact same manner as a potential attacker, more accurate results are best achieved. These can be categorized in many solutions as unsafe vulnerability checks or vulnerability assessment performed by a penetration testing solution.

Without a doubt, there are some merits to this smash-and-grab approach. By using a script to automate an attack, a penetration scenario where machine access is attainable proves that the device was vulnerable to an attack and ultimately could be compromised. However, utilizing this approach is problematic in that the audit trail is incomplete and potentially creates more questions than answers. For example, many attack scripts available on the Internet are flawed and can result in a false sense of security in the form of a false negative.

That is, they do not function as desired even if the system being targeted is truly exploitable. Unsuccessful penetration tests based on potentially bad scripts can give a false sense of security. Vulnerability assessment tools that use intrusive scripts can be harmful because they leave the system open to future attacks that would normally not be exploitable or worse, deny critical business functions from operating correctly. Smash-and-grab vulnerability testing has a propensity to disable services for the duration of the attack. This means that while a service is under attack, that service may not be available for its normal use and an entire network can be immobilized; blue screened; or worse, the attack could penetrate the network and create a new risk surface for real attacks.

Finally, perhaps the biggest argument against smash-and-grab testing is that it creates a corrupt testing environment. By directly performing attacks against a system being audited, the attack script can push the system into an unknown state – or completely disable it – making the remote system useless for further testing and virtually eliminating the possibility of attaining detailed vulnerability reports against this device from future tests. Don't get me wrong, penetration test tools are great, but they take time and expertise to use correctly, they can leave the target systems in an unable state, and they only cover a small portion of known vulnerabilities because they have to possess reliable working exploits. For most commercial penetration testing tools, that is about 10% of all vulnerabilities published for Microsoft Windows operating systems in the last several years. Finally, vulnerabilities assessment audits that are "unsafe" can do everything from account lockouts to leaving the resource vulnerable to other attack vectors after an assessment. This makes intrusive scanning less than desirable on production systems due their risks.

Nonintrusive Scanning

Disciplined attackers often chose to get as much information about a target as possible, using deductive logic to pinpoint potential weaknesses within an organization and information technology assets. Proponents of this stealth and smooth caper methodology rely on the wealth of information from networked systems and infer an even larger amount of information by making logical connections and assumptions based on the available data. This includes everything from social engineering to knowing the applications and vendors a business relies on. With this information, known vulnerabilities and weakness are easy targets for the attacker to attempt an exploit.

In contrast to intrusive scanning techniques, information technology administrators can utilize noninvasive or nonintrusive tests to locate potentially exploitable systems before they become problematic. By performing noninvasive tests, companies can avoid disruption of service while a comprehensive vulnerability assessment is being performed. Attackers utilize comparable techniques to gently probe for vulnerabilities without creating systematic downtime and potentially setting off IPS, IDS, and firewall alert sensors. Organizations can employ the same nonintrusive technology to gather large amounts of information, and follow a best practice dissection of vulnerability data to determine the risk to an environment. This process is often repeated in cycles to further refine and reinforce the findings. Likewise, the same process is used to verify that remediation efforts were successful, and the vulnerability is no longer a threat. By getting a clear picture of the complete architecture, a business can better identify weaknesses in the network, in corporate policies, and proactively prevent intrusions and business interruptions.

Unquestionably, nonintrusive scanning offers quantifiable benefits and dramatically less risk than intrusive scanning. Most organizations are ill-equipped to properly manage an intrusive penetration test scenario, especially those without replicated test networks. The potential damage created by intrusive scanning could outweigh the benefits of an actual detection if the auditors are not careful. Furthermore, the comprehensive audit and remediation trail created by nonintrusive scanning will create a reliable and hardened infrastructure in a much quicker timeframe. Quantifiable and repeatable results will come with a definitive action plan to correct the vulnerability and assist with any patch assessment and compliance requirements.

The bottom line in opting for nonintrusive testing is quite simple. Please consider this statement, ***Except in extreme cases, locating a vulnerability and fixing it is far more important than proving its exploitability***. As a result, administrators and engineers can defend their critical assets without putting them in the line of fire from potentially disruptive tests. By giving network support staff timely and accurate information about existing vulnerabilities, remediation time can be vastly improved, and accurate security states assessed without creating any unnecessary additional security risks or business interruptions. As with all security processes and regulatory compliances, this should be repeated often to keep administrators abreast of the organization's current network vulnerability status and threat level. Nonintrusive vulnerability assessment scanning has become the industry standard for vulnerability management programs and regulations worldwide based on its philosophy and reliability to identify and report on any potential risks within an organization.

Vulnerability Scanning Limitations and Shortcomings

While vulnerability scanners can facilitate network security tasks, they can't replace the expertise of trained personnel. Scanners are capable of returning false positives, indicating a weakness where none exist, and false negatives, in which the scanner overlooks a security risk. Qualified personnel need to carefully check the data their scanners return to detect erroneous results. A scanner's threat assessment is based solely on its database of known risks, and a scanner can't extrapolate upon the data it uncovers to conceive of new and novel methods a hacker may use to attack the network.

One important downside associated with noninvasive scanning is in the way the information is analyzed after performing a scan. Intrusive systems provide immediate results after a targeted attack; successful or nonsuccessful. Hackable or not. Nonintrusive solutions require the results to be correlated and the status interpolated based on the retrieved data. A solid reporting, analysis, and remediation process is needed to turn the results into functional business benefits. Scanning tools that simply provide an unmanageable list of vulnerabilities without proper details and corrective actions tend to complicate the process. For this reason, the act of assessing vulnerabilities is just one of many steps within a proper and robust vulnerability management program. Just knowing the information is not enough.

Finally, vulnerability scanning can potentially take up a considerable amount of bandwidth, potentially slowing the network's performance. When targeting every network node, with tens of thousands of checks, and multiple targets simultaneously, bandwidth consumption adds up linearly. Once vulnerabilities are found, they must be prioritized and dealt with— remediated or shielded from potential attacks. From this perspective, the vulnerability management program within an organization must be orchestrated with other internal processes including patch and configuration management (typically managed by operational teams) to utilize network resources appropriately since a large patch deployment and assessment at the same time could potentially cripple the network. This then becomes an excercise in proper planning and team cooperation.

CHAPTER 6

Configuration Assessment

In recent years there has been an increasing number of legislated regulatory mandates with which organizations must comply with to prove the confidentiality, integrity, and availability of information stored in their systems and provided through external parties. After reading various white papers, websites, and other articles that loosely use the terms "PCI, HIPAA, SOX, CIS, NIST, ISO, CIS, COBiT, FISMA, and FDCC," heads can start spinning. Like many security professionals, we are not auditors or a lawyers but are constantly bombarded with these acronyms on a weekly basis. Feeling dizzy?

The acronyms listed above can be loosely broken down into three categories, or sets of instructions, which help organizations meet their compliance and security goals: Regulations, Frameworks, and Benchmarks. In some cases, the lines between the three can be blurry, but understanding their intent and relationship to one another can help you understand how these pieces can fit together to support an overall security and compliance program.

© Morey J. Haber, Brad Hibbert 2018
M.J. Haber and B. Hibbert, *Asset Attack Vectors*,
https://doi.org/10.1007/978-1-4842-3627-7_6

Regulations

Regulations are legal restrictions created, governed, and publicized by government administrative agencies. Regulations typically do not prescribe detail on how to perform, configure, or manage IT systems, but they clearly indicate the goals a security and compliance program must meet. Examples of these regulations that we will discuss in a later chapter include Sarbanes-Oxley, HIPAA, GLBA, Basel II, and GDPR. To complicate the definition of regulations, there are standards like PCI DSS. Many government and private entities are now required to be in compliance with the Payment Card Industry (PCI) Data Security Standard (DSS) specification. This standard outlines a set of international security requirements for safeguarding credit cardholder data. To comply with PCI DSS, organizations must also perform steps as known as validation requirements, which include a requirement of quarterly vulnerability scanning by a PCI approved scanning vendor. This standard blurs the line between a regulation and mandates and is not legislated by a government but rather the credit card industry itself. This is where people typically start getting dizzy.

Frameworks

Frameworks provide a defined support structure in which a project can be organized and developed. Frameworks are designed to provide a complete security program for an organization. These frameworks may be implemented to support the goals of multiple regulations, and often recommend that hardening best practices, or benchmarks, be used for technical protections. Examples of frameworks include ITIL, CobiT and COSO, NIST 800-53, and ISO 17799 / 27002. It is important to note that frameworks like NIST and ISO are often incorrectly referenced as regulations due to their inclusion in contracts or other standards. When they do, they become regulations, but as stand-alone material, they are not. A contract or other vehicle enables there enforcement beyond their stated best practices and security requirments. Dizzier yet?

Benchmarks

Benchmarks are often used to measure and monitor common elements related to the security and IT infrastructure known as "general computer controls." Benchmarks outline a set of criteria (some of which may be mandatory), voluntary guidelines, and best practices. Whereas frameworks offer nonspecific goals, benchmarks offer prescriptive guidance over tests and settings that should be used to harden the IT environment and protect IT assets against specific risks. This is where the dizziness subsides. Examples of standards include vendor and customer best practices from CIS, SANS, and DISA checklists. These are the settings to actually make your systems more resilient based on configuration settings. Table 6-1 outlines the leading benchmarks from recognized authorities and popular vendors.

It should be noted that not all hardening checklists and benchmark tests are equal. There are various use cases for each from public facing with nonsensitive information to mission critical with extremely sensitive data. Depending on your environment, you will need to select the correct one and ensure that hardening your host does not break the application or mission integrity. As a rule of thumb, always harden a resource as tight as possible but still provide usability, management, and disaster recovery use cases to operate within your internal protocols.

Configuration Assessment Tools

Consider you are a major airline, corporation, or even a local government with thousands of systems that should be identical from a configuration perspective. These could be airline check-in kiosks, a call center handling support calls, or a state or local government agency with a standard image for desktops and laptops. How do (or did) you verify the configuration of these assets on a regular basis?

Table 6-1. Configuration Hardening and Testing Benchmarks

Organization	Name	Public Website URL	Coverage
CIS	Center for Internet Security	https://www.cisecurity.org/cis-benchmarks/	Operating Systems (Multiple), Server Software, Cloud Providers, Mobile Devices, Network Devices, Desktop Software and Multi-Function Devices
	Description	A global community of cyber security experts collaborating on benchmark hardening guidelines for safeguarding the most prevalent technology implementations. It is important to note that many vendors like Red Hat and Oracle, and security organizations like SANS, reference CIS for their own best practices.	
NIST	National Institute of Standards and Technology	https://www.nist.gov	

(continued)

Table 6-1. (continued)

Organization	Name	Public Website URL	Coverage
FDCC (Obsolete)	Federal Desktop Core Configuration	`https://www.nist.gov/programs-projects/federal-desktop-core-configuration-fdcc`	Desktop Operating Systems (Microsoft Windows XP and Vista)
	Description	The Federal Desktop Core Configuration (FDCC) is an OMB-mandated security configuration. The FDCC currently exists for Microsoft Windows Vista and XP operating system software.	
USGCB	United States Government Configuration Baseline	`https://usgcb.nist.gov`	Operating Systems (Microsoft Windows XP, 7, and Vista and Red Hat 5 Desktop), and Microsoft Browsers, Firewalls, and Virtual Machines
	Description	The purpose of the USGCB initiative is to create security configuration baselines (benchmarks) for Information Technology products widely deployed across the federal agencies. The standard is a federal government-wide initiative that provides guidance to agencies on what should be done to improve and maintain effective configuration settings focusing primarily on security.	

(continued)

61

Table 6-1. (*continued*)

Organization	Name	Public Website URL	Coverage
STIGS (DISA)	Security Technical Implementation Guides	https://iase.disa.mil/stigs/Pages/index.aspx	Operating Systems (Multiple), Server Software, Cloud (private and public) Providers, Mobile Devices, Network (Infrastructure) Solutions, Desktop Software and Multi-Function Devices, and Applications
	Description	The STIGs are the configuration (benchmark) standards for United States Department of Defense (DOD) Information Assurance (IA) devices and systems. The STIGs contain technical guidance to "lock down" information systems and software that might otherwise be vulnerable to a malicious computer attack due to poor configurations.	

(*continued*)

Table 6-1. (*continued*)

Organization	Name	Public Website URL	Coverage
MS	Microsoft	https://technet.microsoft.com/en-us/ solutionaccelerators/cc835245.aspx	Operating Systems (Microsoft Desktops and Servers) and Microsoft Applications
	Description	Microsoft provides ready-to-deploy policies and configuration packs that are tested and fully supported. Baselines are based on Microsoft Security Guide recommendations and industry best practices, to manage configuration drift, address compliance requirements, and reduce security threats.	
VMware	VMware	https://www.vmware.com/security/ hardening-guides.html	VMware Hypervisors (VSphere, NSX, and vRealize)
	Description	VMware Security Hardening Guides provide prescriptive guidance for customers on how to deploy and operate VMware products in a secure manner. Guides for vSphere provide checklists and scripts for baseline classifications and risk assessment.	

While the concept may sound simple, checking all of these systems manually is completely unfeasible and using agent-based technology or dedicated configuration compliance scanning appliances were the only choices for verifying individual system settings on a regular basis. These solutions were traditionally very expensive and could be labor intensive to install, configure, and maintain. A rather simple problem for configuration assessment became a complex problem to implement.

Some vendors like Microsoft have released their own solutions for their own software. Microsoft released the Security Compliance Manager (SCM) back in 2010 that allows you to import Security Configuration Benchmarks from Microsoft's own Best Practice Guidelines (or other third-party solutions) and review them using an interactive user interface.

The SCM interface allows you to highlight an operating system or application and review individual recommended security configurations settings by system role. A user can go into any of the settings and change the settings to meet their corporate policy. While this procedure may sound tedious, a user only needs to do it once for each configuration template they need to follow. For the most part, corporate policies match these settings and are similar to standards published by CIS, DISA (in terms of STIGS), and USGCB (NIST). Only minor modifications are normally needed for your organization, and if you are unsure of which settings to choose, Microsoft has given clear guidance into each value in order for you to make an intelligent decision regarding the proper default value.

Once you have completed all of the edits, you are now only a few clicks away from using an agentless network scanner or local SCAP-compliant agent from performing a configuration compliance assessment. This is something that had not been possible before the last few years using an open standard. Microsoft has added to SCM that ability to export all of the settings to a certified SCAP OVAL CAB file. After you save the file, you can import the benchmark into an automated configuration assessment for asset verification.

SCAP

The Security Content Automation Protocol (SCAP, pronounced S-cap) is a suite of open standards that when referenced together, deliver an automated vulnerability management, measurement, and policy compliance evaluation for network assets. The first version of the suite specification focused on standardizing communication of endpoint related data and to provide a standardized approach to maintaining the security of enterprise systems. It provides a means to identify, express, and measure security data in standardized ways such that products from multiple vendors can consume or produce SCAP content for correlation of security information. Each standard, within the SCAP specification, is individually maintained and references specific component versions. For example, version 1.0 of SCAP includes the following standards and versions: XCCDF 1.1.4, OVAL 5.3. CCE 5, CPE 2.2, CVE (no version), and CVSS 2. As the specification has evolved, later versions include new components and revisions to each specification. Below is a summary of each of the revisions since the initial release:

- Version 1.1 of specification expands the specification to include Open Checklist Interactive Language (OCIL, pronounced O-sil) and changes specification to adhere to version 5.8 of the OVAL specification. OCIL is a new component that defines a framework for expressing a set of questions a user must answer and corresponding procedures to interpret responses to these queries. OCIL was developed as a supplement for IT security checklists and is not restricted to IT security alone. It allows an assessment to occur, and vital information entered that not can be observed electronically (i.e., Is there a lock on the server rack door?). This information is then stored with the results to obtain a better picture of the security of the assets.

- Version 1.2 enhances the specification with new and upgraded capabilities including a Common Configuration Scoring System (CCSS), Asset Identification and Asset Reporting Format (ARF), expands the data stream model, and offers options secure and sign SCAP content and results using the Trust Model for Security Automation Data (TMSAD). It also updates support for new versions of included specifications including the Open Vulnerability and Assessment Language (OVAL), Common Platform Enumeration (CPE), and Extensible Configuration Checklist Description Format (XCCDF).

- Version 1.3 is an incremental improvement to the specification and now includes addition components for Asset Identification (AI) 1.1 and Software Identification (SWID) Tags 2015. The AI specification provides the necessary parameters to uniquely identify assets based on known identifiers or information about the resource. The SWID specification, defined by the ISO/IEC 19770-2:2015 standard, provides an important step to inventorying software and provides a transparent way for organizations to track the software installed on their assets. This is in addition to the incremental version changes for other established components.

The two most common implementations of SCAP (so far) are for vulnerability assessment and configuration compliance. Using OVAL definitions, a SCAP compatible (certified) solution can ingest an XML file with vulnerability signatures or configuration benchmark checks and perform a local or network-based assessment for systems that are noncompliant. The product will store the results of the scan in OVAL results and XCCDF results format and have references to CVE, CCE, CPE, and CVSS in the result XML file using standard nomenclature to describe the finding. Essentially, this process defines the check types and definitions using OVAL, and how those checks should be applied and reported using XCCDF, and that the contents of the results all contain the same parameters regardless of product. This makes interoperability between SCAP certified products possible for OVAL content creation to reporting on the end results and storage in a database.

CHAPTER 7

Risk Measurement

IT security is clearly the key business issue of today. The words "threat" and "attack" are commonly used as if they connote some monolithic evil that awaits every organization's infrastructure. In fact, there are many kinds of threats and many modes of attack, and they can originate both inside and outside the organization.

Vulnerabilities in your IT environment can wreak havoc on your business operations. These common weaknesses can be exploited by a variety of external and internal threats, from malicious individuals and "hacktivists," to criminal hacking syndicates and nation-states. The need to proactively address vulnerabilities is accentuated by requirements for always-on business services, cloud-based computing, and regulatory compliance. It's therefore critical to design and implement a comprehensive security management strategy to ensure business continuity and minimize the overall risk across your organization. And vulnerability management is a critical variable in the calculation of overall risk.

$$RISK = IMPACT \times PROBABILITY$$

where:

- Risk: Extent to which an organization is threatened by a potential event.

- Impact: Magnitude of harm that would be expected that results from the consequences of an event.

- Probability: The likelihood that a threat event will occur.

© Morey J. Haber, Brad Hibbert 2018
M.J. Haber and B. Hibbert, *Asset Attack Vectors*,
https://doi.org/10.1007/978-1-4842-3627-7_7

The process of a risk assessment is used to prioritize the risks based on the probability and impact of an event. However, to get a clear understanding of "Impact" and "Probability," we need to dig a little deeper, and this is where vulnerability management can help.

The impact of an event itself can be diverse and can include:

- Proprietary information loss

- Loss of system availability

- Loss or corruption of data or applications

- Loss of productivity

- Regulatory non-compliance

- Damaged customer relations / brand image

The overall impact of an event is a function of the criticality of the asset and the changing threat landscape. The criticality of the asset is determined by the applications or other services, which rely on its existence and proper functioning. The threat is a measure of potential danger to an asset from sources that may regard it as a worthy target, based on user-defined criteria and/or system role. The threat itself is the result of multiple factors including the threat source, the likelihood of an attack, and the probability of success. When calculating the actual threat, organizations can use a mix of qualitative and quantitative inputs. One good indicator of threats is looking at the experience and statistics for the likelihood of an attack. Here security teams should look at how assets in the corporate environment are being exposed to threats and what type of threats challenge their integrity to perform business functions and protect data. Security teams should also measure how open a system is to an attack. This exposure can be based on the number of open ports, shares, services, and users a host contains; the lack of protection such as a firewall or anti-virus solution; and the presence of any illegal or unnecessary applications that have been installed.

The probability side of the risk equation is a function of vulnerabilities and risk mitigation activities. Vulnerabilities represent the quantity and severity of vulnerabilities discovered throughout the organization's IT environment. Measurements are based on such factors as a lack of proper patch maintenance on a host or compliance issues related to current corporate security policy and best practices. Mitigations are the controls that have been employed to eliminate or reduce the risks associated with vulnerabilities.

There are several Risk Management Frameworks discussed in a later chapter that implement these concepts of risk calculation and integrate them with an overall risk management program of an organization. Based on the technical translation to business terms, organizations can have a direct method for understanding the asset's security posture from raw technical data to business impact. For now, a simple analogy can provide a better understanding of this approach to risk management. Consider each asset in your environment to be a castle, as shown in Figure 7-1. Its construction, defenses, location, and treasure are all factors for an impending attack. The castle walls protect an inner sanctum containing a treasure of gold (data, business operations, etc.). Armies (hackers, worms, etc.) are attempting to breach the castle walls and penetrate the inner sanctum to get the gold or disrupt the castle's normal operations. In this case, the security vectors would be defined as:

Vulnerabilities indicate how easy it is for the inner sanctum to be breached and how simple it would be to gain access to the gold.

- Attacks are represented by arrows, bombs, and breach attempts on the walls and inner sanctum.

- Exposures reveal the extent to which the castle walls and openings can be attacked, and how poorly the castle's periphery is protected.

- Threats are the lurking armies on the hills surrounding the castle, and whom are priming for attack.

71

Sitting atop these three vectors is the essential Criticality of the castle itself; in other words, how valuable is the castle and inner sanctum to the empire (your organization). The data contained within can be measured by Infonomics. That is the monetary value of data as an asset to the organization regardless of it is used internally, stolen, sold, or bartered.

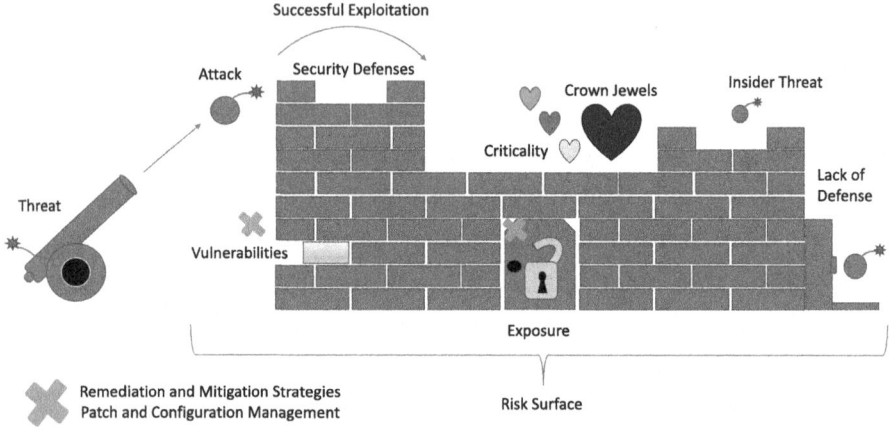

Figure 7-1. *Risk Management displayed as a castle*

Now as you can see, vulnerabilities are a fundamental element when examining and calculating the overall risk associated with your crown jewels. Now shoot your finger in the air. Does this feel similar to how you're attacking your vulnerabilities? If so, you're not alone. You've done a scan and found thousands of vulnerabilities. Now what? You need to quickly pinpoint your most critical threats, and patch the most vulnerable systems – but how?

Not all vulnerabilities are created equal. And finding out which ones pose the greatest danger requires digging much deeper than their CVSS scores. Knowing whether exploits exist, which ones can be exploited remotely or by someone with privilege, whether active malware is using it, and if it can be fixed via a patch or configuration change, are all answers you need before determining risk. Let's take a look at how we can score and compare vulnerabilities across systems and across companies to ensure that risks are appropriately prioritized and remediation tasks appropriately assigned. The basis for this starts with industry standards to describe a vulnerability.

CVE

Common Vulnerabilities and Exposures (CVE) is a program launched by MITRE, a nonprofit sponsored by the federal government, in 1999 to identify and catalog vulnerabilities in software (application and operating systems) and firmware. Organizations can use the vulnerability source to improve their security. The word "common" is the most important portion of this standard. It allows you to know that fundamentally every tool, article, and solution is discussing the same underlying vulnerability.

Organizations identify information systems affected by announced software flaws including potential vulnerabilities resulting from those flaws and report this information to designated organizational personnel with information security responsibilities. Security relevant software updates include, for example, patches, service packs, hotfixes, and anti-virus signatures. Organizations also address flaws discovered during security assessments, continuous monitoring, incident response activities, and system error handling. Related to the CVE database is the Common Weakness Enumeration framework, which provides a common way to report types of vulnerabilities in software. Organizations take advantage of available resources such as the Common Weakness Enumeration (CWE) or Common Vulnerabilities and Exposures (CVE) databases in remediating flaws discovered in organizational information systems.

CVSS

The most common vulnerability scoring system used by vendors and regulatory initiatives is CVSS (the Common Vulnerability Scoring System). It provides a vendor-agnostic, open scoring standard to model vulnerability severity and provides guidance on prioritization of remediation efforts. The basic metrics allows for rating a vulnerability based on the severity of its components like Access Vector, Access Complexity, Authentication Method, etc.

Key components outside of the base scoring for CVSS are the Temporal Metrics. These represent three-time dependent descriptors for the vulnerability. They are:

1. Exploitability provides a measure of how complex the process is to exploit the vulnerability in a specific target system. This is vulnerability specific.

2. Remediation Level provides a measurable level of an available solution. This can be everything from an official security fix to no solution is, and will be, available.

3. Report Confidence measures the confidence in the existence of the vulnerability, as well as the credibility of its existence.

Please note, temporal scores can only **lower** an overall CVSS score, not raise it.

The Exploitability metric is the most important in this calculation. It provides guidance using four different criteria:

1. Unproven: No exploit code is yet available (time dependent).

2. Proof of Concept: Proof of concept exploit code is available at the time of scoring.

3. Functional: Functional exploit code is available.

4. High: Exploitable by functional mobile autonomous code or no exploit required and can be a manual trigger.

This metric allows for a vulnerability to be graded using the CVSS scoring system based on the possibility of exploitation. So why does this matter?

The vulnerability risk score is not enough to prioritize remediation efforts for your environment. The base calculation fails to take into consideration whether someone (or something) can easily exploit the vulnerability, how difficult it will be to mitigate the risk, and real-world confidence at any point in time that the reported vulnerability is credible especially related to assets contained within your infrastructure. This is why CVSS Temporal Metrics are so important and why the Exploitability Metric is crucial for prioritization efforts. It takes into consideration not only the vulnerability severity, but also how real the threat is for exploitation in your environment at a given time.

STIG

Security Technical Implementation Guides (almost always referred to as their acronym – STIGs and pronounced like the character from Top Gear) are the configuration standards for the United States Department of Defense (DOD) Information Assurance (IA) and IA enabled assets and systems. The STIGs contain technical guidance to harden information systems and software that might otherwise be vulnerable to a malicious computer attack based on their default or common settings. They are Benchmarks.

STIGs exist as documentation but also for select platforms and applications, scripts, and INF files to harden the application based on its use cases and mission. For example, different STIGS are available for a Windows Server being used as a web server versus a domain controller and if the resource is on a public network or classified network.

Each recommendation within a specific STIG for hardening comes with a risk severity Category that allows for measuring the risk of a resource based on the number of compliant settings versus noncompliant. Category I violations are unacceptable, and the device needs mitigation immediately, or it should not be allowed to operate on a DOD network.

Vulnerability management vendors have translated these settings into configuration benchmark settings and allow for automated testing of STIGs in order to document and determine compliance. It is important to note, not ever STIG can be automated, and not every platform allows for electronic checks. This requires staff to check STIG requirements manually and may require them to complete forms manually using an OCIL compliant tool for certification as a part of the SCAP standard. Figure 7-2 contains an example of a vulnerability management solutions output from a STIG-compliant assessment against a Windows server used for certification.

Scan Summary

Computer Name:	Serenity.Cricklewood.local
Target Platform:	Windows Server 2012 R2 Datacenter
Benchmark Title:	Windows Server 2012 / 2012 R2 Domain Controller Security Technical Implementation Guide
Benchmark Platform:	cpe:/o:microsoft:windows_server_2012:-
Profile:	I - Mission Critical Classified
Scan Time:	04/04/2018 09:26:25

	Items	
Description	Passed	Failed
1 Unsupported Service Packs	1	0
2 Display Shutdown Button	1	0
3 NTFS Requirement	1	0
4 Legal Notice Display	0	1
5 Caching of logon credentials	0	1
6 Anonymous shares are not restricted	0	1
7 Bad Logon Attempts	0	1
8 Bad Logon Counter Reset	0	1
9 Lockout Duration	0	1
10 User Right - Act as part of OS	1	0
11 Maximum Password Age	1	0

Figure 7-2. *Sample SCAP output from a STIG benchmark assessment*

This data can, therefore, prioritize the asset's risk based on its configuration and is used in conjunction with vulnerability assessment results for the operating system, platform, and application to determine its overall security posture.

OVAL

One of the challenges with vulnerability assessments is that each and every vendor has a different signature (audit) for the same vulnerability and CVE. This produces some false positives, and some false negatives when in fact you would expect the detection to be the same regardless of vendor. Most of the time everything works but from time to time, there are discrepancies; this is where OVAL (Open Vulnerability and Assessment Language) comes in.

OVAL was originally introduced by MITRE and now is managed by the CIS (Center for Internet Security). It is a foundational part of the SCAP (Security Content Automation Protocol) and is an open, free-to-use standard for writing vulnerability and configuration-hardening signatures. By design, any tool can use OVAL checks to detect a vulnerability with the same criteria and expect the same results. It essentially levels the playing field between all vendors to look for vulnerabilities but unfortunately stops there due to the lack of industry-wide support across all technologies. Vulnerability management vendors continue to differentiate their solutions by using proprietary checks and scan engines use OVAL to supplement their assessments when regulatory compliance initiatives require them to present input and output in SCAP format. While OVAL provides standardization for measurement of vulnerabilities, its lack of features, platform support, and technical checks leave it primarily used by DOD clients and related government entities for certification.

IAVA

An Information Assurance Vulnerability Alert (IAVA) is an announcement of a computer application software or operating system vulnerability notification in the form of alerts, bulletins, and technical advisories identified by the DOD and DISA. These selected vulnerabilities are a mandatory baseline that must be remediated across all DOD networks and assets. The United States Cyber Command analyzes every published vulnerability and determines if it is necessary or beneficial to the DOD to release an IAVA. The goal is to secure military assets using the same communications and scoring values and translate each risk to its commercial counterparts using CVE, CVSS, and other public standards.

Just like CVSS, IAVA's contain a risk score that has been determined by the DOD. Based on assets used within the military, these scores can vary from their commercial counterparts to raise awareness or effect prioritization.

As a final note, IAVAs are typically not used outside of the United States' DOD and supporting contractors. If your organization has a requirement to produce IAVA-based reports per contractor or subcontract, you will need to explicitly license additional technology from your vulnerability management vendor to enable these features and the appropriate reporting modules.

CHAPTER 8

Vulnerability States

Vulnerability assessment identifies security risks on assets in the form of software vulnerabilities, missing patches, and configuration weaknesses. It can be used for everything from operating systems and software applications, to Web applications and virtual environments. The data is graded in the form of vulnerability risks. There are many standards for reporting those risks and even more regulatory standards worldwide that grade the results and set service-level agreements for remediation and prioritization.

The act of performing a vulnerability assessment has evolved tremendously since its inception in the late 1990s. Originally, devices were assessed via TCP/IP and network-scanning technology using sequential lists of targets and IP addresses. Today, the technology has evolved to use distributed-state machines, targeting using advanced connectors for technologies like Amazon AWS or VMware, and the ability to assess targets deeply using agent technologies and a variety of credential mechanisms.

An unfortunate absence with all this evolution is that the rating mechanisms (barring CVSS environmental scores) are based on the severity of the vulnerability itself, and unaffected by mitigating controls or criticality of the asset to the services and business processes it provides. Considerations such as how the vulnerability was found and what it actually means to the asset have been ignored.

Take, for example, CVE-2014-160 with a CVSS score of only 5.0. Many of you are familiar with it as Heartbleed. That historic newsmaking vulnerability can be present on many different types of systems, but all of

© Morey J. Haber, Brad Hibbert 2018
M.J. Haber and B. Hibbert, *Asset Attack Vectors*,
https://doi.org/10.1007/978-1-4842-3627-7_8

them have the same risk score. The flaw can be found within a Web service or a local system library, but regardless of whether it is active in memory and potentially exploitable or inactive, sitting unused in a library on the disk, vulnerability assessment solutions will report both as critical despite its industry standard score. The key difference here is *active processes.* Traditional network-based vulnerability assessment solutions do not take into consideration the different "states" of a vulnerability.

This section discusses three potential states for vulnerabilities that are identified with vulnerability assessment solutions and the business ramifications of remediation strategies.

Vulnerability Risk Based on State

Traditional vulnerability assessment solutions rate their findings by risk. Advanced solutions incorporate input provided by end users to rate the risk to the asset (or IP address). Business-ready solutions aggregate that information into logical groups and then rate the entire group compared with others in the organization to gain a perspective of one logical grouping versus another. This view can be used for everything from prioritization to service-level agreements. The fundamental risk-scoring mechanisms within any product follow this methodology:

- **Proprietary Risk Score**—a vendor-defined score that is either numeric or graduated (for example, using terminology such as low, medium, high, critical, or extreme). This mechanism saw its inception at the dawn of vulnerability assessment scanning, before standards evolved to enable all vendors to score vulnerabilities the same way.

- **CVSS**—The Common Vulnerability Scoring System, first developed in 2005 to address the shortcomings of vendor-based rating systems and create a protocol (a mathematical vector calculation) to define the actual meaning of a vulnerability in a standardized fashion. The standard has evolved to include various criteria for temporal and environmental factors. Its scoring calculation continues to drive debate in the industry, and the latest draft versions attempt to address modern technologies and mitigation techniques as a part of the calculation.

- **PCI DSS**—The Payment Card Industry (PCI) Data Security Standard (DSS) includes a modified version of CVSS to calculate risk scoring for PCI ROCs (Records of Compliance). This modified version weights factors such as Denial of Service within the scoring framework to address problems like decreased site availability and outage versus the actual loss of cardholder data.

- **IAVA**—The Information Assurance Vulnerability Alert is not a scoring mechanism in itself. IAVA is an announcement by the United States Cyber Command of a vulnerability of application software or operating systems that should be addressed by participating government agencies. The Defense Information Systems Agency developed and maintains an IAVA database to ensure a positive control mechanism for system administrators to receive, acknowledge, and comply with system vulnerability alert notifications. Within the IAVA database, and vulnerabilities are given a Category Score of I to IV to rate the risk. The DISA assigns the values, but in general, those values follow suit with CVSS recommendations.

81

The rating mechanisms above are fundamentally important to understand because they ensure that, no matter what a vulnerability looks like on an asset, it is graded the same way. For example, on a Microsoft Windows asset, if the system has multiple Internet browsers installed, and only one of them is being used by end users, the vulnerability assessment score for all three browsers is exactly the same regardless of whether a browser is actively being used, is dormant and just installed on the asset, or was shipped as a part of the operating system and not even fully installed.

Vulnerability management guidelines require that all critical vulnerabilities be remediated. In this case, we have a clear prioritization of the "in-use" browser but cannot accurately quantify the risk metric in any of the standard vulnerability reporting systems currently available.

In addition, current risk scoring mechanisms fail (outside of manually excluding a vulnerability or modifying CVSS scores per asset and vulnerability) to address the case of vulnerabilities that have been properly mitigated by having associated services disabled. That is a valid mitigation technique, but a vulnerability assessment solution cannot necessarily differentiate between the potential of a vulnerability and the flaw actively running on a system.

Therefore, vulnerability assessment techniques must evolve to compensate for the state of an asset and the applications being used, versus just checking for files, registry keys, banners, and installed packages. This leads us to a strategic future for vulnerability assessment technologies and the three potential states for a vulnerability.

The Three Vulnerability States

As mentioned earlier, there are three quantifiable states of a vulnerability on any given asset:

- **Active**—The flaw is actively running on the asset and consuming resources. An active vulnerability means successful exploitation would compromise the system (depending on the limitations of the vulnerability).

- **Dormant**—The flaw resides on the host but is not actively consuming any resources at all. A dormant vulnerability might be anything from a disabled service to an installed application that is not being used at a specific time. If the application is executed, the vulnerability is no longer dormant and would be reclassified as active for the duration of its runtime.

- **Carrier**—This flaw is by far the most nebulous classification because it contains a "what if" component. A carrier's binaries are on an asset but not configured—*yet*—to be either dormant or active. An additional step is required to change the state, but there is no need for external media or an Internet connection. For example, adding features to a Windows asset can be done with proper credentials and without any external resources. Once the configuration change has occurred, a vulnerability may be present in a dormant or active state until remediation occurs.

Not one of these concepts is addressed during a vulnerability assessment, although basic common sense tells us—correctly—that active or potentially exploitable vulnerabilities should be remediated first. Current standards do not take the three states into consideration when reporting, so it is up to a security vendor's proprietary implementation to make these workable models for a successful implementation. In that way, the status quo is very reminiscent of early scoring techniques in the 1990s. The following are important details about each of the three states that should always be considered.

Active Vulnerabilities

Active vulnerabilities clearly represent the largest threat to any organization. They are vulnerabilities that are actively executing in the operating system or application (in everyday working code), and they are potentially vulnerable to exploitation. In vulnerability assessment tools today, all vulnerabilities are classified as active regardless of the mitigation steps performed by the end user. It is left to the tool administrators to know they should exclude a vulnerability because of mitigation or to manually change the risk score knowing a vulnerability's inherent dormant state. Scanning technologies simply find a file version, a hash, a registry key, or a package and do not consider the state of the program. This is the basis of the state problem.

Dormant Vulnerabilities

Dormant vulnerabilities represent an unknown risk to an organization – a real one that could be just as critical as an active vulnerability. It is not uncommon for a program to remain dormant for long periods of time but then be executed and represent a real risk to the organization. Consider desktop applications like Microsoft Help, WinZip, or Adobe Acrobat, which like many others may not be run very often. The application is not a risk when it is not being used, but it has the potential to be a risk. A dormant vulnerability is an unknown risk until it is used and its usage quantified. At any given point, applications are "Dormant," but the files associated with them (such as PDF ➤ Acrobat Reader) can be prioritized as well. Clearly, if a program and its accompanying files are never used *at all,* then the risk is zero. Common sense would then dictate uninstalling, disabling, or placing another mitigating control around such a program, but in the real world that might not always be possible. You cannot uninstall Microsoft Help, for example, or in the case of Red Hat Linux, leave a copy of the previous kernel on the disk as a backup. Therefore, just finding the vulnerability is reasonable within scoring systems we generally accept today. How the application and associated vulnerability are actually being used, however, represents the change from a dormant vulnerability to an active one, and no scoring system has addressed that to date. It is up to each security vendor to display and prioritize the information in its own proprietary way.

Carrier Vulnerabilities

Carrier vulnerabilities are like a virus in the human body. They are always present, not always detectable, and could be activated a variety of ways to cause real harm. The most common form of a carrier vulnerability is cached installer files. For example, modern versions of Microsoft operating systems and applications cache the installer files on the hard drive in case features are added or even just requested for the first time. The installation could potentially install vulnerable components that would then be flagged by a vulnerability assessment scan. The changes could then be in either a dormant state or an active vulnerability state. A real-world example would be to install the .net Framework or even Microsoft WSUS from a cache installation. A user would need to run Windows Update or use a patch management tool after the fact to remediate the newly introduced vulnerabilities. The problem lies in the dormant installation files (vulnerable to begin with if scanned for) and backup files residing on the system that created the vulnerability in the first place.

While this concept may seem borderline, it is very common with bloatware installed on default images and mobile devices. In many cases, programs are not fully installed until the first time they are used (and a EULA potentially accepted), and therefore an assessment solution may miss them because of unique vendor packaging.

State Prioritization

We developed the terminology used to classify vulnerability states for the purposes of this book. The prioritization of states is clear based on the discussion, but it still leaves a void when translated into regulatory standards. For example, the PCI DSS clearly states that all critical vulnerabilities should be remediated in 30 days. While this makes perfect sense for a system in the scope of the PCI, it does not take into consideration many of the systems that are outside of PCI scope but that are managed by an organization using the same processes. You might even argue that a dormant vulnerability represents the same risk (because of standard scoring) and that a carrier vulnerability should be managed through proper change control and patch management. In reality, however, that rarely happens. Placing definitions around these states of vulnerabilities assists organizations by:

- Prioritizing the highest risk vulnerabilities first – regardless of standardized scoring deficiencies;

- Expediting remediation on vulnerabilities that represent real-world active risks – regardless of whether an exploit is publicly available;

- Quantifying vulnerabilities based on their real-world application usage and not just theoretical exploitations;

- Raising awareness of additional steps that may be required for change control when operating system or application changes are made that could affect security; and,

- Identifying partially configured or installed vendor software that could represent a risk if allowed to execute.

To coin a potentially useless acronym, consider "ADC": Active, Dormant, and Carrier vulnerabilities, in order of their priority. When reviewing a vulnerability report, consider these a vital part of the risk prioritization and determine whether you can accurately detect the different types. If an application is actually running (active), it should always be a higher priority than if it is never used (dormant).

CHAPTER 9

Vulnerability Authorities

Since the late 1990s, vendors, end users, and governments have struggled with classifying and communicating vulnerabilities in a coherent fashion. The results produced a variety of standards for communication and governing bodies to store, process, and perform public announcements outside of the vendor community. While a wide variety of organizations have been created to communicate findings, a few provide the backbone for publicly disclosed information. The most popular are defined in Table 9-1, Vulnerability Authorities. These are the organizations that communicatie and reference all of the attributes and metrics about a potential risk.

© Morey J. Haber, Brad Hibbert 2018
M.J. Haber and B. Hibbert, *Asset Attack Vectors*,
https://doi.org/10.1007/978-1-4842-3627-7_9

Table 9-1. *Vulnerability Authorities*

Abbreviation	Full Name	Description	URL
US-CERT	United States Computer Emergency Readiness Team	US-CERT strives for a safer, stronger Internet for all Americans by responding to major incidents, analyzing threats, and exchanging critical cyber security information with trusted partners around the world.	https://www.us-cert.gov/
CERT	Software Engineering Institute at Carnegie Mellon University	CERT is a division of the Software Engineering Institute (SEI) that studies and solves problems with widespread cyber security implications. CERT collects, analyzes, and validates emerging vulnerabilities to common computing platforms, and will broadly notify operators of vulnerabilities as well as provide mitigation and remediation guidance.	https://www.cert.org

(continued)

Table 9-1. (*continued*)

Abbreviation	Full Name	Description	URL

DISA	Defense Information Systems Agency	DISA is a combat support agency of the Department of Defense (DoD). The agency is composed of military personnel from the Army, Air Force, Navy, and Marine Corps; and defense contractors. The agency provides, operates, and assures command and control and information-sharing capabilities and a globally accessible enterprise information infrastructure in direct support to joint warfighters, national-level leaders, and other mission and coalition partners across the full spectrum of military operations.	`http://www.disa.mil`
			`http://www.disa.mil/`
			`Cybersecurity`
			`http://www.disa.mil/`
			`Cybersecurity/Secure-`
			`Configuration-Guidance`

BUGTRAQ	Bugtraq or Bugtraq Identifier	SecurityFocus has been a mainstay in the security community since 1999 and supports the back end for Bugtraq IDs. Their technology provides a high volume, full-disclosure mailing list for announcement of new vulnerabilities; and a database to view history and discussions on each potential threat.	`http://www.securityfocus.` `com`

(continued)

Table 9-1. (*continued*)

Abbreviation	Full Name	Description	URL
MITRE	Mitre	The MITRE Corporation is a not-for-profit company that operates multiple federally funded research and development centers. It provides standards for vulnerability classifications and scoring like CVE that is used throughout the industry.	`https://www.mitre.org` `https://cve.mitre.org`
NVD	National Vulnerability Database	The NVD is the U.S. government repository of standards-based vulnerability management data represented using the Security Content Automation Protocol (SCAP). The NVD includes databases of security checklist references, security-related software flaws, misconfigurations, product names, and impact metrics.	`https://nvd.nist.gov`

CHAPTER 10

Penetration Testing

One of the finer arts in protecting assets from threats is penetration testing. While beginners, and sometimes news media, confuse vulnerability assessments with penetration testing, they are distinctly different disciplines. The confusion, however, is sometimes justified. Vulnerability assessment solutions can sometimes use exploit code in order to determine if a vulnerability is present (typically referred to as an "unsafe" or intrusive check). and penetration solutions can have network scanners to identify hosts for targeting. These two are more of a feature overlap in commercial solutions than a substitution or replacement for one discipline over the other.

To make this perfectly clear, a vulnerability assessment determines if a threat exists through an inference and some form of detection. A file is present, a port is open, a Windows registry key indicates an update has not been applied, and then the vulnerability is present. For the most part, it cannot detect if any mitigating controls are in places to prevent an exploit. A penetration test takes it to the next level. It will attempt to run exploit code against a vulnerable asset and prove it can be compromised – by actually doing it. The target is therefore no longer in a pristine state; exploit code is executing, and the asset is in far worse shape than just a

© Morey J. Haber, Brad Hibbert 2018
M.J. Haber and B. Hibbert, *Asset Attack Vectors*,
https://doi.org/10.1007/978-1-4842-3627-7_10

vulnerability assessment. It has been compromised even though the test was initiated. Leaving an asset in the state could leave to future attacks and must be fully remediated (or reimaged) before resuming production.

As discussed, there are a variety of commercial penetration-testing tools from Core, Canvas, and Rapid7, but as powerful as they are, they only contain about 10% of the actual exploits available for a modern Windows device. This makes their capabilities quite limited but still an absolute requirement to prove that an asset, resource, or an organization can easily be compromised using easily mitigatable vulnerabilities. It is therefore natural to have integrations between vulnerability management solutions and penetration-testing tools. Vulnerability management solutions safely detect the presence of flaws and penetration-testing tools consume the results to target potential targets for exploitation. Figure 10-1 is a sample screen from vulnerability assessment scanner integration from the Retina Network Security Scanner by BeyondTrust into MetaSploit by Rapid 7.

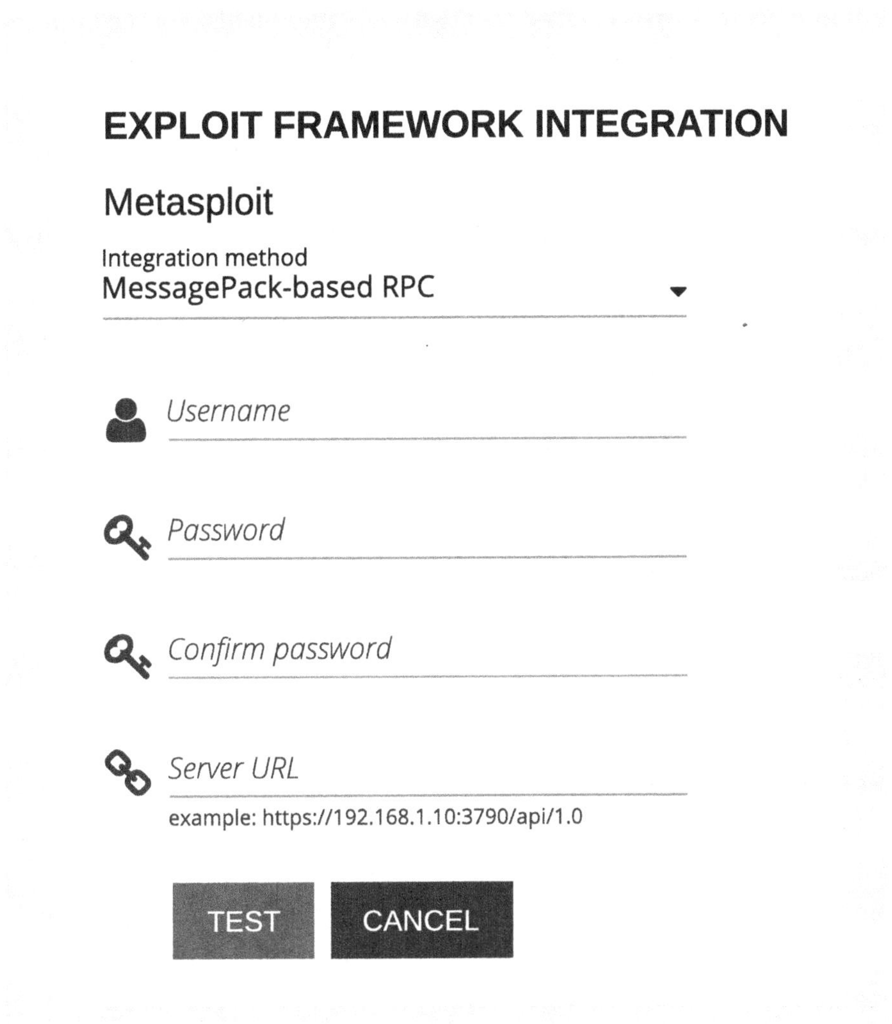

EXPLOIT FRAMEWORK INTEGRATION

Metasploit

Integration method
MessagePack-based RPC   ▼

👤 *Username*

🔑 *Password*

🔑 *Confirm password*

🔗 *Server URL*

example: https://192.168.1.10:3790/api/1.0

[TEST] [CANCEL]

Figure 10-1. *Vulnerability Assessment and Penetration Testing Integration User Interface*

This allows you to integrate the requirements of vulnerability management and penetration testing together electronically so information between the tools can be shared for a streamlined user experience.

While it is recklessly careless to target every identified resource from a scan for a penetration test, strategically targeting a few as part of a controlled test can prove the overall risk to an organization. And, if the test does not work, it just means the automated test did not work. A good security professional engaged in white hat hacking can understand the output and many times customize the test to be successful. This means a threat actor could potentially do the same, and without your permission. This is why relying on the automated output from a penetration testing solution alone is not a good security practice.

One last note on penetration testing and regulatory compliance initiatives. Standards like the PCI DSS require that penetration testing is performed on assets in scope of the specification. These tests go beyond running automated tools alone and looking at the results. Organizations specialize in performing penetration tests using tools and seasoned security professionals to "pentest" clients to meet these requirements (mercenary hackers). The results are designed to mimic a threat actors attack on your organization and see how far they can breach the environment using a trusted source versus potentially being a victim of a hacker using similar techniques.

Conversely, it is not a recommended practice to use internal resources for these activities. They know too much about your environment. Contract out for these services and use a different vendor each time. This gives you a variety of talent to perform the "pentest," and details about your environment necessary for a breach have to be learned from the outside. These mimic a foreign threat actor posing as an external threat, and most importantly, there should be no restrictions on their attack vectors, staff, or resources. A threat actor attempting to gain access will not honor the safety controls you put in for a "pentest." They will try every technique they can to breach your environment. While there are use cases to scope a legitimate penetration test to specific resources, an actual attack will not be limited and not have rules. Therefore, consider for regulatory compliance and internal tests the difference between your knowledge and testing and what a threat actor might actually do in order to compromise your assets.

With this in mind, the concept of risk acceptance forms the foundation for business decisions and budgeting of information technology security. If you understand the risk, accept that incidents could and will occur, the amount of resources and money spent to minimize threats becomes justifiable and quantifiable. Spending more money and resources, however, does not necessarily mean that the risks will linearly, or even exponentially, decrease. There is an inflection point where decisions are made and state, "I can accept that risk," or "I do not have enough budget to do so." There is, however, another philosophy to help offset resources, budget, the real results found from a penetration test. It is called the Mean Time to Breach. Similar to MTTR (Mean Time to Repair) or MTBF (Mean Time Between Failures), the concept documents the average time it takes a threat actor to breach the environment. If the known risks are critical, and exploitation method trivial, the MTTB (Mean Time To Breach) is very small. This means that any detection and prevention solutions in your security arsenal will have to alarm quickly and teams will have to respond in an extremely timely manner to mitigate the threat. If the risks are difficult, complex to exploit, but known, then the MTTB should increase. Controls can be placed around the known risks and teams have a little more luxury, in terms of time, to respond and mitigate the threat. If security teams can quantify the risks in terms of critically and ease of exploitation, then MTTB is something that can be used to help in cost and risk assessments. The problem is, that is not always a trivial task to accomplish due to complex architectures and unknown risks— organizations have plenty of them. While vulnerability management solutions can help build some of that foundation, another empirical approach may help as well; penetration testing. Consider how you perform penetration testing on your organization today. Do you employ red test teams, hire outside consultants, or even look for the cream of the crop in the form of hacker mercenaries who get paid bounties based on how deep they can penetrate your organization (the latter is a relatively new contractual approach that has incentives for ethical hackers based on their findings). For all methods, their results can be measured in the form of a MTTB and they should report a timeline based on each successful or thwarted attempt in their mission. Why? Because a successful mitigation strategy can map to these attacks as if they were real, ensure controls are in place to stop movement and malware, and that alarms, prevention, and workflow are responding each step to increase the MTTB to as long as possible. This ensures that security teams can be notified and react to the threat in a timely manner versus a quick smash and run scenario. The end goal, make the MTTB as long as possible with as many alarms necessary for security teams to understand the breach and respond accordingly. This balances a real-world attack "test" with the known risks covered during vulnerability and configuration assessments. An extended MTTB with security alarms is therefore desirable and replicatable using penetrating testing and can help determine how much money is spent based on a successful attack vector to mitigate the threat. Some threats realistically, are just too costly to mitigate and thus making them extremely difficult to exploit is desirable. For example, end-of-life servers and applications with known and unpatchable vulnerabilities. While MTTB is a relatively new term for cyber security, its meaning has been well established and is generally thought of in terms of when detection (and a breach) has actually occurred within an organization. As a new term, it should be thought of from the opposite perspective. How long did it take a threat actor to successfully breach the environment, and could my business detect the steps and techniques they used along the way? If I can detect the intrusion, and make the MTTB relatively long, then I have found a good balance for risk assessments, budget, and future security spending that leverages my existing solutions and time to respond. Penetration testing helps quanitfy this metric. We should all assume a breach will happen. Just make sure you have plenty of time to detect and respond to it and linking MTTB to your pentests is a great way to start.

CHAPTER 11

Remediation

While the cyber security community struggles with identifying vulnerabilities, classifying them, and providing remediation, vendors have taken on the problem with their own methodologies, service-level agreements, and public disclosure policies. As we have seen, it is one thing to identify a vulnerability and an entirely different problem to apply a remediation or mitigation strategy. To compound the problem, vendor implementations of public disclosure vary greatly, and the technologies they implement, even on similar platforms, to deploy security patches are not always consistent. To that end, we need to look at the leading vendors first and their patch remediation strategies and disclosure schedules.

Microsoft

Microsoft officially provides security patches for its solutions on the second Tuesday of every month. This has been affectionately labeled "Patch Tuesday" by the security and information technology community. This process has been operating under this paradigm since 2003. Security updates are available via a manual download, Microsoft Windows Update, and bundled with licensed third-party patch-management solutions.

© Morey J. Haber, Brad Hibbert 2018
M.J. Haber and B. Hibbert, *Asset Attack Vectors*,
https://doi.org/10.1007/978-1-4842-3627-7_11

While there are tons of details regarding Microsoft's patch process, there are a few tidbits every information technology professional should be aware of:

- Outside of the second Tuesday of every month, Microsoft will issue out-of-band security patches on an as needed basis depending on threats in the wild.

- Windows Update originally started as a feature within Internet Explorer and moved to a dedicated feature within the Windows Control Panel (now Settings in Windows 10) as the operating system evolved. This means the operation for older end-of-life operating systems is different than modern versions and continues to evolve. Older technology, while technically is not supported, has seen out-of-bound patches (EternalBlue) to mitigate real-world threats (WannaCry) on Windows XP and Server 2003. This means that even if a device is at end of life, you still need a method to provide updates and configuration changes because the unknown may very likely require you to manage the resource just like any other modern system.

- Modern versions of Windows 10 (not server-based versions yet) automatically opt-in for security updates and are bundled together on a monthly basis. Older Windows solutions are allowed for the selection of individual patches in order to manage change control and prevent incompatibilities. This means that based on operating system age, applying security updates varies not only in techniques but also the selection of what can be applied.

- Microsoft provides a free solution, Windows System Update Services (WSUS), to manage patch deployment for Microsoft solutions only. While this is a basic solution that works for many environments, it cannot manage many advanced use cases including third-party patching required for enterprise environments. This limitation has grown into a mature industry for patch-management solutions from IBM, Ivanti, and Tanium (to name a few).

In all fairness, Microsoft is one of the most mature vendors in the market for vulnerability identification, disclosure, and patch management. While there are nuances with obtaining and deploying patches, the transparency and tools for obtaining them exceed the remaining vendors in the market. The latest security updates for Microsoft solutions can be found here: `https://portal.msrc.microsoft.com/en-us/security-guidance`.

Apple

Apple updates for MacOS (formerly OS X) and iOS are available via the Internet and App Store updates and manually downloadable for air gapped systems and third-party application deployment. Each release is listed on their website, but the details, actual fixes, and identification are often lost in the marketing Apple overlays on everything. This is contrary to the Microsoft approach. Microsoft will provide you details on the security flaw and why it is deemed an issue: sometimes in great detail. Apple will do the bare minimum with a description, CVE number, and only high-level information. This can be viewed as a consumer-friendly approach, a method not to disclose too many details to a potential threat actor or a minimalist approach to acknowledge and patch the vulnerability based on

Apple's long-standing stature that they are "safer" than other platforms. With these in mind, here are a few things regarding Apple Updates that all information technology professionals should be aware of:

- End of life for MacOS is typically five years. Apple does not provide a formal end-of-life schedule for their operating systems, but empirically, new security patches are always included for the latest version of MacOS and two previous versions. While this does not equate to five years (since Apple releases a new OS every year), older versions receive critical updates only and then enter end-of-life status.

- iOS versions typically receive updates over the air (cellular) or via WiFi. While initial releases are a manual opt-in, as the version matures, Apple forces adoption via a nagware approach to install updates. Users are forced to take the latest release after Apple concludes it is necessary.

- Apple, like Microsoft, allows for preferences to be set to automatically install security patches when available and control via third-party solutions such as JamF to manage the remediation portion of the life cycle. This is required for change control and business continuity within most organizations.

To that end, Accessing the Preferences for Apple Security Updates on MacOs can be found at: `https://support.apple.com/en-us/HT204536`. This will allow you to control the updates on MacOS. Please note, Apple has been to known to overwrite these settings to their defaults inbetween OS upgrades. Administrators (or end users) may need to reset them to desired parameters after an upgrade in order to avoid an unexpected outage or incompatible upgrade. If you are a Mac user, you have seen this before with 32bit applications, third party display drivers, and even compatibility with USB devices.

Cisco

While Cisco does not provide a desktop or server-based operating system, they provide an operating system for switches, routers, firewalls, and tons of other infrastructure called IOS (not to be confused with Apple iOS). On top of this, they provide a variety of commercial applications for collaborative working, automation, the cloud, and analytics. Above and beyond the problems of patching one platform like Apple or Microsoft, patching Cisco applications and infrastructure requires multiple tools since the foundations are fundamentally different. In our vulnerability management life cycle, you will see that ownership and workflow for remediation will differ based on the vulnerability and method for remediation or mitigation. Cisco is one of those vendors, in the extreme, that will test those workflows and policies. For example, patching a vulnerability in Webex (a collaborative web application sharing solution) will require application-patch deployments for potentially Windows and MacOS. This is compared to a switch, firewall, or router flaw that will require an IOS update using dedicated management tools from Cisco (or third party). To that end, there are a few traits about Cisco updates every information technology professional should be aware of:

- Cisco advisories and updates are released on an as-needed basis without a set schedule like Microsoft. This means security, information technology, and network professionals must always be on guard because a new advisory and/or patch could come out at any time and on any day.

- Next to Microsoft, Cisco is the most thorough in vulnerability reporting and patch disclosure. Advisories go through extraordinary details to educate teams to explain the flaw, mitigation strategies, and the importance of the advisory.

- Cisco has the upper hand in advisories and alerts compared to all other vendors. They have provided a simple website to research any product, any risk, and any date to determine a threat. For every other vendor, this is a model we hope they would adopt. The latest Cisco updates can be found at: `https://tools.cisco.com/security/center/publicationListing`.

Google

The patch release schedule and advisories for Google Android solutions and Chrome OS are fragmented depending on the solution. As technology professionals, hopefully, you are aware of the fragmentation problems with Android and that each hardware vendor is responsible for certifying and deploying patches. To make matters worse, cellular phone carriers must approve and deploy the updates Over-the-Air (OtA) creating a third layer of complexity in maintaining security for their products. Mind you, this is just for the operating system and not for any applications manually installed or downloaded from Google Play (formerly Google Marketplace). This makes maintaining Android the hardest operating system in the industry and a consistent problem for vulnerability management programs.

As a shining light, Google does very well for solutions like Chrome. Their security updates are well documented, and patches are released in a timely manner. In addition, since most of their products are based in the cloud, security updates are completely transparent to the end user, making them very efficient for vulnerability remediation. The latest Google security updates can be found here:

- Android: `https://source.android.com/security/bulletin/`

- Chrome: `https://chromereleases.googleblog.com`.

Oracle

Oracle provides a well-established hybrid approach for patch updates, security alerts, and bulletins available in quarterly updates. Their implementation of the remediation cycle is based on the actual flaws listed by CVE and the patch updates needed to remediate flaws. While the public-user experience is not as mature as Cisco, it does provide the details needed for information technology and security professionals.

The hardest part for any user of Oracle technology is not necessarily finding an advisory nor applying the security patch, it is just as complex as Cisco or Microsoft, but rather accurately identifying all the places to apply the patch. Vulnerability assessments for Oracle applications typically require authenticated vulnerability assessment scans on the operating and many times, the database itself. With this in mind, these are some things information technology professionals should consider when remediating the risks for Oracle solutions:

- Change control for Oracle patches is critical. Any patches for databases or custom implementations of their solutions should be tested in a lab first. Oracle has the highest risk of any vendor from security patches causing production issues.

- Oracle desktop products like Java should be treated just like any other client based third-party application requiring patch management. However, there is a huge caveat. Deploying Java desktop client patches MUST be tested thoroughly to ensure functionality in the application or the browser does not break. This is a major problem for Java applications and environments that have regulatory compliance requirements to remediate a vulnerability in a timely manner. Many times, end users are forced to use older and vulnerable versions since their applications are not compatible with maintenance and security releases. Java is the highest-risk desktop application for these types of problems.

- Fragmentation of Oracle solutions is the last consideration for all information technology professionals. Like many other large organizations that have grown organically and through acquisitions, the deployment of patches can vary from product to product even on the same platform. Other vendors like CA (old Computer Associates) suffer from similar problems and should be considered in your workflow when building out your vulnerability management program.

Details on the latest Oracle patches can be found here: `https://www.oracle.com/technetwork/topics/security/alerts-086861.html`.

Red Hat

Red Hat has a mature release and notification format for their security advisories. They provide a user interface similar to Cisco for finding and investigating security flaws. The latest security updates can be found here: `https://access.redhat.com/security/security-updates/#/`.

Details regarding each flaw is a simple click for each entry and provides collateral for the most security-conscious team members. This view is also available in a pivot table referencing flaws by CVE. This makes it easy to correlate a finding to a vulnerability management report and formulate a strategy for remediation. Deployment of security patches can either use the native tools within the operating system or third-party patch management vendor.

Adobe

Adobe solutions from Adobe Reader to Adobe Flash have been the target for threat actors for years and have unfortunately been some of the lowest-hanging fruit to successfully exploit an asset. Adobe has taken these threats seriously in recent years and publishes extensive details regarding each finding, security update, and platform affected on their Security Bulletin web pages. Their security issues have unique significance within the industry since their solutions typically are supported on multiple platforms from Windows to Linux and MacOS and within multiple browsers from Chrome, Edge, to Safari. This makes an identified vulnerability potentially exploitable (with the proper coding) on more than one type of system and can affect more than one type of persona. From a vulnerability management perspective, the same CVE can, therefore, exist almost everywhere, but the remediation will be different depending on operating system, browser, etc. The latest Adobe security updates can be found here: `https://helpx.adobe.com/security.html`.

Open Source

Open source vulnerability and remediation management is a significant problem within an enterprise. Open source can be incorporated as source code, compiled libraries, or embedded in existing commercial or custom solutions. All of which are subject to potentially critical vulnerabilities. The problem with vulnerability detection is the reliance on signatures to identify a flaw. The path of a file or compiled code may not be considered by a vulnerability management vendor when they create signatures and thus create a false negative and a false sense of security. Therefore, open source code needs to be considered on a per-use case basis:

- Compiled Libraries – It is up to the distributing manufacturer to document the use of precompiled libraries in their solution and provide disclosure if any of them are affected by a vulnerability. This provides a challenge for vulnerability management solutions to incorporate the most popular solutions and consider that the library can appear in non-default directories or paths in a typical installation.

- Source Code – Incorporating source code within your custom application or embedded within a commercial compiled application is also a risk. Outside of code review solutions and web application scans, there is little chance of a vulnerability management solution detecting the flaw. This is especially true for an application-layer vulnerability compared to a service operating at the network layer. End users are dependent on the manufacturer to provide disclosure, and development teams need to stay aware of vulnerabilities posted for open source code in order to remediate their own applications.

If you consider that major vendors like Red Hat, Cisco, and Microsoft (to a lesser degree) use open source code and libraries in their solutions, public disclosure of a vulnerability is critical for their security advisories. They are in effect the "messenger" of the flaw and providing a service to update their solutions based on someone else's prior art. This is why building defenses for assets can be difficult. Information regarding a security flaw is dependent on the developer incorporating the open source and not necessarily the creator themselves. The open source developers will post a CVE and perform public disclosure too but typically not reference all the vendors that have chosen to embed their technology.

Everyone Else

Remember, vulnerabilities can be present from firmware and microcode all the way up to web applications, and everywhere in between. Any place code can be written allows the possibility for a vulnerability to exist. Therefore, for everyone else, it becomes policy and procedures for public disclosure. There is no vulnerability assessment vendor on the market today that covers everything and every CVE. There is none and end users should not be fooled in thinking this is true. Considering there are thousands of new vulnerabilities per year affecting tens of thousands of applications, no one vendor can incorporate all of the threats as signatures and provide full historical context. While it is not unreasonable for a vulnerability management vendor to have tens of thousands of active checks in their audit database, it still does not cover everything and the size alone does not dictate accuracy, manage obsolete checks, and honor patch supercedence. For every other application, operating system, and asset you have deployed, you need to consider the coverage of your vulnerability management tool and their ability to handle custom audits for your custom applications. And yes, for custom or homegrown applications, you will need to write those checks yourself.

The diversity of these just leads to the complexity that organizations face in getting patches and mitigation deployed to their resources. While we have coalesced on standards for risk score and notifications, there ultimately is no standard that vendors follow for release schedules and notification. Just the contents of the release itself and that varies greatly between vendors. This is where standards like CVE and IAVA become important because they abstract details away from the vendor and actually allow risk measurements in a consistent fashion.

If your environment would benefit about knowing about every one these alerts, bulletins, advisories, and notifications, consider using the Threat Intelligence built into your vulnerability management solution or subscribe to the RSS feeds available from every major vendor.

Finally, the more vendors you use within the environment, the more potential research, tools, and workflows will be needed for remediation. Vulnerability management vendors include the relevant details in their reports but as you move downscale from the major vendors, the maturity curve for security updates weakens and getting relevant information can become problematic. There is no law that a company has to issue a CVE for a discovered flaw nor any law requiring public disclosure. Some vendors just do not participate. This is contrary to the laws for breach notification that are present in various degrees worldwide and very public in the form of regulations like GDPR.

CHAPTER 12

The Vulnerability Management Program

With the recent spate of high-profile data breaches, security-conscious organizations realize that their financial viability and business continuity depend on effective IT security risk management. Given the potential fallout of a breach, many organizations rely on vulnerability and compliance management initiatives to keep their critical information secure, protect sensitive systems, and demonstrate compliance with regulatory requirements. These efforts are further complicated by burgeoning new security exposures introduced by a proliferation of applications, employee-owned devices, mobile computing, social networks, cloud, and other expanding attack surfaces. As well, critical compliance regulations, such as PCI, HIPAA, and Sarbanes-Oxley, also mandate specific security controls pertaining to vulnerability management. Unfortunately, there's no way around the harsh reality that noncompliance results in penalties, lost business, and other indirect costs. Additionally, aligning internal security processes with regulations and providing meaningful reports to management and auditors are notoriously time-consuming and costly exercises.

While an organization generally cannot control the threats faced by the organization, they can respond to threats by mitigating the associated risks to either reduce the vulnerabilities or the potential impact on the business. To implement such a program, there are four phases – Design, Develop, Deploy, and Operate as illustrated in Figure 12-1.

© Morey J. Haber, Brad Hibbert 2018
M.J. Haber and B. Hibbert, *Asset Attack Vectors*,
https://doi.org/10.1007/978-1-4842-3627-7_12

Phase	Objectives	Task Items
Design	Requirements, Goals, Budget	➤ Review business requirements for the vulnerability processes ➤ Create a VM strategy with timelines, priorities, measurements, and goals ➤ Determine a budget and cost analysis for the VM program
Develop	Requirements, Plan Creation, Selection	➤ Translate business requirements into technical requirements ➤ Vulnerability plan creation & validation ➤ Selection and procurement of supporting technologies
Deploy	Deployment, Team Training, Handoff	➤ Install, test, and validate VM program ➤ Educate and train key stakeholders ➤ Transition VM plan to operational and security staff
Operate	Operate, Measure, Expand	➤ Operate VM program – (Assess, Prioritize, Report, Remediate) ➤ Measure effectiveness of program versus stated goals ➤ Expand scope and mature VM program over life cycle

Figure 12-1. *Four phases of a vulnerability management program*

Design

The role of an information technology security team is to work with key individuals throughout the organization to develop business cases and implementation plans for new security projects and perform risk assessment of existing controls and planned information systems. So where does one start? Common sense would dictate that one should start with the most critical resources that would have the biggest impact if they were compromised. Those would be the ones that you want to protect first. But how do you prioritize these resources? How do you protect them? How do you measure the existing and planned controls? The devil is the details and we will explore the design and planning in subsequent chapters.

Develop

During the development phase, the security team assigns security and vulnerability engineers to translate the business-level strategy and design into technical requirements that can be implemented and enforced across departments.

As the plan takes form and sign-off for technical requirements is secured, the team should collaborate with other departments to examine opportunities for integration and automation with existing information technology processes including asset management, security monitoring, audit reviews, and change control. The goal of the design should be to help *operationalize security* into the daily decisions made throughout the organization. One of the best ways to accomplish this task is to integrate with existing processes and systems to embed vulnerability management as a normal course of doing business.

Deploy

The development, proof of concept, and deployment of any new technology should be tested, code reviewed (if applicable), and assessed for risks before product implementation. That includes even the vulnerability management process and applications itself! This not only includes vulnerability assessments but also configuration hardening and placement within secure zones within the environment.

Often during the deployment phase, organizations will work with vendors or contractors to execute against a deployment on a subset of the environment. During this time the deployment team may perform training for internal deployment resources who will complete the larger deployment, and to the operational staff who will take over ongoing management and maintenance post implementation. It is also during the deployment phase where refinements to the operational procedures may be finalized and security holes identitied and mitigated in the deployment.

Operate

Now that the assessment process is well defined, asset owners updated, training complete, and processes transitioned over to the vulnerability engineers who will be overseeing the daily operations, the hard work begins.

Too often we find organizations trying to jump to the 4th phase – "Operate" without proper planning, training, or "buy-in" from executives and asset owners. This often results in misaligned expectations and contention between security and other teams impacted by the vulnerability process. When planning a successful vulnerability program, plan not only for what it will take to procure and implement the program, but also what it will realistically take to manage the systems and perform the appropriate remediation on an ongoing basis. This is required for proper sustainment of the program and how to mature the solution beyond these four steps.

Maturity

The goal of any implementation is to mature into a state that makes the processes, procedures, and workflow seamless with everyday business. For a successful vulnerability management program, this includes making the life cycle operate independently of department and regulations. Table 12-1 outlines this concept.

Table 12-1. Vulnerability Management Maturity

Maturity	Solution	Assessments	Patch	Reporting	Ownership
			Descriptions		
Business and Regulatory Mapping	Assessments are security, business, and regulatory compliance-driven	Assessments drive compliance requirements	Patch is measured in compliance terms	Regulatory compliance reporting	Auditors are included in ownership
Attack Mitigation and Strategic Remediation	Dynamic response based on multiple data sources	Assessments are evaluated for business partners and third party technology	Service level agreements are generated internally and for third parties	Reporting expands into risk and threats for the business units	Team response is included in ownership tasks
Threat Intelligence and Risk Prioritization	Vulnerability solution integrates with bi-directional with third party solutions	Assessments have multiple data feeds and sources	Resources are segmented or isolated until patching occurs	Reporting and events are present in third party governance and security solutions	Ownership between departments is documented and followed
Continuous Monitoring and Active Risk Assessment	Network scanners are supplemented with agents and third party tools	Assessments can be triggered by events or API	DevOps processes can remediate as needed	Reporting is scheduled and provided to teams ad-hoc	Clear ownership and fully documented policies
Periodic Assessments	Centralized enterprise vulnerability management with network scanners	Assessments are scheduled (null session and credential)	Remediation workflow is defined	Vulnerability and patch management reporting is consistent	Base policies and SLA's are in place
Ad-Hoc Assessments	Vulnerability assessment solution partially deployed	Assessments on an as needed basis	Reactive remediation and patching	Simple reporting on coverage generated ad-hoc	Basic directives to minimize risk
No Risk Assessments	Minimal or no assessments, tools, or policies	Targeted or manual checks only	Incomplete remediation and mitigation	No measurement or reporting	Inconsistent management directives

115

Maturity Categories

- No Risk Assessments – The lack of any procedure and policy for vulnerability management and how to mitigate any threats that are detected.

- Ad Hoc Assessments – Solutions may be available to the team and assessments are conducted on an as-needed basis depending on the threat of the day or regulatory inquiry. There is no established procedure or policy overseeing the security initiative.

- Periodic Assessments – Established procedure and policies for scheduled assessments. Results have a workflow for remediation but only provide a snapshot in time based on scheduled assessments.

- Continuous Monitoring and Active Risk Assessment – Policies and procedures are mature and allow for real-time vulnerability assessments and active vulnerable applications detection. All results are treated with traditional scoring and not prioritized based on real-world threats nor active exploits.

- Threat Intelligence and Risk Prioritization – Real-world security threats are blended with detected vulnerabilities regardless of source: ad hoc, periodic, or continuous monitoring. This information allows for the prioritization of threats-based relevancy to the business and applications.

- Attack Mitigation and Strategic Remediation – Based on all the vulnerability and threat intelligence collected, remediation and mitigation strategies can be automated. This is a basic step for integrating vulnerability and patch management solutions regardless if patching still requires change control approval before deploying an update. The maturity is the automated linking and staging of a patch or mitigation to current the flaw with minimal interaction.

- Business and Regulatory Mapping – All of the data provided in the maturity model is technical and based on real-world threats. The final step is translating the data into regulatory information that the business can understand and prioritize. For example, if the business has ISO 27002 requirements, then the vulnerability data is represented by threats to safeguard the implementation of the regulation. Figure 12-2 illustrates this type of mapping. This allows the business to allocate resources above the technical aspects of the threat.

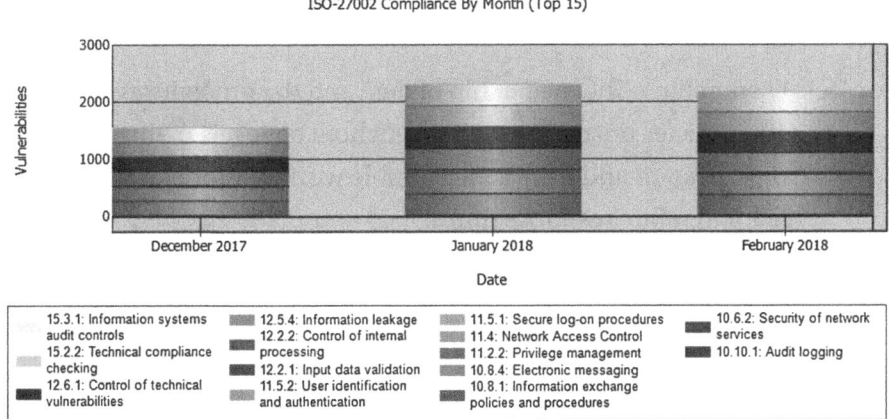

Figure 12-2. *Vulnerability information mapped to ISO 27002 regulatory compliance by requirement*

Descriptions

- Solution – The maturity of the deployment and potential usage of features and capabilities within the solution.

- Assessments – The technical sophistication and requirements needed from the business in order to successfully perform a vulnerability assessment and establish a vulnerability management program.

- Patch – Remediation and mitigation strategies are not only based on the threat, criticality, but also the potential impact to the business based on objectives and real-world threats.

- Reporting – Reporting of vulnerability information matures by line of business and relevance to stakeholders versus being technical and targeted only to security and operation teams.

- Ownership – The ownership of data and the procedures and policies are established throughout all levels of the organization and have a measurable workflow for each team to refine response times.

CHAPTER 13

Vulnerability Management Design

A key requirement for any Security Officer is reducing the risks of a cyber attack by finding and closing off holes in the IT infrastructure, and this is exactly what a sound vulnerability management (VM) program should do. An effective VM program should be designed to ensure that the people, processes, policies, and selected technologies work together to proactively protect, shield, and defend the enterprise from cyber threats. As threats cannot be completely eliminated, and as the Security Officer does not have unlimited resources, his/her job to ensure the associated security and compliance risk is well communicated, understand, and falls within an organization's tolerance levels.

To ensure alignment of prioritizes across IT, business, and an organization's risk, several frameworks and methodologies have been developed including NIST SP800-30, FAIR, ISO20005, ISACA, ISF, and OCTAVE. Some of the frameworks promote top-down analysis, other promote bottom up; whichever is selected as the starting point, most organizations use elements of multiple methodologies to determine acceptable risks levels across the asset base and ensure the IT systems are adequately protected. As organizations begin the process of defining their overall vulnerability management program, they should link the risk assessment and measurement activities with these existing control

M.J. Haber and B. Hibbert, *Asset Attack Vectors*,
https://doi.org/10.1007/978-1-4842-3627-7_13

frameworks. Not only does this ensure alignment of priorities, but also enables the security team to communicate risk across both business functions and management levels more effectively.

To accomplish this task when defining the VM program, the Security Officer oversees a number of typical tasks during the design phase of the program as shown in Figure 13-1.

Phase	Objectives	Task Items
Design	Business Requirements Program Goals Program Budget	➤ Review the needs of the business to help prioritize risks and criticality of assets ➤ Review the compliance obligations of the business ➤ Determine which assets are to be included in the scan process ➤ Determine the types of frequency of the scanning process ➤ Identify all stakeholders, define roles, and responsibilities ➤ Identify stakeholders and data owners that will need to be consulted and included in the vulnerability process ➤ Collaborate with stakeholders on requirements, process integration points and potential risk or constraints ➤ Securing general agreement of obligations, measurements and success criteria from IT and asset owners ➤ Create a VM strategy with timelines, priorities, regulations, and goals ➤ Define and secure an upfront and ongoing budget to support the vulnerability management process

Figure 13-1. *Vulnerability Management Design Phase*

It is important at this early stage to begin discussing and educating business and asset owners on the importance of the vulnerability management process and the roles that they, and their teams, will play in securing the organization from internal and external threats. Reviewing and formalizing high-level processes early on with lead to better understanding of stakeholder needs, and it will reduce the likelihood of creating supporters rather than detractors as the program is developed and deployed. Time and time again we see scenarios where the vulnerability process is implemented in isolation. For a program to be effective, appropriate departments and team members must be mobilized to address the issues with an understanding for how those activities will be tracked and measured, and why these activities are critical to the security and compliance posture of the organization. As with other security projects, the implementation of a vulnerability solution is not simply to automate the discovery of vulnerabilities to promote compliance adherence. Implementing a sound vulnerability management program focused on business risk, and benefits, provides an opportunity to examine and improve existing processes across departments. Stakeholder inclusion earlier in the process is critical to success and should be positioned as an enabler for the business.

Operationalizing and improving risk-based decisions and driving a security aware culture across the organization is a theme that should be common across security projects. Assessment and remediation activities must be prioritized based on threat, likelihood of an attack, and potential business impact. To ensure alignment of the program with the business, the Security Officer and team need to realize that the definition of business impact should not come from the Security Officer or security team. Business Impact of a cyberbattack should be determined by the business stakeholders who can more readily define the importance of the business service or data that relies on the IT systems. During the design phase, the Security Officer should collaborate and provide a framework and approach for classifying the value of the data and systems, which can then be used to prioritize risk and ensure the VM program and stakeholder activities are aligned.

In a large complex environment with global teams, mobile workers, cloud migrations, DevOps operations, and more, knowing where to start can be a challenge. If you find yourself in this situation, consider the following guidelines when first designing your vulnerability management program.

Crawl, Walk, Run, Sprint

You don't need full coverage with complete systems integration from day one. Remember that a successful program can always be expanded. Start by identifying the most critical assets and services at risk. Demonstrate value and expand the program in accordance with the overall plan.

Starting with a smaller scope introduces other stakeholders to the vulnerability and remediation processes without overwhelming them with thousands of "to dos." It also provides a defined time frame to iron out deficiencies, uncover additional resource or technical constraints, prove value to secure additional budget; and it enables asset owners to address critical items without being overwhelmed.

Implement for Today, But Plan for Tomorrow

Even though some departments or assets may be out of scope for the first integration of the vulnerability program, you may need to include them in the future. Whether it is simply planning for scale to handle more assets or shifts in business or technology direction, plan for growth day one. Typical implementations may start with a specific asset class, business service, and department. They may initially focus on externally vulnerability systems, on-premise systems, and cloud data centers. Again, where you should be the result of a risk analysis determined by prioritizing critical business functions and mapping these to the assets, threats, and risk tolerance levels of your organization. To start, learn where your crown jewels are and what you need to protect within your castle.

It's All About Business Value

Implementing a vulnerability process on time and on budget is hard. Unfortunately implementing the program on time and on budget does not demonstrate success. Spend time looking deeply into how the team will report success. That is, how do we demonstrate that this project delivered value to the business?

Security and risk are now considered a "board level" as executives are increasingly held accountable for breaches that damage they cause. This level of raised visibility calls for a higher degree of C-level involvement. This involvement is best sought at the onset of planning a new (or improved) vulnerability management process and not after you hit barriers and conflict executing the plan. Determining the best way to communicate the threats and risks associated to your business at the asset owner, manager, and executive levels is a way that they can understand and see the value of the VM program. If you are showing a chart that you now have 4,000 vulnerabilities across the organization, I would say – so what. The challenge with designing a vulnerability program is how can you quantify the value of "the spend" and the impact in the departmental resources in a nontechnical and informative way. Here are some suggestions:

1. Use comparative analysis. Indicating that we had a risk score of 98 last month comprised of 10,000 vulnerabilities and are now at a risk score of 72 comprised of 4,000 vulnerabilities.

2. Where possible, tie risk levels to applications or business processes that the executives and business leaders understand. The current risk level to our Payment System is "Medium."

3. When high-risk vulnerabilities are covered in the media, be prepared to demonstrate if you are, or are not, at risk. If you were at risk, demonstrate how quickly your team identified the risk and responded with appropriate remediation activities.

4. Use a Service-Level Agreement (SLA) analysis. Use SLA reports and dashboards to demonstrate how IT and asset owners are performing in general and compared to one another to drive accountability.

With this general strategy, priorities, budget, responsibilities, and measurements now defined, the Security Officer and their team can work to secure approval and executive commitment to the overall plan and move into the development stage.

CHAPTER 14

Vulnerability Management Development

A well-planned vulnerability management program that aligns with the overall organization's risk management program can assist in this process by reducing the overall attack surface by:

1. Identifying and prioritizing assets across the organization;

2. Identifying the vulnerabilities that can be exploited by attackers;

3. Prioritizing vulnerabilities by their potential impact on the business;

4. Communicating the associated risk to key business owners, executives, and auditors;

5. Measuring the effectiveness of shielding and remediation activities.

So where do we start?

© Morey J. Haber, Brad Hibbert 2018
M.J. Haber and B. Hibbert, *Asset Attack Vectors*,
https://doi.org/10.1007/978-1-4842-3627-7_14

The following are a set of typical tasks that are undertaken by the engineering team during the development stage of the program (Figure 14-1):

Phase	Objectives	Task Items
Develop	Technical Requirements / Vulnerability Plan Creation / Vendor Selection	➤ Translate business needs into technical requirements for assessment, reporting, and remediation ➤ Translate business goals into measurable activities including SLA targets for remediation ➤ Managing appropriate RFP and/or "proof of concept" activities for solution\vendor selection processes ➤ Identifying opportunities for automation, process integration, and value creation with other systems/processes ➤ Identifying detailed resource requirements, skills and/or resource gaps for initial deployment ➤ Identifying detailed resource requirements, skills and/or resource gaps for ongoing vulnerability processes ➤ Identifying possible constraints including coverage and/or possible exceptions to remediation activities ➤ Identifying possible risk to program success (technical, financial, political, operational) ➤ Work with Security Officer to update plan details regarding risks, constraints, budget & timelines ➤ Defining appropriate training programs for key personal supporting the vulnerability process

Figure 14-1. *Vulnerability Management Development Phase*

Vulnerability Management Scope

While developing your vulnerability management plan, end users need to determine what is in the initial scope and what will be added at a later date. A blanket statement of developing a plan for everything within a network, directly from the start, rarely succeeds. Therefore, consider your scope. What needs to be developed for the first set of assets within your vulnerability management program and what will it ultimately grow to. It is not uncommon to start with just Windows Servers, but in reality, at some point, everything needs to be discovered and assessed. This will help with plan creation during the initial phases and allow you to grow the solution over time to meet your business objectives. It is important to note, that as the solution grows, you may need to revisit the "Development" phase multiple times to validate your priorities and adjust the scope and goals in order to be successful.

Operating Systems

When thinking of the scope of the vulnerability management processes, the first assets classification that comes to mind are the desktops and servers. This is a natural reaction as patching vulnerabilities has become common routine from basic home users, to power users running their own home networks, and to security professionals. Across all of these user types from the unknowledgeable to the highly skilled, the importance of keeping their machines up to date is pervasive. This level of awareness is largely driven by the hacking stories published daily by the media, but also by the promotion of good security hygiene by the hardware and software manufacturers who want to make sure their customers are protected. And while this may seem like common sense, many organizations do not include all servers or desktops within the scope of their vulnerability management programs. Here are some of the reasons behind this fragmented approach to scanning operating systems:

1. Some may assume, wrongly, that they only need to scan externally facing servers as those are the only ones that pose a threat to the organization.

2. Some may only scan a subset of servers based on classification or perceived risk.

3. Some may limit their scan scope based on the requirements for specific regulatory mandates. For example, PCI mandates that organizations must scan all Internet-facing external IPs.

4. Some may believe that only servers should be scanned as desktop themselves do not contain any sensitive applications or data.

5. Some may not scan laptops or roaming devices due to connectivity, complexity, or the perceived low-risk impact of compromise associated with these devices.

With today's disintegrating network perimeter combined with the sophistication of attackers, ensuring zero gap visibility across your server and desktop asset inventory should be the minimum baseline requirement for your vulnerability program. Attackers from outside and within your organization can target any asset. This is the basis for lateral movement. Whether that asset is a critical application or database server, or whether it is providing a noncritical service when if compromised only provides a means for a hacker to hide and move laterally within the organization, these attack vectors must be closed.

Client Applications

For many organizations, deploying patches to user's desktops and laptops is old news. Microsoft's System Configuration Manager (SCCM), Windows Server Update Service (WSUS), and Windows Update enable information technology administrators to deploy the latest Microsoft product updates. For some companies, this is seen as good enough but does not consider any third party applications. That is a critical mistake. The reality is that not all organizations have the means to quickly identify, test, and deploy all patches quickly and easily. Additionally, limiting the assessment and patching process to Windows-specific applications may open the door for attack. Whether your organization is leveraging Windows, Macs, or both, third-party applications present serious security risks and have been the target for many phishing, drive by and ransomware attacks.

Incorporating client applications within the vulnerability management program helps organizations gain visibility in the risks associated with missing patches, as well as support for third-party applications. Information technology teams can prioritize remediation activity more quickly, fix the most impactful weaknesses for Microsoft and third-party applications appropriately, and track measure the overall effectiveness of the patch program.

Web Applications

Web applications have traditionally been one of the biggest threats to an organization's security. Inherently, they are much more difficult to defend versus traditional applications that benefit from the security infrastructure that has been already deployed. In order to detect and properly defend against web application threats, you must first have the capability to identify these vulnerabilities. This includes performing web application vulnerability assessment scanning.

The best way to identify web application security threats is to perform web application vulnerability assessment. The importance of these threats could leave your organization exposed if they are not properly identified and mitigated. Therefore, implementing a web application scanning solution should be of paramount importance for your organization's security plans in the future.

By definition, web application scanning is an automated vulnerability assessment solution that crawls a website (either automatically or has been trained) looking for vulnerabilities within web apps. The solution analyzes all web pages and files that it finds, and it builds a structure of the entire website. The scanner then performs automated checks against security vulnerabilities by launching a series of common web attacks and analyzes the results for vulnerabilities.

Web Application Scanners can perform Static Application Security Testing (SAST) or Dynamic Application Security Testing (DAST). DAST testing takes the point of view of an attacker and examines an application in its running state trying to compromise the application. SAST takes a different approach and looks "inside" that application, reviewing source code for evidence of potential vulnerabilities.

When selecting an appropriate web scanning methodology and solution, also take into consideration the operator of the scanner itself. The application scanning market has two primary sets of solutions:

1. Enterprise Vulnerability Assessment solution that scans a broad array of assets classifications typically offer coverage of web applications. As the operators of these scanners tend to be more generalists with respect to security, these tools often offer good coverage heavily weighing on DAST, or black-box scanning to find vulnerabilities. Many of these scanners do a pretty good job of detecting the most common types of web vulnerabilities as described in the OWASP top 10. Examples of such scanners include Retina, Nessus, QualysGuard, or Nexpose.

2. For organizations creating their own web applications that have in-depth knowledge of web development, there exists more capable and dedicated web application scanners. A typical use case for these scanners is for web application teams to scan software builds in development and QA environments before they are deployed into production. SAST can also be integrated into the secured development life cycle of Agile development and DevOps automation to tighten security controls and detect and promote early detection and remediation of vulnerabilities across a Continuous Integration Continuous Development (CICD) environment. Examples of such scanners include Acunetix, AppScan, Burp Suite, or WebInspect.

As web application scanners and associated technologies have matured with more advanced interactive interfaces and a combination of DAST and SAST capabilities, a new class of web application scanners known as IAST (Interactive Application Security Testing) has emerged.

Protecting the production environment from web application vulnerabilities is not only good practice, but it is also a compliance requirement for standards such as PCI and FedRamp covered later in this book. Many organizations will solely rely on the results of network scanners to perform limited DAST scans against production applications. These scans may enable an organization to pass a compliance audit but may leave gaps to risk visibility. If you are also creating your own applications, using a combination of dedicated Web Application Scanning in the development and QA environments, complemented with network-based scanners across the production environment, assuming that you have the resources, may provide them with a good alternative.

Network Devices

Unprotected network devices can also have devastating impacts on an organization from enabling lateral movement, data exfiltration, and service disruption. Network Devices include a broad range of IP-based devices that connect to your network including routers, switches, gateways, printers, IoT, and much more. Commercial vulnerability scanning solutions include support for thousands of vendors and can be used to examine missing patches, weak configurations, poor password management, open ports, and more. Attackers can compromise these assets and use them in a variety of ways including service disruption, gaining an attack foothold, moving laterally, and exfiltration information.

Databases

When it comes down to it, business is data. It has an asset value in the form of Infonomics. This includes everything from customer data, employee data, product data, medical data, and financial data (and more) — which needs to be secured and monitored effectively. As databases house the company's most vital asset, they should be rated with high priority when planning the scope of your vulnerability program. Like other asset types, databases are prone to flaws that can expose your corporate data. Database vulnerabilities can include:

- Missing security patches
- Default accounts and passwords
- Weak passwords (simple to guess)
- Unmanaged passwords (shared or infrequently rotated)
- Misconfigurations
- Excessive privileges

To protect the database assets, an organization should inventory all database platforms to validate appropriate vulnerability scanning coverage. Additionally, the corporate databases reside on, and rely on, other IT components including hypervisors, operating systems, databases management applications, and Web applications. Weaknesses in these components can also expose the underlying data. When examining database risk, ensure that you include all related components and potential attack vectors in your analysis.

Flat File Databases

A lot of focus has been placed on database scanning; however, users tend to ignore flat file databases used for applications and local data files that are produced as subsets. Very little information is present on best practices for securing flat file-based databases and how to mitigate the risks of data contained within them even though there are strict regulations on PII and data leakage.

It's a valid argument to suggest that database application servers are not as secure as flat files. To some this may seem reasonable, as standard database solutions may have more visibility as an attack vector. And if you consider that any file contained on a host could be sensitive with regard to the information contained within, flat file databases are more secure because of local permissions and the operating system itself.

However, flat files are only as secure as the permissions, operating system, and application services that protect the files. Unlike widely adopted RDBMS solutions that provide built-in auditing, event notification, encryption, and granular access controls, applications that utilize flat files may rely on the application developer(s) to provide these services.

When deploying any new application or reviewing existing ones, we would like to propose a process for investigating the data storage capabilities of the application. The Microsoft operating system does a good job keeping MS Office documents and MS Access database files in the My Documents directory. This makes it easy to secure by the user but is awful if the application is shared on the network. It should not be installed within an end users profile.

So, what about applications that store flat file databases in nonstandard locations? What if the application uses nonstandard file extensions to mitigate the association of the files? What if your web application needs a flat file database? What if the application managing the data provides another layer of granular access control to the data?

As a part of the security model when reviewing a new or existing application, consider the following:

1.   How does the application store data?

2.   What file format is the data stored in?

3.   Can the file system be secured with permissions to isolate the files?

4.   Does the local user need to be an administrator in order to access the files?

5.   Can the files contain a different permission set then the user login?

6.   Can you secure the services for the application with different permissions than the logged-in user and the files?

7.   Are temporary files created containing flat file data and are they purged when the application is complete?

8.   Are the data files password protected or encrypted?

9.   What is the location of the files and can they be moved to a standard location for backup, deletion, and security?

10.   What auditing facilities are available to track access and changes to the file data?

If your organization stores critical data that may be a violation of regulatory compliance initiatives, be mindful. You will need to find this data and secure it just like any other secure process within your organization. Also, consider that if these files are not secure what liability you may have if they are exposed. An HR spreadsheet can be considered a sensitive flat file database depending on the data it contains too. Your vulnerability assessment process should consider this and be capable of PII (personally identifiable information) discovery.

Hypervisors

Hypervisor technology (VMware, Microsoft Hyper-V, XEN based) enables organizations to consolidate physical servers and data centers into virtual images running in a virtual container, on top of a virtual network, to reduce cost and gain strategic flexibility across development, testing, and production IT environment. If a hypervisor is compromised, it can have widespread impact across all of the servers and services that it is housing. In summary, hypervisors need to be managed, patched, and configured like any other asset.

The images running within the virtual environment include servers, desktops, network components, applications, or services that the organization relies on. In addition to scanning these virtual images, organizations should also include the underlying hypervisor. Note that some variation exists between the commercial vendors with some vendors offering more advanced techniques to scan offline images and advanced APIs. This is important to consider in your design phase for targeting and operations.

IaaS and PaaS

When enterprise applications and services migrate from the physical data center, organizations begin to lose visibility and control as the shared infrastructure model of the cloud forces IT to give up their traditional control over the network and system resources. As a result, many organizations and cloud providers will tell you that security continues to be a source of concern and confusion.

In a public IaaS deployment, customers can manage the operating systems and applications, and they can implement controls and processes on that level. In these shared implementations, the providers typically implement security layers at the network and hypervisor layers that may include firewalls, encryption, IDS/IPS, VLANs, and vulnerability and penetration testing. However, the details of these internal security programs and their output are not always visible to their customers.

Additionally, many times the cloud providers do not provide an OS or application-level security solution, which of course should include vulnerability and scanning for enterprise images and applications running on their shared, multitenant infrastructure. With respect to vulnerability scanning, the customer must often rely on the claims of the provider with respect to the network and hypervisor layers. Customers must then, assuming that they are permitted, perform their own scanning to assess their virtualized OS and application risks. As such, core security responsibilities, including vulnerability and penetration testing, are more heavily shared between the provider and the customer, which can result in some confusion and "gray areas" when attempting to implement a solid end-to-end security strategy. As an example, this is why Spectre and Meltdown are preceived as a higher threat. A virtual machine could jump between hosts and the hypervisor based on information scraped from memory and even between clients in shared cloud resource environment. The end user has no visibility into other instances or hypervisor to determine if resources have been remediated to prevent this threat. It is after all, not your computer.

Giving these IaaS challenges, many organizations may opt to adopt the Private Hosted Cloud, as a way to balance security and compliance requirements with the benefits of a managed infrastructure. In a private hosted cloud, the data center is virtualized on dedicated hardware and managed by the cloud provider. Much like the public cloud, the provider manages physical, network, and hypervisor security, but is often more willing to make these programs and processes more transparent to the end customer. Some private cloud vendors also allow customers to perform vulnerability and penetration testing directly against the isolated network and systems, which is a critical component in these virtualized environments.

In SaaS and PaaS, organizations have limited visibility into the underlying infrastructure and again depend on the provider to properly secure and manage the network and systems. In these deployments, customers rely on the provider's security claims of scanning, patching, configuration, and vulnerabilities.

Though these challenges differ depending on the delivery model –Infrastructure as a Service (IaaS), Platform as a Service (PaaS), or Software as a Service (SaaS) – ultimately, organizations must understand their responsibilities and design the vulnerability management program with these environments in mind. While many vulnerability programs initially targeted their on-premise assets, more and more organizations are now expanding their vulnerability management programs to include servers, applications, and data assets that reside in the cloud.

Mobile Devices

Attackers are increasingly targeting mobile and remote machines. For example, blended threats (which exploit several different flaws simultaneously, such as sending a virus via an email attachment or SMS text message (SMShing) along with a Trojan horse embedded in an HTML file) are specifically targeting laptops outside the firewall to gain unauthorized access to the corporate network during an ISP connection.

As the number of mobile and remote workers has exploded over the past few years, so too have the security risks they pose. With the rise in new and blended threats that use multiple vectors of attack, these workers are increasingly vulnerable. They also pose a growing threat to the corporate network when hackers use vulnerabilities on these machines as conduits to the corporate network once these workers reconnect. Even as the number of mobile and remote users increases, so too does their risks. Today, the number of attacks and their complexity are growing, along with their associated risks. While in the past, there were only a few primary types of well-understood attacks, it is now impossible to keep up with the number of threats organizations face today.

Today, industry experts agree that the best method for securing mobile and remote machines, and the corporate networks they access via a virtual private network (VPN) or within the perimeter firewall, is an integrated, defense in-depth strategy. One component of this strategy is assessing the attack surface through robust inventory, assessment, prioritization, and remediation of vulnerabilities across the mobile environment.

For information technology to be confident mobile and remote machines are secure against latest known threats, they require a solution that guarantees that the necessary fixes or patches are in place and the machines are in compliance with latest corporate policies: for example, requiring that machines contain the latest anti-virus software.

Two types of tools are available to assess vulnerabilities and status on mobile and remote devices. Network-based security tools, which reside inside the corporate network and report on the status of installed security agents; and network scanners, which detect open ports, identify services running on these ports and reveal possible vulnerabilities associated with these services. These solutions can report on mobile devices after they connect to the corporate network, and they escalate findings to the appropriate administrators.

Host-based vulnerability assessment tools reside on the mobile or remote machine and audit the machine for system-level vulnerabilities including incorrect file permissions, registry permissions, and software configuration errors. They also ensure that the system is compliant with predefined company security policies.

As stand-alone tools, they can verify the risk of an asset while on the network but do nothing to protect against an infection and the initial connectivity of the device to the corporate environment. Network Access Control solutions have been developed to address some of these problems but do not effectively perform a risk and vulnerability assessment unless they are tied to other tools. To address this gap, many organizations are integrating their vulnerability management assessment results into their network access control policies and their mobile device management (MDM) solutions.

IoT

The Internet of Things (IoT) devices are not new. We have had cameras, alarm systems, and door locks IP-enabled for years. They have always had risks and vulnerabilities. However, with the recent introduction of verbal digital assistants, thermostats, lighting systems, etc., that are all TCP/IP-enabled, we have grouped them into a definition so we can manage them: just like we did for BYOD (Bring Your Own Device).

IoT devices are simply just another network device connected to our home or business networks. Their primary difference is that they are single purposed, generally do not contain features for security best practices like least privileged or role-based access, and they can be notoriously difficult to patch or even monitor.

In fact, if businesses allow IoT devices to be connected to wired or wireless by users, this just represents an extension to the BYOD concept to now include purpose-built devices users can bring into work. Unfortunately, MDM solutions have not caught up to this premise, and the risks of these devices are quite significant unless unmanaged on the business network. Many IoT devices require patches, use default or hard-coded passwords, or are misconfigured, making them easy prey for attackers. A new generation of distributed denial of service (DDoS) attacks (think Mirai) have emerged, and they want your IoT devices.

While the convenience of these devices is currently outweighing the security risks, government, companies, and consumers are taking note of their risks and potential long-term threats. In order to manage any new problem, the first step is to include these devices within the vulnerability program to identify all of the moving parts that contribute to the risk. This includes establishing acceptable use policies, security standards, and identifying any shadow IT that may already be occurring by IoT devices that are present on the corporate network.

Industrial Control Systems (ICS) and SCADA

Modern life depends on the automation of large-scale systems. Almost every time we turn on a faucet, switch on a light, or jump on a train, we are relying on industrial control systems (ICS) or supervisory control and data acquisition (SCADA) systems to manage processes like water purification, electricity generation, and mass transit signaling. But relying on computers for such essential tasks requires absolute trust in their security since attacks that disrupt these basic necessities could trigger catastrophic economic and public health and safety collapses.

Industrial control/SCADA systems have traditionally operated using proprietary protocols and remained "air gapped" to protect their mission-critical functions and to ensure the safety of the surrounding communities and the environment. As manufacturing technologies have matured, organizations have realized the scalability, centralized management, and cost savings of streamlining IT operations by connecting ICS endpoints to the corporate network. This shift toward connectivity, the transition from proprietary protocols to TCP/IP, and high-profile attacks on critical infrastructure, have raised significant concerns to the highest levels.

Additionally, many ICS vendors now use standard IT technologies within their solutions – common operating systems, databases, security modules, and protocol drivers, etc., making them more susceptible to attacks. To address such concerns, the ICS-CERT (Industrial Control Systems Cyber Emergency Response Team) provides ICS-CERT alerts to assist owners and operators in monitoring threats and actions that could impact ICS/SCADA systems.

For organizations that have industrial control\SCADA systems, these systems and the surrounding assets that could provide an attack vector for hackers must be considered when designing the vulnerability management program. Most commercial grade vulnerability scanners provide robust feature sets to proactively identify vendor vulnerabilities with prescriptive remediation options.

DevOps

When examining the scope of a vulnerability management programs consider all risks across all assets that may be targeted by attackers from both outside and inside the organization.

Devops (short for development operations) is an Agile-based software development and delivery process that aims to provide automation around the building, testing, and deployment of software rapidly, frequently, and more reliably. IT organizations seek to employ greater levels of automation and DevOps processes to increase the level of innovation and speed to market to achieve competitive differentiation.

As DevOps brings together development and operations together to provide both agility and productivity, it can also introduce additional risks from a security perspective. DevOps usually requires IT to grant administrative access not only to multiple development staff but also to configuration management and orchestration systems, meaning there must be tighter controls over privileges, patching, and configuration management. Without the proper controls, risks can include:

- Insiders leveraging excessive privileges or shared accounts to compromise code;

- Inadvertent vulnerabilities, misconfigurations, and other application weaknesses may get introduced into the production environment;

- External attacks on insecure code and other security exposures;

- Automation tools and scripts that deploy malware, sabotage code, or do other damage.

Organizations cannot fully embrace DevOps without appropriate controls to support security and compliance objectives. Therefore, organizations must enable DevOps securely (SDevOps) without inhibiting the velocity and agility of the business. For these reasons it is recommended that organizations expand the scope of their vulnerability management programs beyond the production information technology environments and assess all aspects of automation included in DevOps.

Docker and Containers

Tied to the increasing trends in DevOps, componentizing applications and running them inside containers rather than on virtual machines is gaining popularity. This approach allows organizations to isolate the dependencies that the application requires, thereby reducing the maintenance and security overhead of the container itself. It sits within a container and is separate from the host. The host itself could be a Windows or Linux machine that is managed, secured, and patched separately than that application itself.

This container approach enables more flexible and rapid deployment of the application without worrying about the compatibility and security aspects of the underlying host. Additionally, as it only contains software that the application depends on, the attack surface of the application environment itself is smaller. While the number of vulnerabilities within the container may be reduced, it is not eliminated and should be included within the scope of the broader vulnerability management program. However, a container-friendly approach to vulnerability scanning, and patching should be considered.

Many application containers are based on "container templates." That is, the application container itself is simply an instance of a template. If one can be assured that all active containers are instances of approved templates that have to make their way through testing and release controls, a more appropriate and nonintrusive approach to vulnerability scanning may be to scan the template library to detect which have vulnerabilities. Once detected, the organization can update the container template and redeploy the application containers into production.

If all running containers cannot be tied to approved templates, or if running containers allow for local configuration changes or updates to be made within the container itself, then it may be more appropriate to scan each production image for vulnerabilities.

Lastly, there are several steps that must take place before containers are deployed in the production environment. This includes development, testing, and staging the containers and their associated libraries. To ensure that all container and/or containers are included in the assessment, organizations may consider scanning both active and offline containers.

Code Review

Waterfall or Agile – whatever development methodology an organization uses, code reviews and more specifically, secure code reviews, are a critical step in the process, especially for custom software development. To maximize the benefit of code reviews, security teams should participate and educate development teams on secure coding techniques so that they can include this aspect of coding into their reviews. In addition to manual code reviews, many security vulnerabilities and coding flaws can be uncovered using Static Code analysis tools as part of the build process. This enables manual and automated inspection of the source code or a partially compiled version of the source code to detect potential vulnerabilities before the code is compiled and deployed. This type of vulnerability assessment is typically performed by development and should be a part of any organizations processes if they are writting, deploying, or even selling custom code.

Tool Selection

A vulnerability management program is typically seen as a long, complex, burdensome project to deploy across an enterprise. There are a number of factors that affect this that should be identified and discussed during the planning and development stages as discussed previously. When architecting the vulnerability program, it is important to ensure the technology, integrations, and processes implemented are flexible to handle yet unknown, or out-of-scope requirements, which may be absorbed into the project over time. It is also recommended the architected solution minimize the amount of customization, utilize standard protocols for possible integration points, and be constructed to handle a wide range of assets and use cases to future proof the security investment where possible.

In order maximize success, consider this sample list of 20 high-level selection criteria that may be considered when performing a vendor(s) selection:

1. Asset discovery, profiling, and management capabilities

2. Heterogeneous Asset Coverage

3. Virtual desktops, servers, and application support

4. Cloud inventory and scanning support

5. Mobile and IoT support

6. Scalability

7. Deployment Flexibility

8. Delivery Model

9. Ease of Use

10. False Positives

11.   Vulnerability Updates

12.   Threat Intelligence

13.   Consolidated Risk Visibility

14.   Reporting

15.   Risk Prioritization

16.   Patch Integration

17.   Ticketing & Workflow Integration

18.   Other Third-Party Integrations

19.   Technical Support

20.   Pricing

Adding the relevant selection criteria to a scoring to objectively measure the benefits of potential solutions is a common approach that can help ensure features selected are prioritized and in alignment with business requirements. Appendix B has a sample questionnaire (RFP) that can be used to assist with a tool-selection and vendor-scoring process.

Selection of the appropriate tools can ensure that the vulnerability program has the appropriate level of risk coverage, prioritization, reporting, and remediation. However, what is also important is to evaluate the ongoing maintenance and operational requirements to support the overall program. Many times, organizations do not plan ahead to ensure appropriate levels of staffing are allocated to perform, analyze, and react to the assessment activities. These skills and resources required to manage the ongoing operation of the solution should be identified and if possible, included, in the vendor-selection process. This is required for successful soluton sustainment (operations).

The Vulnerability Management Process

Once the development of the solution is complete and validated, responsibility to manage the systems is transitioned to the vulnerability engineers (deployment) and the initial vulnerability scans are scheduled and begin the cyclical portion of a vulnerability management life cycle (Figure 14-2).

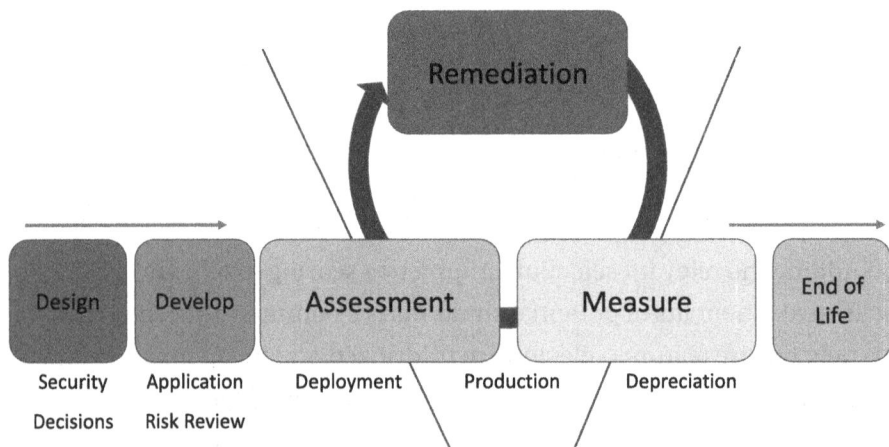

Figure 14-2. *Vulnerability Management Life Cycle*

Assessment

As resources are placed in production, periodic vulnerability assessments are required. An assessment is the act of actually looking for risks through any vehicle like a network scanner or patch management solution. Vulnerability management is the life cycle of an assessment including remediation (mitigation) and re-measurement. For the sake of this book, we will be focusing on the vulnerability management aspects of the life cycle implemented within an organization.

Measure

The vulnerability management life cycle requires periodic and frequent measurements to determine if new vulnerabilities are present and if mitigation and remediation strategies are effective. Typically, measurements are performed using service-level agreements to age a vulnerability:

- Date of public disclosure

- Date of Audit Release in an Assessment solution

- Discovery date of vulnerability

- Date of mitigation or remediation

- SLA measurement for date of discovery to closure

- Age of outstanding risks critical to the business

- Number of acceptable Exclusions or deviations

There are a variety of acceptable methods for reporting and SLA measurements. Methods that are automated with a high degree of accuracy are obviously preferred. However, there are times that manual invention will always be required. These include:

- Verification of an exception

- Identification of a false positive or a false negative

- One-time correlation with external sources

Remediation

The action for a vulnerability can come in multiple forms:

- Remediation – the actual application of a security patch (update) to fix a vulnerability;

- Mitigation – the removal of software, changing of a configuration, or the intentional modification of a resource to block the vulnerability (local HIPS for example) and potentially its corresponding exploit (if available);

- Exclusion – the acceptance of the vulnerabilities risk (also called a deviation) due to remediation or mitigation strategies that will impact the business.

These are currently the only acceptable classifications for a vulnerability remediation. Any identified vulnerability that does not fall into these categories is aging and considered open.

Rinse and Repeat {Cycle}

The vulnerability management life cycle requires that assessment, measurement, and remediation be implemented by policy and enforced periodically. This process is continuous and is expected for every asset in scope, resource, and application throughout the environment.

End of Life

End-of-life technologies represent an exceptional risk to any business regardless of the mitigation strategy. The underlying risk will always exist until the technology is removed and replaced with supportable business resources. Vulnerability management solutions will continue to identify new threats present on end-of-life resources, but there is no longer a remediation path from the originating vendor. Therefore, end-of-life assets are an exception and the last phase of the life cycle when measurement of the risks and cost will ultimately determine your next steps. Therefore, ask the following questions: When is risk too high to continue the usage of the asset? When will it be cost and time prohibitive to continue and not replace the asset?

Common Vulnerability Lifecycle Mistakes

Vulnerability management programs make up the front lines of risk reduction for security-conscious organizations worldwide. However, despite widespread deployment of vulnerability management technologies, many security professionals still struggle to decide how best to protect their organizations, achieve compliance, and communicate risk enterprise-wide.

The fact is, most vulnerability management solutions do little to help security leaders put vulnerability and risk information in the context of business. Saddled with volumes of rigid data and static reports, the security team is left to manually discern real threats and determine how to act upon them.

Read on to learn how to avoid the top five vulnerability management mistakes to improve your security posture and protection of critical IT assets, while reducing costs.

Mistake 1: Disjointed Vulnerability Management

The job of protecting corporate assets would be challenging enough, even without new attack vectors being exploited through desktop applications, employee-owned devices, mobile computing, and social networks. Every day you face new network devices, operating systems, applications, databases, web applications, plus numerous IP-enabled devices (laptops, servers, printers, etc.), and increasingly, IoT.

Clearly, as your environment gets more complicated, so too does vulnerability management. Many organizations piece together disparate, stand-alone solutions to accomplish the key aspects of vulnerability management – assessment, mitigation, and protection. However, this leaves them with a disjointed picture of security, which is not only more difficult to manage, but also more expensive.

Solution

TAKE A UNIFIED APPROACH. With security budgets and resources under pressure, you need to take the most efficient approach possible, one that brings the key pieces of vulnerability management together in a single solution. The answer is Unified Vulnerability Management, which delivers a consolidated solution for assessing, mitigating, and protecting your environment while reducing the overall cost of security and compliance.

ASSESSMENT. Vulnerability assessment must deliver unified configuration and vulnerability scanning across network devices, operating systems, applications, databases, and web applications using a scalable, nonintrusive approach. It's critical that vulnerability management includes configuration assessment, not just patches. Poorly set internal configurations can be as harmful as security violations from an outside source. Ideally, assessment should include unified reporting over all of these assets as well.

MITIGATION. You need prescriptive guidance and recommendations to effectively remediate critical vulnerabilities and strategically prioritize the rest. Make sure your solution adheres to broadly accepted standards, which include integration with both SCAP and ASV (PCI) for assessment, risk scoring, and reporting. In addition, look for alert and notification capabilities so you can take immediate action on critical issues.

PROTECTION. You need zero-day protection in cases when a vendor has not yet created patches for vulnerabilities in their operating system or application. Your solution should also reduce risk with intrusion prevention, application control, and USB and FireWire controls. Bringing assessment, mitigation, and protection together under one roof, in the form of a single solution, will ultimately save you countless hours and dollars.

Mistake 2: Relying on Remote Assessment Alone

Running remote vulnerability assessments works for many systems, but what about those blocked by firewalls or segregated from the network? What about cloud and virtual environments, and mobile and IoT devices? These are potential gaps that could be exploited.

In most environments, not every system can be reached. Thus, they can't be updated immediately without impacting stability, introducing operating incompatibilities, disrupting business processes, or negating internal or regulatory compliance. Relying solely on remote vulnerability assessments is not enough—and may, in fact, give your organization a false sense of security.

Solution

CLOSE THE GAPS WITH REMOTE AND LOCAL VULNERABILITY ASSESSMENT. For truly complete security, you need remote vulnerability assessment as well as local assessment for assets that are disconnected, unmanaged, or "exception" systems. Using a lightweight agent is the best way to get at these types of systems. It serves to augment your remote scans and makes it easier to meet stringent regulatory compliance requirements, where local credentials and more frequent scans are required.

With combined local and remote vulnerability assessment, you'll:

- Strengthen your security posture and ease the burden of regulatory compliance;

- Close the security gap on assets that are disconnected, unmanaged, or "exception" systems;

- Get a true picture of your enterprise-wide risk Lastly, you need full visibility via a single console to view the combined results of all scans to ensure complete security.

Mistake 3: Unprotected Zero-Day Vulnerabilities

Zero-day vulnerabilities continue to increase as attackers find new ways to penetrate your network. Clearly, you need safeguards to protect against these exploits and other complex attacks. Of course, like nearly all companies, you have anti-virus and anti-spyware in place. These signature-based technologies work well, but they must be augmented with zero-day vulnerability management to protect systems when vendor-supplied patches do not yet exist for an operating system or application. Continuous zero-day vulnerability monitoring and protection is a must-have in today's threat landscape.

Solution

ADD A LAYER OF PROTECTION. Augment foundational security components like anti-virus and anti-spyware with an additional layer that stops zero-day vulnerabilities. The ideal solution leverages a host-based intrusion prevention engine to dynamically collect and incorporate new threat data in real time. With this, you can enforce policy and secure your organization from targeted email or Internet attacks that could compromise your systems and data. Zero-day protection helps you:

- Reduce risk with intrusion prevention and zero-day protection where a vendor has not yet created patches to protect against vulnerabilities in their OS or application;

- Improve system protection by setting policy over which applications are allowed to function and preventing modification of specific registry settings;

- End data theft and leakage by regulating USB and FireWire access, and preventing the transfer of sensitive or confidential data to personal storage devices.

Mistake 4: Decentralized Visibility

Decentralized security visibility is one pitfall that trips up many organizations. Many organizations perform assessment, mitigation, and protection activities at individual locations but lack centralized management across the enterprise. Quickly identifying which assets are most at risk is imperative for the overall health of an organization. But, the challenge is finding a solution with a strong distributed architecture and the ability to provide a single point of management and visibility across the enterprise.

Solution

CENTRALIZE VISIBILITY. To achieve centralized visibility, look for a fully integrated, completely web-based security console product. An easy add-on to some vulnerability management solutions, this will dramatically simplify the management of distributed, complex infrastructures while providing true end-to-end protection. The key is becoming more efficient at finding, fixing, and protecting against the most urgent vulnerabilities and strategically prioritizing the rest. Look for a workflow-oriented console to make it easier to meet regulatory and security compliance requirements. Also, one that offers an asset-driven architecture will enable you to make logical groupings of assets regardless of their IP address and business function. But, you should also be able to view and prioritize risks grouped by business function or event, as well as by asset.

Mistake 5: Compliance at the Expense of Security

Yes, you need to meet regulatory compliance. Many organizations place a heavy focus on meeting requirements, which is certainly a wise approach. Especially for regulations such as HIPAA and PCI, audit failures (in the form of fines) are not only expensive but potentially devastating to customer confidence. Some high-profile, highly publicized breaches serve to highlight what can happen if an organization takes their eye off the ball. However, a truly comprehensive security initiative requires focus not just on compliance, but also on the broader management of security and vulnerabilities.

Solution

CREATE A SECURITY BASELINE AND MEASURE AGAINST THOSE STANDARDS. Institute comprehensive, strategic security initiatives that include compliance. This can be facilitated by finding a solution that lets you easily create a security baseline and then measure against those standards. From there, you should be able to measure against internal security policy and regulatory compliance. In other words, implement a solution that gives you the tools to meet compliance regulations, and then go beyond those requirements to actually improve security posture and reduce risk.

Common Challenges

Despite the technology challenges of a vulnerability management deployment, the business itself can have challenges. The following are a few common challenges an organization may face.

Aging Infrastructure

Defending an organization's systems and data against threats of growing complexity requires a defense in-depth strategy that can be as sophisticated as the campaigns launched by attackers. However, as we have discussed, a necessary component of any cyber security program includes tackling the low-hanging fruit—that is, basic tasks such as patching vulnerabilities and updating old software. The challenge for many commercial organizations and government agencies is the existence of legacy IT systems that create an environment with increased risks. These risks range from outdated components and software on desktops to network devices, which provide an attractive target to outside hackers and insiders.

Upgrading infrastructure and legacy applications is a costly undertaking and requires downtime and funding, so when prioritizing security spending, it is understandable why many organizations continue to put this investment on the back burner. As well, many organizations may simply not have viewed aging systems and applications as a priority, especially if they are not hosting sensitive applications or data. However, even in these scenarios, they can provide an attacker a foothold and the costs of ignoring the problem of aging infrastructure can run much higher than losing the use of a Windows XP workstation – namely, in the form of a devastating attack. As such, organizations and federal agencies need to recognize the risks associated with aging assets and properly prioritize the risks of not upgrading components and software. Additionally, organizations need to proactively plan for appropriate maintenance and system hygiene as a component of their ongoing security strategy:

Depth and Breadth of the Program

Gaining visibility into risk across large, heterogeneous IT environments comprised of network, Web, virtual, cloud, and mobile assets requires the following:

- Consolidated View of Risk – Making sense of multiple risk data inputs from decentralized, stand-alone security tools;

- Quantifying the Risk in Business Terms – Discerning the unique implications of security exposures on business operations;

- Multiple Regulatory Mandates – Demonstrating compliance with multiple regulatory mandates;

- The Output's what matters – Building and customizing reports for management, auditors, and other stakeholders;

- Zero-Day & Client-Side Exploits – Ascertaining the risk potential of zero-day threats and client-side exploits;

- Program Oversight – Confirming that security controls are in place and operating effectively;

- The Remediation Process – Researching remediation options and gauging their potential impact and related costs;

- Vulnerabilities and Patch Management – Effectively bridging vulnerability and patch management processes;

- Handling Exceptions – Accounting for "exception" systems, as well as changing network and configuration profiles;

- Complex Architectures – Assessing remote office infrastructure and complex network architecture;

- Coordinating Global Teams – Mobilizing local, global, and delegated administrative administrators.

Building the Plan

Now with an understanding of the business and technical requirements, challenges, and common mistakes, let's walk through a process to build the framework for a vulnerability plan. This is the final piece in understanding the Development phase.

Step 1: What to Assess?

The first step in any successful vulnerability management process is the determination of what to assess. This includes the following criteria:

- Logical grouping of assets by function, business unit, operating system, mission critically, storage of crown jewel data, etc.

- Assessments into technology stacks such as databases, hypervisors, virtual machines, containers, BYOD, IoT, IIoT, SCADA, ICS, etc.

- Geographical organization based on region, country, or regulation.

- Logical network and zone grouping based on DMZ, firewalls, zones, subnets, or business function.

- Asset Inventory based logical groupings used in Active Directory or Asset Management systems such as ServiceNow.

Step 2: Assessment Configuration

Equally as important as what to target for an assessment, is what should the parameters be for a proper, detailed scan assessment. These include the following criteria:

- Null session scanning provides a "hackers" perspective – performed on a regular basis to provide rapid assessment and network visibility of remotely exploitable vulnerabilities.

- Credentialed scanning provides an in-depth view of all existing vulnerabilities by remotely logging on to a target regardless of platform.

- Use network scanners for remote assessments and assessing for open ports.

- Use agents for hard-to-reach or hardened systems.

- Perform perimeter scanning.

- Web application scanning.

- Configuration compliance.

- Code analysis during development.

Step 3: Assessment Frequency

There are many factors that can determine scan frequency from regulations, internal SLAs, all the way through environments embracing automation and DevOps. In general, scan frequency should be determined by:

- The frequency of asset or environmental changes;

- The frequency of new threats;

- The frequency of remediation and mitigation schedules.

Any one of these variables can impact the need for a more frequent (or even less frequent) assessment. The question is what is the best technique to adopt an assessment to these requirements? Consider the following:

- On-demand assessment for validation or adaptive response;

- Scan new assets (specifically for DevOps and automaton) prior to moving them to production;

- Frequent discovery scans (recommended);

- Automated/recurring vulnerability assessment (recommended);

- Programmatically triggered by an event (SIEM, NAC, etc.).

Step 4: Establish Ownership

One of the primary problems experienced in most organizations is the ownership of assets, assessments, and remediation activities. This includes the entire stack from firmware, patches, operating system, and any applications.

Step 5: Data and Risk Prioritization

No one likes to read the dictionary or a phone book for work or for fun. Vulnerability assessment solutions can produce a plethora of meaningful data akin to a phone book. Due to the common requirement for frequent assessments, full reports are virtually unusable on a daily basis unless reduced down to a meaningful and concise format that can be prioritized. The real world of data prioritization takes into considering the following threat intelligence:

- Risk scoring is more than CVE and CVSS vectors

- Malware Toolkits present for the vulnerability

- Penetration Tools that have working exploits

- Exploits available in the wild

- Zero-Day vulnerability intelligence

- Data feeds from the dark web or other intelligence providers

- Successful mitigation and remediation recommendations

Step 6: Reporting

As a part of the vulnerability management life cycle, communications of an assessment are critical. They need to be accurate, concise, and have clear guidance for actionable remediation or mitigation. As with any solution and worldwide business requirements, there will be gaps in using reporting to communicate the response no matter how much a vendor tries to anticipate the requirements. The goal for all reporting should encompass:

- Reporting should be automated and available in a timely manner for delivery;

- Allow for custom and ad hoc report creation to satisfy unique requirements;

- Provide role-based access to reports and the data contained in the reports;

- Detail user access in logs to prevent data theft;

- Provide access via third-party solutions for custom integrations.

Step 7: Remediation Management

The remediation process (including mitigation and exclusions) is defined as the actionable guidance and execution performed in a vulnerability management life cycle. The success of this step ultimately determines the success of the entire vulnerability management program. While you can identify vulnerabilities, if they are documented and not resolved, your vulnerability management process is in jeopardy. In addition, as a reminder, this is not a one-time process. This must work repeatedly and like clockwork to truly be effective in mitigating risks. In order to govern the remediation process, please consider the following when applied to resource owners:

- Establish SLAs by vulnerability severity and asset criticality (crown jewels)

- Manual Remediation

- Automated Remediation

- Patch management Integration

- Mitigation

- Outsourced Remediation

- Managing Exceptions

- Documenting Risk

Without sound remediation practices that can reduce risks across the stack, the process is analogous to plugging only holes in a dam that you can reach. Ones outside of reach could lead to the next breach. The remediation process is the highest-risk step in the life cycle that is currently not functioning as expected based on vulnerability assessment data.

Step 8: Verification and Measurements

The closed loop process of vulnerability management requires continuous reassessment of risks and documentable measurements to determine their age, remediation (fixed), mitigation (closed), or excluded. This process draws on reporting to demonstrate activity. Basic measurements can include:

- Confirm vulnerabilities were patched, closed, fixed, or no longer present (for example software no longer installed)

- Service-Level Agreement (SLA)

- Risk Analysis

- Return on Investment (ROI)

- Support and Change Ticketing

Measurement and verification are the final steps in the closed loop vulnerability management process. Without these working correctly, threat reduction initiatives cannot be measured, and the risk to the business can escalate out of control. In addition, this can impact the vulnerability assessment process itself since the number of vulnerabilities will increase over time due to new public disclosures and the remediation process never keeping up.

Step 9: Third-Party Integration

Vulnerability assessment data is not an island. It is best shared with teams from operations and security to audits and executives to understand the risks to the business in various perspectives. No one vulnerability management solution can do this on its own. Therefore, all vulnerability assessment technologies depend on extensive third-party integrations to raise visibility into other disciplines and instrument additional workflows.

The most common integration points with the highest return on investment include:

- Security Information Event Managers

- Help Desk and Call Centers

- Identity Access Management (IAM)

- Threat Intelligence

- Cloud (Private and Public)

- Mobile Device Managers

It is very important to note that the architecture for your vulnerability management program will vary greatly from vendor to vendor and based on your own internal architecture. Some vendors are SaaS based, some on-premise, some hybrid, some use a client-server architecture, and others are more mesh or peer-to-peer based. It is out of the scope of this book to recommend one design over the other since technically they all could work in almost every organization. The difference will be how well they perform, cost to deploy and maintain, and other deployment issues covered in Chapter 15. The best recommendation we can make is to ask each vendor for their Reference Architectures and see how they overlay to your organization. This will help determine compatibility and costs.

CHAPTER 15

Vulnerability Management Deployment

Now that the vulnerability process and associated technologies have been thoroughly tested and validated in a lab and/or pilot deployment, it's time to roll it out to the production environment where it will be run on an ongoing basis. It is recommended that enterprise deployment of a Vulnerability Management solution and supporting processes be implemented in a phased approach. This controlled approach enables the deployment team to uncover and address challenges using managed approach. From years of experience, doing it all at once rarely succeeds. Figure 15-1 highlights the tasks for a successful deployment.

Phase	Objectives	Task Items
Deploy	Technical Implementation / Operational Hand-off / The Assessment Lifecycle	➤ Deploy solutions in the production environment ➤ Conduct required training to stakeholders including remediation, exception handling and SLA reporting ➤ Coordinate with IT and security teams on the scheduling of asset scans ➤ Initiate the Assessment Lifecyle within a pilot implementation ➤ Meet with Asset Owners to review results and guide through the remediation process ➤ Address technical, process, political and/or resource issues ➤ Perform a formal hand-off from the security engineering team to the vulnerability engineering team

Figure 15-1. *Deployment tasks for a successful vulnerability management program*

© Morey J. Haber, Brad Hibbert 2018
M.J. Haber and B. Hibbert, *Asset Attack Vectors*,
https://doi.org/10.1007/978-1-4842-3627-7_15

To ensure long-term success and to gather personnel support during the deployment phase, it is recommended that the vulnerability management program be rolled out incrementally. This approach ensures that issues and risks related to implementation, scanning, scans results, third-party integrations, remediation, and training are mitigated and manageable. The incremental versus "big bang" approach takes into consideration the sensitivity of vulnerability information and the cautiousness of performing network scans on targets that may be susceptible to faults and could negatively impact the business.

While the implementation phases for an organization may vary greatly, we will discuss three approaches for an initial deployment that can be implemented to discover the health of the environment in manageable steps.

Approach 1: Critical and High-Risk Vulnerabilities Only

In this model, the organization can configure their vulnerability scanners to only check for critical and high-risk vulnerabilities. This approach has several advantages over full audit scanning:

- Audits that could have adverse effects on user accounts or websites are not executed.

- Vulnerabilities that could be exploited with little to no user intervention will be accurately identified.

- The volume of potential compliance data and information messages will be eliminated.

- Business units and security teams can focus on the highest priority items that could interrupt normal business operations.

- The organization can expand the vulnerability program once the critical and high-risks vulnerabilities are remediated to a tolerable level.

This approach allows for targeted scanning of devices with only the most severe vulnerabilities included in the audit. This approach helps determine:

- How well patch-management functions meet remediation service level agreements;

- If devices with sensitive data can be compromised with minimal to no intervention;

- Devices that contain severe vulnerabilities and are potentially discontinued can be identified for replacement.

This approach has a few disadvantages:

- Low severity compliance related audits will not be included.

- Basic audits for usernames, groups, rogue services, and processes will not be identified.

- Application-based vulnerabilities may be excluded.

Approach 2: Statistical Sampling

Many regulatory compliance initiatives including the PCI DSS allow for statistical sampling of assets to perform an effective vulnerability management strategy. In order for this approach to be successful, a sample of all types of devices must be represented in a group of approximately 10% of the environment. In addition, proof of image standardization for hosts like desktops is required to validate the statistical sampling approach.

Please consider the following:

- All operating systems in the environment

- All applications in the infrastructure

- All hardware and network devices and printers

All of the devices above must be included in the target group. No version or platform can be excluded. The sample can be scanned with all audits or targeted vulnerabilities to report on the trends within the environment. Proof of standardization with no baseline drift is absolutely critical for this approach in addition to imaging procedures.

Statistical Sampling has several advantages:

- Limited targets and risk to production devices;

- Validation of compliance management initiatives and image standardization;

- Rapid scan times compared to evaluating the entire infrastructure;

- Consolidated reports based on samples;

- Results of scans and remediation activities can be completed and measured providing the information required to expand the scope of the vulnerability program at a manageable rate.

In contrast, the disadvantages to this approach:

- No rogue asset identification;

- Bottom "n" vulnerabilities and "one offs" are not identified but are still susceptible to an attack;

- Changes in ports, services, process, and users due to an attack may be missed.

Approach 3: Targeted Scanning Based on Business Function

Many devices in an environment provide supporting functions to a business but have no direct connectivity to critical information. Consider a web application. Only the web server and supporting infrastructure should have access to any middleware and databases. A web application vulnerability assessment scan will reveal any flaws, and which flaws could potentially be leveraged to penetrate the target through this entry point. Therefore, assessing every workstation that only interfaces with critical data via the web is overkill, that is, scanning the web application and web server as opposed to scanning all the machines that access it. A better approach follows the "where are the crown jewels in the castle." The business must identify where all of the critical business systems are and group them accordingly. Scans of these devices will target all possible entry points and should only occur during a predefined and acceptable scan window. This must also take into considersation any potential lateral movement in order to be successful.

This approach informs all parties that a network scan is going to occur (in case of a fault or outage) and that all critical systems are free from high-rated risks.

Advantages to this approach:

- Scans occur only at acceptable times.

- Systems housing sensitive data are validated to be risk free.

- Results of scans and remediation activities can be completed and measured, enabling the team to expand the vulnerability program to additional applications and services at a manageable rate.

- Scans and attacks outside of the scan window may be indicators of compromise.

Disadvantages for targeted scanning:

- Noncritical systems are not assessed and could be used as a beachhead to infiltrate an organization.

- The manual process of identifying hosts may lead to missing systems for targeted scans.

- Minimal or no rogue asset detection.

- Real attacks during scan windows may be ignored and deemed a part of the assessment.

These three approaches outline a conservative rollout for a vulnerability management program. The methodologies presented take into consideration the sensitivity of vulnerability information, the cautiousness of performing network scans on targets that may be susceptible to faults within an organization, and teams that may have little to no experience with vulnerability assessment scanning. These approaches differ slightly from traditional methods that may focus more heavily on asset classifications (start with servers, then workstations, then network devices etc.), or by geography. Whatever model is employed, it is important to realize that there are several other technical, process, and human elements that will need to be monitored and refined along the way. To that end, we have included an inventory of other best practice elements to consider during the deployment phase. After the deployment is complete, a full ramp up of complete assessments is obviously a function of maturity and the ability to manage remediation cycles and the influx of data. This maturity model for vulnerability management was covered previously in this book.

Team Communications

The most common approach to communicating vulnerability findings is through reports, an integrated ticketing system, or through custom spreadsheets (typically end-user customized). These can be generated automatically, delivered via email, warehoused in a repository, or hosted via tools like SharePoint. The main point is to communicate the threats, risks, and remediation strategy to all team members in order to enact a timely response. Often times, discussions arise around mitigation strategies, false positives, and exclusions in order to prioritize the risk or defer actions. These are completely acceptable, and the workflow and asset owners must accommodate these conversations. These can occur via meetings but in most modern organizations occur via email. Email, unfortunately, weakens our communications through complacency and a lack of organized structure. If threat and risk communications must occur via email, consider the following guidelines and suggestions to resolve this chronic cliché, "Didn't you read my email?" (The truth of the matter is, I didn't read it and I probably won't. It was unreadable.). Therefore, if your vulnerability mamagement program does rely on email, consider this guidance on how to craft a threat and risk email that is acknowledged and acted upon by the solution owners.

- Goal – The goal of an email or meeting invite is to clearly communicate information with an economy of words.

  - Avoid telling a story.

  - Focus on needs and expectations.

  - Set deadlines clearly.

- Brevity

  - Avoid long paragraphs and blocks of text. If you find you've written several, you're including too much detail.

  - Focus on the issue, not backstory or related situations unless absolutely relevant.

- Focus

  - Bullet points or numbered lists are great for focus and readability.

  - Numbers are helpful to provide a reference point for responses.

- Clarity

  - Use full and correct names. Abbreviations, nicknames, and first names only can cause confusion.

  - Be sure to include clear expectations for resolution, including specific action items for named team members, partners, clients, and all parties.

- Subject

  - The subject line should be as short as possible but clearly summarize the discussion. There should be no ambiguity.

  - Ensure the subject line is pertinent to the discussion and do not change it.

  - If you change the subject line, delete unnecessary portions from the body and consider it the beginning of a new thread.

- Use BCC

  - When emailing externally, avoid including internal resources such as developers.

  - BCC them if you need to, but some team members in every organization should not be forward facing.

  - BCC can also be considered an informal method of escalation when including management and can be reviewed as rude or subversive when used in this manner.

- Use Action Items

  - Clearly indicate questions and action items (including dates and names).

  - Do not ask general requests; no one will ever own them.

  - If you don't know what the action items are, perhaps a meeting is better. That might be a better purpose for the email request in the first place.

- Summarize – If you forward a long email chain to someone, add a quick summary in at the top.

- Meeting Invite emails

  - Ensure the meeting title captures the intent. See email subject line guidance above.

  - Attendees:

  - Invite only those that need to be there.

  - If you're not sure who should be on there, find out. Talk to managers and leads.

- If an attendee is not going to talk or be responsible for any actions, they probably don't need to be there.

- If someone is there "for visibility," it is better to get them caught up afterward with a summary or minutes.

- Include an Agenda

- Vital to focus the meeting

- A quick reminder of what the meeting is about, essential for busy people

- Allows pre-meeting preparation to be performed by attendees

- Avoids meeting subject creep. "While I've got you here...."

- Clearly state goals of the meeting:

  - What is its purpose?

  - Where do we want to be?

  - What do we want to solve?

  - Tie goals or discussion points to owners where possible.

Improving our security communications and making them more clean and concise will help our overall security posture. Having good writing skills will help, but being able to express them in an email everyone will read, understand, and can act upon is even better.

Network Scanners

There is one basic rule that should be followed for any network-based vulnerability assessment scanner, to be as electronically close as possible to the target. Any bandwidth, latency, packet shaping, QoS, port filtering, or access control lists can impact the performance of a network-based scan and therefore the accuracy of the results. While this may be easy to overcome by just deploying more network scanners, the cost of appliances, remote locations, and physical security may be deciding factors in your overall architecture. In addition, perimeter scans must allow full-unrestricted access (non-credentialed) to assess public address spaces for regulatory compliance such as PCI. Therefore, you must whitelist the IP range of the vendors scanning solution in order to have accurate results. This "simple" configuration change must be applied to firewalls, load balancers, and any other infrastructure and security solutions protecting your forward-facing websites and Internet applications. This now sounds not as simple as the initial request to "whitelist" scanners. It can be a fairly involved process, especially if you need scan windows. Unfortunately, this may be a real requirement for your organization, and the same principles may apply to your internal network as well. The same devices and policies internally can impede an assessment and cause errand results. The architecture for your organization needs to consider them. If not, your vulnerability assessment solution could be a packet canon and cause everything from a denial of services to account lockouts.

Firewalls

The purpose of a firewall is to block or redirect unwanted network traffic by port, application, and source and destination. Regardless of anyone's marketing that the perimeter of your network is dissolving, a firewall is still your first line of defense from malicious Internet traffic and a threat actor's toolkits. Whether the firewall is external and internal, it should now be obvious why it poses a problem for network scanners. A network scanner needs a clear line of electronic communications from the scanner itself to a target and should be able to assess every port on the target unrestricted. Typically, information technology administrators will whitelist a scanner through the firewall to achieve this goal, but there are other inherent problems with scanning through a firewall that team members are habitually not aware of:

- Total TCP Session Limitations – Most firewalls have a limit of around 64,000 or 256,000 concurrent TCP connections. For an all ports and all audits scan, a single target can exhaust all the resources on the firewall by attempting to open all 65,535 concurrently. This will cause a denial of service or outage on the firewall itself. On older devices, it has been known to cause the firewall to reboot spontaneously.

- Raw Packet Discards – Firewalls are designed to accept traffic via rules and pass them through to the proper destination. This can involve Network Address Translation (NAT) or simple IP forwarding. If the packet is malformed and does not adhere to RFC specifications, it will likely be discarded. That is a problem. Most vulnerability assessment solutions generate raw malformed packets and review the results from the target to determine if a vulnerability is present. While this is typically used as a part of a null session scan to determine in a network-based vulnerability is present and may or may not contain portions of exploit code, the malformed packet would be dropped by the firewall and the vulnerability not detected due to the lack of results.

It is, therefore, a best practice recommendation to never perform a vulnerability assessment through a firewall unless you absolutely need to. Many times, you may not even be aware that it is impacting your assessments and potentially will give you a false sense of security.

IPS/IDS

Intrusion Prevent and Detection Systems are designed to identify and block potentially malicious network traffic generated by malware, bots, a threat actor, etc. Their design digs deep into network traffic and packets looking for signatures, patterns, and network and user behavior to determine when something is suspicious and when something is categorically wrong.

If you consider a threat actor may:

- Use a network scanner or similar toolkit to infiltrate an environment and look for vulnerable hosts to infect.

- A worm-based ransomware or bot may leverage the network to propagate its infection.

- Malicious traffic may originate from an untrusted source.

- Communications may be occurring on untraditional or previously unused ports.

- An infection can spread laterally using existing trusted connections.

An IPS/IDS solution can provide a good identification and defense against a myriad of these types of threats. Unfortunately, a typical network vulnerability assessment will trigger these solutions as well. The results could be:

- Blocked or incomplete network traffic to a target

- An automated quarantine of network scanner traffic

- False alarms from the solution to a SEIM or other stakeholders

- The masking of real threats due to log noise from a scanner

For information technology teams that must perform network-based vulnerability assessments over a network with an IPS/IDS, the scanners and all their traffic must be whitelisted, and most importantly, teams should be notified when scans are occurring to separate expected traffic from a potential threat.

Packet Shaping

Packet-shaping solutions are designed to optimize network traffic and bandwidth. They are a very effective solution to control the flow of packets on a network and can perform advanced functions like delaying packets in order to favor other traffic based on priority. Since network-based vulnerability scanners need unaltered and unrestricted access to a target to perform an assessment, it is obvious that packet shaping or traffic altering technologies can skew the results of a test. It is therefore recommended not to use packet-shaping technology in line with a network scanner. A simple traceroute will help determine by IP address if a packet-shaping solution is in line with your network scanning traffic provided you know it exists in the first place. Hopefully, your network architects can help you identify these devices, firewalls, and IDS/IPS solutions prior to the design of your vulnerability management architecture. They will impact your design by either requiring more scanners or policies to exclude their traffic from modifications.

QoS

Quality of Service (QoS) technology is conceptually similar to packet shaping, but instead of storing and forwarding of packets to meet traffic requirements, TCP/IP packets are tagged with prioritization information and processed by routers, switches, and hosts to meet business and network requirements. Similar to packet shaping, any alterations to traffic and timing can impact the results, and typically strict QoS policies will impede an assessment. Vulnerability based network scanners should be excluded from QoS policies and allowed to flow unrestricted on a network.

Tarpits

A tarpit is a service on a computer system or network that purposely delays incoming connections from initiating and responding. The technique was developed as a defense against computer-based worms to slow detection, infection, and propagation from occurring at the speed a network computer can operate. Which is typically really fast. Essentially, it introduces a lag in network communications to slow things down to a human sustainable level. The term is derived from real tarpits, in which animals can get bogged down and cannot easily escape.

If you consider the basic requirements again for a network vulnerability assessment scanner, a tarpit will grind a network scanner to a halt. Scanners will never complete assessing targets correctly, and scan jobs will therefore never complete. Tarpits need to be disabled, detectable by network scanners, or infrastructures must allow for scanners to operate (whitelist) in order for vulnerability assessment scans to complete successfully.

Honeypots

A honeypot is a computer or network technology implementation designed to detect, deflect, or counteract attempts at unauthorized resource access. It does this by providing a "fake" set of crown jewels or services a threat actor will be drawn to an attempt to profile or compromise. This may also be called "Deceptive" security defense technology. A typical honeypot consists of data that appears to be a legitimate part of the environment but is actually isolated and monitored for attacks. Traffic to the honeypot can be IP based or port routing from many addresses to a single destination. For example, port 25 – SMTP, should not be open on client networks. All traffic destined to port 25 on end-user workstation subnets may be rerouted to a honeypot for capturing and investigation.

For the deployment of any vulnerability assessment scanners, honeypots should be:

- Excluded from any vulnerability assessment scans. Only the supporting resources of the honeypot should be assessed, and hopefully, they can be targeted securely through a separate IP address and designated management network.

- Subnets that include port routing to a honeypot should allow for scanner whitelisting or for all audits on a given port to be disabled. It is important to note that if ports are excluded, certain vulnerability signatures will not execute and potentially create false negatives about the environment.

- The security of the honeypot is just as important as the security of other resources. If a threat actor determines they have been targeting a honeypot, they may choose to target it with exploits since it is already known to be under attack. If compromised, it can provide a beachhead for future attacks and leverage a security solution against the organization.

Authentication

A network-based vulnerability assessment scan can operate successfully in two different modes of authentication: null session or with administrator or root privileges. Any privileges used to perform a network scan with privileges somewhere in between can result in false positives, false negatives, and a plethora of errors in the resources log files regarding denial of privileged access. While many organizations safeguard their administrative and root credentials like gold, they are required in order to perform a proper assessment remotely. With that in mind, a target must be "unhardened" to allow for a remote privileged connection. This includes the following capabilities depending on the platform:

- Remote SSH login as root
- Sudo access to root
- Privileged Access Management (PAM) least privileged elevation
- Complete access to the remote file system
- Remote registry access
- Authentication via NetBIOS
- WMI and/or SNMP access if enabled

- Web application credentials

- SA or equivalent database access

None of these are suitable for resources connected to the Internet or a potentially hostile environment. This is where agents and alternative technologies become viable. Based on your organization's requirements, you may decide on different frequencies as well per scan type, but performing a credential scan from time to time (frequently) is always recommended to get a true perspective of your security risks.

Null Session

Null session (with no credentials) vulnerability assessments will provide administrators an anonymous perspective of the risk profile for an asset. It is akin to a threat actor targeting an asset from the network with no foreknowledge of the resource. While this is valuable, it will only document vulnerability findings from a network or network-facing application perspective. Any vulnerability that does not have a network facing service will be undetectable. If you consider a modern scanner can detect less than 5% of an asset's vulnerabilities with a null session scan, the results will be disturbingly skewed from the actual risks if this is the sole source of information. It is therefore only recommended to run a null session scan to get a hacker's perspective of resources and privileged assessments for dictating actual remediation workflows. For example, which external resources or services are susceptible to WannaCry. Null session scans will be a subset of these scan results anyways, barring any false positives. With these characteristics in mind, here are a few best practices for null session scans:

- Targeting external assets with null session scans forms the basis for regulatory compliance initiatives like PCI DSS.

- Null session scans can help find vulnerable assets quickly that are remote susceptible to worms and certain bots.

- Null session scans are much faster than their credentialed counterparts since they will only apply a portion of the vulnerability signature database to a scan job.

- Null session scans are ideal for identifying rogue assets and rogue network services and applications like FTP, SMTP, VNC, RDP, etc.

Credentials

Credentialed scans, regardless of target platform or application, will provide the most accurate and best-detailed vulnerability assessment results. They provide the ability to log in as an administrator, root, or root equivalent to interrogate the entire operating system, registry, file system, ports, processes, services, and users for vulnerabilities. As discussed previously, using credentials requires a target to allow remote authentication and unrestricted access. If you plan to use credentials, there are some best practices you should follow for assessing resources:

- Use a dedicated privileged credential for vulnerability assessments. This account should not be shared by with any interactive users or services.

- Monitor for privileged activity using dedicated assessment credentials and escalate if they are being used outside of scan windows.

- Ensure prerequisites are met for remote access. If they fail, review assessment report findings to determine which services, like remote registry access, are not enabled for a target.

- If hosts are typically hardened and do not allow remote access, consider using one (or all) of the following techniques to get privileged access:

- Install, enable, or configure a second management network that has the proper services enabled for a credentialed scan. This management network should have strong access control lists prohibiting any forward-facing access or network bridging.

- Enable settings or group policy that allows for credentialed scans on a time basis and reference a scan window. For more details on scan windows, please see the section later in this chapter.

- Consider alternative approaches for a credential scan using local or dissolvable agents.

- Clone the environment, exactly. This is highly viable for virtual environments where images can be cloned to a lab, unhardened, and a credentialed assessment performed. This approach is common in mission-critical high-availability environments and sensitive government installations.

- All resources should be subject to a credentialed assessment and not just servers nor assets with crown jewels. Hopefully, we have already made this case based on ransomware attacks and threats to infrastructure, cloud, and IoT. If a team tries to justify why they should not be subjected to some form credentialed assessment, they are wrong and the risks explained to them.

Privileged Integration

One of the risks of credentialed scans is entering enterprise-wide administrative and root credentials in a single solution that can access the entire environment; your vulnerability management solution (Fair). A second, high risk is that once this is done, organizations tend not to change the password and it ages out of acceptable policy (Poor). The simple mitigation is to change the password frequently (Good) or to use unique credentials per target that frequently change too (Best). This can be accomplished by linking your vulnerability management solution with a Privileged Access Management solution. This can be done via API calls or dedicated connectors in each solution that allow for the retrieval of the current managed password on a per scan job or per asset basis. Figure 15-2 illustrates how a vulnerability management console enables a managed account for this use case with a network security scanner.

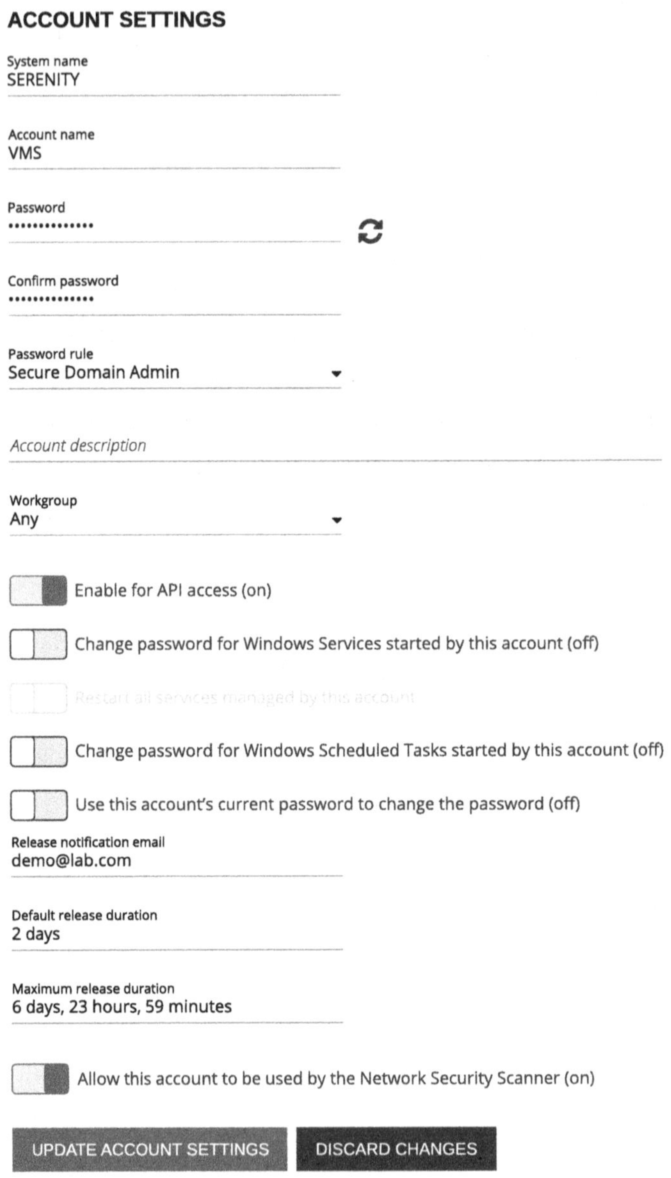

ACCOUNT SETTINGS

System name
SERENITY

Account name
VMS

Password
•••••••••••••

Confirm password
•••••••••••••

Password rule
Secure Domain Admin ▾

Account description

Workgroup
Any ▾

▮ Enable for API access (on)

▯ Change password for Windows Services started by this account (off)

Restart all services managed by this account

▯ Change password for Windows Scheduled Tasks started by this account (off)

▯ Use this account's current password to change the password (off)

Release notification email
demo@lab.com

Default release duration
2 days

Maximum release duration
6 days, 23 hours, 59 minutes

▮ Allow this account to be used by the Network Security Scanner (on)

[UPDATE ACCOUNT SETTINGS]   [DISCARD CHANGES]

Figure 15-2. *Enabling a network scanner to use a managed privileged account*

While there are risks that use the same credential everywhere, and over and over (like memory scraping malware that can steal hashes and passwords), the benefits do outweigh the risks. If you can monitor and manage the privileged credentials themselves in the first place, then risks are managable and ultimately acceptable.

Agents

Agent technology is nothing new. In fact, many organizations wrestle with quantity, conflicts, and updates for the wide variety of agents they have today. So why should a vulnerability assessment agent be anything special? It is not except that the usage is not widespread and not all vendors are equal in their agent offerings and their accompanying management capabilities. Some use cases in support of agents in lieu of network-based vulnerability assessment scanners are:

- Platform support for agent technologies (Windows, Linux, and MacOS) that are air gapped, hardened, short time to live, cloud, virtual, etc.;

- Immediate assessment results via API or CLI to support context aware integration initiatives;

- Deployment architectures that do not easily support network scans from remote devices to cloud and mobile (notebooks and tablets);

- DevOps certification of assets before deployment;

- Stand-alone assets like point-of-sales systems or embedded devices that require assessments for security best practices or regulatory compliance.

With these use cases in mind, there are two types of vulnerability assessment agents:

- Local – Agents are installed persistent on the asset and managed. Key management features include:

  - Binary version updates

  - Signature or audit database updates

  - Job scheduling

  - Ad hoc assessments via the management console, API, or CLI

  - Store and forward scan results

  - Scriptable installation and minimal resource consumption

- Dissolvable – Agents are installed on demand via a script or trigger. Once the assessment is complete, the agent automatically uninstalls. Key management features include:

  - Installation is complete with latest versions. No need to update before an assessment

  - Minimal resource consumption

  - Uninstall does not leave any files or fingerprints behind

  - Installation, operation, results, uninstall, and fault analysis is available via API or CLI

Agent technologies for vulnerability assessments offer a viable alternative to network scans. The results will be similar to credential scans and offer a method to obtain results without the potential problems and nuances of traditional network scanners. If you are migrating to the cloud, have a DevOps strategy, or prefer maintaining the hardening of your resources in lieu of network credential scans, agents are recommended approach.

Third-Party Integration

Vulnerability assessment information does not have to come from scanners and agents alone. Many third-party security products report vulnerabilities via CVEs and provide reports based on their own detection capabilities. For example, next-generation Palo Alto firewalls capture potential vulnerabilities and exploit information based on traffic and established rules. They can be considered a form of passive vulnerability scanners. These vulnerabilities are associated with a source and destination IP address and can easily be correlated to existing assets that may be in scope for vulnerability management. Typically, this data is sent to a SIEM, but there is no reason it cannot be included in your vulnerability management tool as an additional data source. If the data appears alongside other assessment results and can leverage the same reporting and alerts, the better. Your vulnerability management implementation should be the center of all your vulnerability information regardless of how it is gathered. This provides a holistic approach to the problem and a single pane of glass and system of authority to track vulnerability information.

If this use case is not in line with other corporate initiatives, the same approach could be overlaid to your governance solution like RSA Archer. The data is still relevant from each source, but in lieu of your vulnerability management solution being the record of authority, your governance solution becomes the focal point. This raises the bar and allows the introduction of other asset information and lifecycle data to be managed as well for a bigger perspective within the organization. The point is, do not ignore other security solutions and their identification of vulnerability information.

Patch Management

Patch-management solutions inherently are designed to apply missing patches regardless of type. Based on each vendor, patches may classified differently but they all follow a similar model outlined below:

- **Critical Updates** - A widely released fix for a product-specific, security-related vulnerability. Critical updates are the most severe and should be applied as soon as possible to protect the resource.

- **Definition Updates** – Deployed solutions that need signature or audit updates on a periodic basis in order to perform their intended mission or function. Anti-virus definitions are an example of these types of updates.

- **Drivers** – Non-security-related driver updates to fix a bug, improve functionality, or support changes to the device, operating system, or integrations.

- **Feature Packs** – A collection of new or updated features applied to the operating system or application. These commonly enhance functionality and provide new capabilities once installed. Feature packs can be free, or a paid add-on depending on the application.

- **Security Updates** – A widely released fix for a product-specific, security-related vulnerability that is noncritical. These updates can be rated up to a high and should be scheduled for deployment during normal patch or remediation intervals.

- **Service Packs** – A collection updates, fixes, security updates, and enhancements delivered in a single consumable update. It is considered a minor update required for cumulative or update rollups and many times drivers.

- **Tools** – A package of tools to aid in the usage, deployment, or troubleshooting of a solution.

- **Cumulative / Update Rollups** – Is similar to a service pack but it provides the latest updates for a specific solution including bug fixes and compatibility. It differs from a service pack in that it is targeted in nature and is used in addition to the service pack. For example, the service pack may be required as a prerequisite before the rollup.

- **Updates** – General bug fixes and corrections that can be applied that are not security related.

- **Upgrades** – Major operating system or application upgrades that can be automated for deployment.

In order to protect your assets, Critical Updates, Security Updates, and Service Packs contain a plethora of information regarding the patches and their corresponding CVEs published by each vendor. Similar to third-party integrations, patch-management solutions can, therefore, detect a vulnerability by inferring its corresponding CVE. Since a comprehensive CVE library is also present in vulnerability management solutions (signature and audit databases), a reverse mapping of the data allows for solutions to identify missing security patches and their corresponding vulnerabilities without performing any type of scan; network or local. A third-party patch-management agent, including Microsoft Update Agent, has at least partially identified vulnerabilities within the asset based on what it can detect is missing. While this is no subsitution for a vulnerability scan, it does provide a perspective on what known security patches are missing. It does not always take into consider if the patches have been correctly or fully deployed. It is therefore only a partial list and limited by the coverage of the patch management agent. This concept also highlights the overlap between the two disciplines and is another source for vulnerability data.

Virtual Patching

There are times when a security solution (or team) identifies a vulnerability that cannot be patched or cannot be patched within an acceptable time frame. These scenarios can vary from the risk of downtime or service disruption in patching critical applications and services, to end-of-life systems no longer being patched by the vendor. In these circumstances, the security team can opt to employ a virtual patch. A virtual patch does not remediate the underlying vulnerability but rather shields the asset by blocking the attack vector that could exploit it.

While remediating the actual vulnerability should be the ultimate goal, virtual patching does have a place and has gained in popularity. Such shielding techniques are often employed and positioned among Web Application Firewalls, Network-based Intrusion Prevention Solutions, and Endpoint Protection Platforms. And while the virtual patch can reduce the risk surface of an asset or application, it does not guarantee that it can block 100% of the attack vectors that could be used to exploit the vulnerability. Furthermore, by using a virtual patch, you must now be confident that the virtual patch mechanism is operational and effective on an ongoing basis. The long-term solution should always be to remediate the vulnerability through appropriate patching, configurations, or system upgrades.

Threat Detection

Threat detection is the art of identifying a potential active threat, correlating it to an appropriate set of risks, collecting Indicators of Compromise (IoC), and initiating the appropriate action. Organizations perform threat detection every day with solutions like anti-virus all the way through behavior and artificial intelligence analytics. Threat detection occurs at almost every layer within an organization and is one of the primary functions of every single security solution.

Threat detection within vulnerability management solutions satisfies the basic use case for identifying vulnerabilities everywhere along an infrastructure stack. To that end, these solutions collect a wide variety of other asset data that can be correlated automatically (or manually) for advanced threat detection use cases:

- Operating System – Identification of Shadow IT, end of life, or unsanctioned (rogue) assets

- Hardware – Potentially illegal devices such as USB removable media or hardware configurations that may have been compromised

- Ports – Network services that are operating that are not sanctioned like FTP or SMTP

- Processes – Inappropriate processes executing due to malware or rogue application

- Scheduled Tasks – Scheduled automation that does not conform to organization guidelines or privileges

- Services – Inappropriate services executing due to rogue software and their associated accounts and privileges

- Shares – Inappropriate shares for accessing an asset and their corresponding access control lists

- Software – Software inventory to verify appropriate applications, identification of rogue software, and incorrect version

- Users – Identification of local user accounts, privileges, and any misappropriation of user and group resources

- Certificates – The identification, expiration, and ownership of system certificates

- Personally, Identifiable Information (PII) – The identification of PII within user files and logs

- Malware – the association of hash information from processes and services with known malware

Vulnerability assessment solutions provide threat detection above and beyond missing security patches and flaws. The data can be used to supplement additional indicators or compromise and even form the basis for malicious activity. Consider processing this additional information locally or within a SIEM to bolster your security awareness.

Continuous Monitoring

Vulnerability assessment continuous monitoring is the process and technology used to identify vulnerabilities associated with an asset or resource in real time (or near real time) in contrast to a scheduled scan job or periodic assessment. The goal is to close the gap in vulnerability detection and not allow a threat to be present for a finite period of time, in between assessments, which can be leveraged by a threat actor. In order to implement continuous monitoring within an organization, there are several technology approaches:

- Network-Based – A vulnerability assessment-based network sniffer is placed on a span port and monitors all traffic. Based on the contents of packets, vulnerabilities are identified based on headers and packet contents. This includes things like identifying vulnerable network services based on banners and browsers broadcasting their versions. Network-based continuous monitoring only works on unencrypted traffic and cannot manage vendor backporting of patches. This leads to both a high rate of false positives and false negatives and requires all appropriate traffic be replicated through the span port. In highly segmented environments, multiple network-based devices will be needed in upstream locations in order to properly assess the environment. This is also called passive scanning.

- Application Control – Dedicated agents that work in conjunction with application control solutions to identify vulnerable applications as they are executing on a resource. These are detected as "Active" (as previously defined in Vulnerability States) since they are being used versus "Dormant" and just present on the host. This will provide continuous monitoring based on actual user activity and report the findings just like a local vulnerability assessment agent.

- Agents – Vulnerability assessment agents can provide continuous monitoring via frequently scheduled assessments or triggered via changes in the operating system, logon, or other criteria. The goal is only to send changes and perform assessments frequently so the gap for malicious activity is minimized. Configuring a local scan agent to run nearly continuously (looped) with minimal resources will meet these objectives.

Each of these solutions should consolidate its findings into your vulnerability management infrastructure and be a foundational component if you require continuous monitoring.

It is important to note, however, that continuous monitoring concepts can be applied to other security strategies and should be applied across your organization to avoid gaps in detection that are batch or scheduled based. For example, if you import logs on a daily basis for analysis, it will take up to 24 hours to detect the last threat. Continuous monitoring goals apply to the same process to eliminate that gap and make detection of entries and correlate the results as fast as possible.

Performance

The performance of a network or agent-based vulnerability assessment scanner can be dependent on a variety of factors. While meeting the minimum requirements for operating system, CPU, and RAM are critical, they are typically not the reason for poor performance. Vulnerability management vendors prefer you use their appliances to overcome these simple shortcomings but the environment 9 out 10 times is the problem;

not the scanner. Please consider these issues in your design and resolving performance issues with your network scanner(s):

- Network services such as NTP, DHCP, and DNS should operate reasonably well in order to resolve hostnames, track IP address changes, and accurately control the clocks on scanners for timely jobs and results.

- Scan targets should be electronically closed, and targets across a distant WAN should be targeted by local scans and not across the world or through firewalls. Low latency will help the performance of any network scan.

- The slowest link to the target will always be the bottleneck. If the scanner is on a gigabit network, but the target must traverse an old 10mps half-duplex network in order to communicate, every target downstream through that link will suffer performance issues during a scan.

- Network saturation and available bandwidth is key. Vulnerability assessment scanners can be packet cannons. If a link is saturated, or the pipe is too thin, scans can time out, and other services may experience a denial of service. Slowing scans down in terms of the number of targets and the number of connections (namely, checking simultaneous signatures and ports) will help links that are already overprovisioned.

- Reporting is associated with scan performance all the time. While you may be able to review an individual asset as results are being identified, it does take time for the entire job to complete and the results to be processed (normalized) in order for a report to be generated. A typical Class C network with all ports and audits can easily take 30 minutes. For an enterprise using limited scanners, it obvious to see how this can take days.

Threads

The number of threads (also called simultaneous targets) allows vulnerability assessment scanners to process more than one resource at a time during a given scan job. Depending on bandwidth and the environment, it is not uncommon to process up to 64 targets at a time on a 10GB network. If you consider an all ports scan again, it's easy to see why a network scanner can also be considered a packet cannon. If you consider the bandwidth required, the following recommendations are applicable to the slowest network pipe in a scan job (Table 15-1):

Table 15-1. *Number of Scan Targets Based on Slowest Available*
Network Link

Slowest Trace Route Link	Scan (Targets)	Ping Retries
10 GB Full Duplex	64*	1
1 GB Full Duplex	48*	2
100MB Full Duplex	24	3
100MB Half Duplex	12	3
10MB Full Duplex	10	4
10MB Half Duplex	5	4
256k Frame Relay	3	5
128k ISDN	2	5
56k Dial Up	1	5

* - Increasing network speed by 10x multiples does not translate into 10 times more capacity for scan targets. Other factors like TTL, latency, saturation, and remote target response time limit the number of targets that can be targeted by a single scanner.

This is applicable if the target is an operating system, database, or even web application and network scanning technology.

Time to Complete

Time to complete has different variables for the scan completion of a workstation, server, database, domain controller, or even web application. Each one will vary greatly based on their traits and knowledge about the target will help determine how long a potential assessment could run:

- Workstation – A workstation is typically the second fastest resource to complete an assessment even if it is fully loaded with vulnerable applications. Assessment times can typically run from a few minutes to 15 minutes maximum per target.

- Server – A server is generally around the same time as a workstation but can have extended times due to local accounts and additional applications. If a database is present or web application, the thread will be tied up with the server but supporting assessment of the application. This ties back to how many threads are allowed to occur simultaneously regardless of the target type.

- Database – Database assessments are typically the second longest targets for an assessment. This is not due to the signature-based checks that are included but the potential enumeration of the database, tables, stored procedures, etc., that need to be verified for privileges, misconfiguration, and vulnerabilities.

- Domain Controller – Domain Controllers are just Role-based servers. They can have extended scan times if the vulnerability assessment scan is configured to enumerate users and their associated groups and password age, login dates, etc. Scanners have features to limit enumeration to a certain quantity or disable the collection of information to minimize excessive scan times and potentially loads on the network and server to process each request.

- Web Application – In general takes the longest to enumerate and some scans can easily last days depending on the number of pages, complexity, and technology used to host a website. Typically, scanners for web applications have crawling engines and use signatures and machine learning to process the responses and vulnerabilities on a website. Web application assessments are normally done as separate scan jobs and do not follow the same thread model as vulnerability assessment scans. This is because threads are used to open and process multiple web pages simultaneously as targets versus entirely different web applications. It is important to note that while most vulnerability assessment vendors have a "lightweight" web application assessment engine built into their network scanners, some have dedicated tools for this sole purpose and perform a much more comprehensive assessment. These tools are typically used by developers for custom applications to ensure that they do not have any latent risks.

- Infrastructure – Are typically the fastest devices to process for a vulnerability assessment unless they allow connections to time out versus reporting an error or closed / filtered port. The signature list is significantly smaller for these devices compared to a modern OS and thus require fewer checks.

Bandwidth

Bandwidth is one of the critical factors affecting scan performance and overaccuracy of a scan assessment. There can never be too much bandwidth for an assessment, but too little bandwidth will affect everything from the number of threads you can spin up simultaneously to target resources to false negatives due to connection timeouts.

In order to ensure bandwidth does not become a limiting factor in your deployment, infrastructure and network teams should be engaged to overlay network diagrams with scanner deployments to determine if bandwidth will be an issue based on network design or empirical network performance data. This supports our previous conclusions that network scanners should always be electronically close to their targets.

Ports

The success of a network-based vulnerability assessment scan requires that a scanner be able to open a connection to any TCP/IP port on the target via TCP or UDP. While some regulatory compliance initiatives like PCI require enumeration of all ports, oftentimes this is overkill for routine assessments and internal workflows. Scanning all 65,535 ports takes time, but assessing default associated with audit signatures, typically the first 1,024, will give accurate results and a good baseline to work from. Granted, it will need to find rogue network services potentially running on high ports, but a credentialed vulnerability assessment scan is more about what needs remediation then threat detection. Therefore, in order to improve scan performance and time to complete, consider only testing relative ports and leave all ports for certification assessments and their accompanying follow-up.

Scan Windows

A scan window is the time and date a scan job is allowed to operate. Since network-based vulnerability solutions can be network and resource intensive, organizations generally plan for assessments during change control windows or dedicated maintenance time. Scan windows can be applied to scan jobs, the scanners themselves, or to the targets in an assessment. Times outside of these windows will suppress activity. Scan windows themselves can be configured to perform the following:

- Start and pause a job when an assessment exceeds a scan window. For example, if a scan window is specified for 1 am to 3 am every night, a scan job that is still operating at 3 am will be paused until the next evening and resume at the same place the next evening at 1 am and continue this cycle until the job completes during the scan window

- Start and abort a job when an assessment exceeds a scan window. For example, a scan window may be configured for the second Saturday of every month for 24 hours. If the job runs longer than 24 hours, it is automatically terminated.

If you consider the sensitivity of ICS devices and security for mission-critical systems, scan windows are a mandatory requirement in order to ensure there are no errand effects from a scan and that any network traffic to assets is not malicious.

Scan Pooling

Scanning pooling (or sometimes referred to as scanner grouping) allows environments to group scanners together for scan jobs. The purpose is to take the entire target range and split the load equally among all the scanners in a group. For example, if there are 1,000 targets (host names, IP addresses, CIDR, etc.) in the scan job and 4 network scanners in the scan pool, each one will get 250 assets to scan in order to complete the job. This allows you to minimize the time it takes to complete the job by using more resources, more threads among multiple scanners, and distribute the load on multiple network interfaces versus trying to run everything with a high thread count that could saturate the network and cause performance issues.

Target Randomization

Target Randomization is a simple concept. In lieu of running the target list sequentially, including IP addresses in a range, the target list is shuffled like a deck of cards and processed by the scanner. This means that one subnet will not experience the heavy load of all threads operating simultaneously and when used with scan pooling, the distribution of targets is also randomized as well. Target Randomization helps keep the vulnerability assessment scan load balanced across the network by never targeting too many resources in the same network at the same time.

Fault Tolerance

If you consider all the potential restrictions on a scan job from scan windows to performance, and if a scan job fails to start or hangs during an assessment, the results will be deferred or lost until the next opportunity to run a scan job and correct the fault. Fault tolerance for scan jobs allows for scanners to be linked as a fault-tolerant pair. If one scanner experiences a fault, its fault-tolerant peer can be assigned to pick up the job after a user-specified period of time. Figure 15-3 illustrates this configuration.

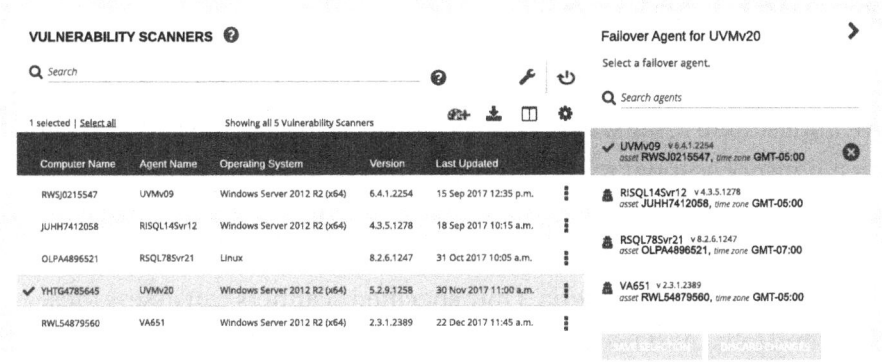

Figure 15-3. *Vulnerability assessment scanner failover configuration*

For more advanced environments, clients may choose to do the following:

- Designate one or more network scanners to a single purpose-built fault-tolerant scanner. All other scanners point to it in case of a fault, and by itself, it does not have any periodic scan jobs assigned. Its sole purpose is failover.

- Designate a round-robin failover using three or more scanners. Each scanner failovers over to a peer and if you follow the settings, you have a round-robin loop of assignments.

- Scanners follow a buddy system and are paired to each other for fault tolerance.

205

Scanner Locking

As we have previously discussed, scanning across a firewall or WAN can have undesirable results. For users setting up scan jobs, they need to know which network scanner to use in order to avoid potential problems. In order to avoid mistakes, there is a simple concept called scanner locking. Scanner locking assigns the targets to a scanner by IP range, group, or other asset-designated criteria. Only specified scanners can assess these targets and jobs must use them when running a job. The end results are simple, pairing the targets for assessment with the network scanners that can perform the work and ensure users do not make a mistake that could cause a business impact or faulty data. This is a common practice for managed service providers and multi-tenant installations.

CHAPTER 16

Vulnerability Management Operations

You have a vulnerability scanner, but where's your process?

Most organizations are rightly concerned about possible vulnerabilities in their systems, applications, networked devices, and other digital assets and infrastructure components. Identifying vulnerabilities is indeed important, and most security professionals have some kind of scanning solution in place. But what is most essential to understand is that a vulnerability scan represents just a single snapshot of your infrastructure at a fixed moment in time. Figure 16-1 illustrates Operation tasks that must now be accomplished in order to make this a repetitive sustainable process.

Phase	Objectives	Task Items
Operate	Technical Implementation / Operational Hand-off / The Assessment Lifecycle	➢ Expand assessment scope and scale the assessment processes ➢ Perform quarterly reviews with key stakeholders to adjust for changes in the business or risk environment ➢ Work collaboratively with various teams and departments to improve the program and risk posture of the company

Figure 16-1. *Operating a successful vulnerability management program*

© Morey J. Haber, Brad Hibbert 2018
M.J. Haber and B. Hibbert, *Asset Attack Vectors*,
https://doi.org/10.1007/978-1-4842-3627-7_16

The fact is, your infrastructure is constantly changing, and vulnerabilities may appear at any time. Attackers may appear at any time, as well. That's why you need to build a comprehensive vulnerability management plan that ensures frequent coverage of your environment – but also includes a sustainable process for analyzing, prioritizing, and remediating vulnerabilities when they are found. This covers the Production loop of the life cycle as illustrated in Figure 16-2.

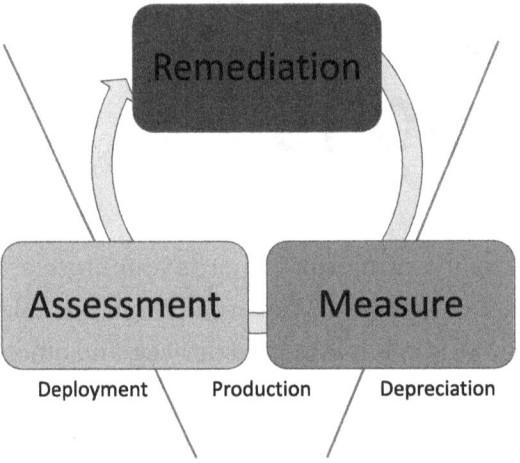

Figure 16-2. *Vulnerability management production portion life cycle*

Only with a consistent, repeatable vulnerability management process that covers all assets and provides regular reporting so that informed decisions can be made quickly – shortening the window during which you are vulnerable – can you be assured your solution is providing the protection you expect. As a part of the assessment step however, we need to explore Discovery, Analysis, and Reporting (not shown) as three sub steps. Remediation and Measure complete the lifecycle before any exit paths are considered.

Discovery

In terms of discovery, the question is how often you should scan? Again, that will depend on the size and nature of your digital assets. At the very minimum, low-risk or low-value assets should be scanned at least once a quarter. At the opposite end of the spectrum, high-risk/high-value assets can be scanned as often as several times a day. It all depends. There are other factors to consider as well; for example, patches from some vendors are released on the 1st of every month and others the 15th of the month like Microsoft. That is, therefore, a good time to schedule scans of servers and sensitive hosts based on remediation availability and in order to meet SLAs.

The scope and frequency of scanning should be well defined and documented as responsibility for the ongoing assessment is passed over to the vulnerability engineers. At this point, it is up to the vulnerability engineer to schedule and validate scan job health, performance, and that remediation activities are proceeding on schedule.

Analysis

The challenge here is that you might be generating an enormous amount of data through your scanning solution, and being able to analyze it in an efficient way is essential for remediation activities. This is a key capability of a robust vulnerability management solution, as there will be too much information to sift through it all manually. You need to be able to configure a solution to identify the highest-value information that each scan yields. Through ongoing collaboration with the security teams, information technology teams, asset owners and auditors, the vulnerability team can work to ensure appropriate levels of reports are delivered to the "right" people, at the "right" time. This is an analysis and reporting excerise and benefits the most from threat intelligence.

Reporting

The reporting sub step is where the data becomes actionable. The vulnerability assessment process will generate a variety of reports, focusing on such things as threat analysis, service-level agreement status, regulatory compliance, and exceptions and expiration dates. Reports should be reviewed by the security team, system owners, and system administrators, all of who will work to create a schedule of what actions must be taken and what the priority of each action should be. The vulnerability engineer must ensure that the appropriate levels of reports are being generated and distributed accurately and on a timely basis. This includes not sending the same list of 10,000 vulnerabilities to all asset owners every week. This is when reports and emails get ignored. Filter the reports and only send asset owners vulnerabilities for which they are responsible. For example:

- Vulnerabilities on Desktops to the Desktop team

- Vulnerabilities on Windows Servers to the Windows team

- Vulnerabilities on Unix Servers to the UNIX team

- Vulnerabilities in the DevOps staging area to the Development and QA teams

- Vulnerabilities on the Web Servers and databases to the application team responsible for those assets

- Vulnerabilities on network devices to the appropriate network teams

Remediation

This leads to the second major step in production, remediation. Depending on the asset and the vulnerabilities found, remediation can be done quickly and remotely, or it may require a more complex, hands-on fix that may require taking some systems offline, using redundant systems, and implementing additional components. As noted earlier, such contingencies should be identified in advance so there is no delay in eliminating the vulnerability. Ultimately the decision to remediate or accept risk should be made by the asset owner and coached by the security team. The vulnerability team must ensure that appropriate steps are followed to mark exceptions within the vulnerability solution to ensure appropriate risk, audit, and service level agreement reporting are all documented.

Measurement

Finally, measuring the overall vulnerability attack surface and effectiveness of the remediation processes is a critical component of any successful program. Measurement is used to ensure risks fall within accepted levels, ensures that compliance mandates are not violated, and can be used to provide positive (and negative) motivation for information technology and asset owners responsible for remediation and other supporting activities.

During the operational phase of the vulnerability management system, it is likely that asset owners will require, and demand, specific and sometimes custom reports to report on risk and streamline remediation activities with existing processes. Successful vulnerability management programs are the ones where the vulnerability engineers work with the various stakeholders to understand their information needs to try and optimize the process. Here are some recommendations:

1. Do not send the same raw vulnerability report to all stakeholders and ask them to filter and find what they need.

2. Understand what assets, what vulnerabilities, and what level of detail that each stakeholder requires and provide pre-canned reports to simplify and automate the process.

3. If possible, automate report generation and allow self-service reporting at the technical, management, and executive levels.

4. Select a vulnerability scanner that provides a flexible reporting framework that enables customization to satisfy incoming requests.

5. Do not attempt to satisfy ongoing report requests manually. That is, do not get into a routine of hand jamming spreadsheets and other reports for stakeholders. As the number of refinements increases, more and more time will be spent trying to keep up with incoming requests, increasing the overall cost of the program and delaying access to critical risk information.

CHAPTER 17

Vulnerability Management Architecture

Once a vendor has been selected for vulnerability management, the process of an actual implementation will vary greatly from one vendor to another. The simple question is why? Each of the leading vendors has taken a different technology approach to instrumenting vulnerability management at the console or management layer but is actually very similar at the scanning layer. This is why you hear security professionals state, "a network scanner is a network scanner" or that "vulnerability assessment is a commodity." The truth is that scanners are definitely a commodity but how the data is aggregated, scans are performed, and the type of reports available are what differentiate each of the vendors. They all have false positives; they all have false negatives; some are faster at scanning one type of asset over another; and in the end, it's the people and support that will make the difference with results and integration from the management console. Some security professionals will have a favorite solution but the deployment of each, from a management console perspective – not scanner, will vary due to on-premise technology, hosted solution, peer-to-peer databases, air gapped networks, appliances, agents, etc. All deployments need the traits discussed in this book, but

© Morey J. Haber, Brad Hibbert 2018
M.J. Haber and B. Hibbert, *Asset Attack Vectors*,
https://doi.org/10.1007/978-1-4842-3627-7_17

the architectural topology from one vendor to another will be different. Some will connect to the cloud, some will use a spoke-and-wheel tiered hierarchy, and others peer to peer. Which architecture fits your network best is a decision only you can make. Consider the following:

- A hosted solution works best when all scanners have a routable network connection to the cloud as an SaaS offering.

- An air gapped or isolated network can only work with a peer to peer or on-premise installation of vulnerability management technology since the Internet is not accessible.

- A centralized database and management console is required (typically in a data center or cloud) for any vendor proposing a tiered architecture.

- Peer-to-peer installations distribute vulnerability results and require almost all nodes to cross communicate. This may not be practical for some environments with strict segmentation.

With these in mind, the following questions should be answered for any deployment regardless of architecture:

- Does the installation require software, appliance, agents, or a hybrid approach?

- What are the prerequisites for the operating system, databases, and network for a successful architecture and deployment?

- What additional hardware and software will I need to acquire?

- Where will my scanners be logically and geographically placed? How many will I need?

- Which modules out additional features like regulatory reporting or configuration management will I need to license?

- What modifications will be needed to IDS/IPS and firewalls for a successful architectural deployment?

- What is my scan and remediation policy? Have all the stakeholders signed off?

- Do I have the necessary credentials for an authenticated scan? For all assets? Will this integrate into a Privileged Access Management solution (PAM)?

- What third-party integrations do I need to implement?

- Who are the stakeholders for reports?

- What are my regulatory compliance deliverables?

- What additional resources need assessments from the cloud to mobile devices?

- Who is being trained and how do I accommodate personnel turnover?

Once you have answered these basic questions, you literally have your deployment model to apply to any architecture. As an illustration, Figure 17-1 contains a basic architecture for any vendor, while Figure 17-2 contains a reference architecture for a typical enterprise environment with an on-premise solution.

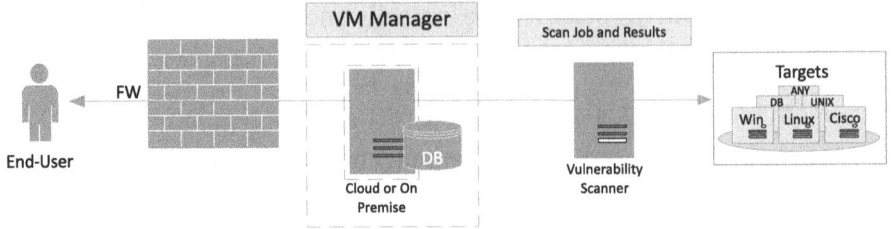

Figure 17-1. *Basic vulnerability management architecture*

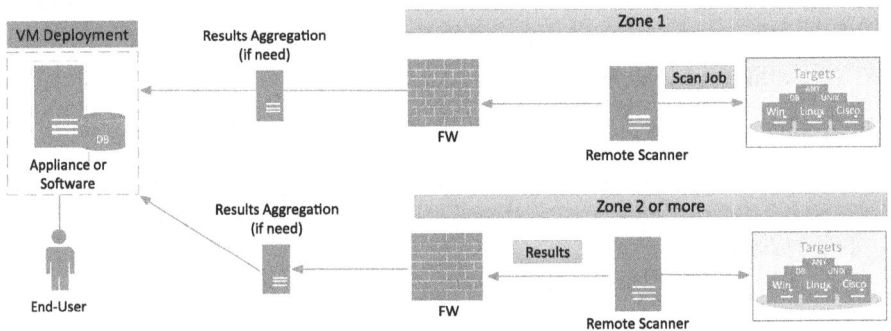

Figure 17-2. *Enterprise Architecture for an on-premise implementation using a tiered model*

The questions will decide which technology to place in which locations and how the solution will be interconnected once you consider all the parameters necessary for a successful assessment.

CHAPTER 18

Sample Vulnerability Plan

This chapter outlines the vulnerability management policies and controls required to maintain high levels of system and application security in a diverse IT environment. It details the technology and procedures necessary for implementing a comprehensive, integrated program to detect and remediate vulnerabilities in operating systems, applications, mobile devices, cloud resources, and network devices to maintain maximum levels of security. It forms the written procedures and policy necessary for the Operations phase of a deployment. Consider it a sample of what you will need to document for your own program and requires the sign off of all asset owners in order to be successful.

Vulnerability Management Solution and Remediation Service Levels

A typical vulnerability scanner will scan the network infrastructure for devices on a scheduled periodic basis and generate a variety of reports highlighting the vulnerabilities identified across all in-scope assets.

Upon receipt of the reports, the Operations Team is responsible for:

- Reviewing the results;
- Distributing results to appropriate stakeholders and asset owners;

© Morey J. Haber, Brad Hibbert 2018
M.J. Haber and B. Hibbert, *Asset Attack Vectors*,
https://doi.org/10.1007/978-1-4842-3627-7_18

- Monitoring asset-owner activities, which may include providing remediation via configuration changes or deploying security patches, or implementing other mitigating measures;

- Working with asset owners to properly documenting any exceptions.

Vulnerability remediation is to be completed as soon as possible following these guidelines (Table 18-1):

Table 18-1. *Vulnerability Severities and Service Levels*

Severity	Description	Service Level
Critical	Critical vulnerabilities have a CVSS score of 8.0 or higher. They can be readily compromised with publicly available malware or exploits.	2 Days
High	High-severity vulnerabilities have a CVSS score of 8.0 or higher or are given a High severity rating by PCI DSS v3. There is no known public malware or exploit available.	30 Days
Medium	Medium-severity vulnerabilities have a CVSS score of 6.0 to 8.0 and can be mitigated within an extended time frame.	90 Days
Low	Low-severity vulnerabilities are defined with a CVSS score of 4.0 to 6.0. Not all low vulnerabilities can be mitigated easily due to applications and normal operating system operations. These should be documented and properly excluded if they can't be remediated.	120 Days
Information	Information vulnerabilities have a CVSS score lower than 3.9. These are considered risks but are generally reference information for the state and configuration of an asset.	Flexible–180 Days

Any findings that need to be mitigated later than the service level must be approved by management and documented as exceptions. These are to be reviewed and approved by the operations manager and director of security.

Team members may also use specialized scanners to identify specific vulnerabilities or gain a deeper level of analysis, such as through the use of dedicated web application scanners, static source code scanners, etc.

Vulnerability Scan Targets

All devices connected to both public and private segments of the network are scanned. Device scans are organized by the individually defined address spaces, active directory queries, cloud resources, and locally installed agents.

Assets to be scanned should be grouped together in logical units named for the "commonality" that it holds for assets. A logical name also identifies its classification or a general description of the hosts/devices on the network and is used for role-based access for team members to restrict unauthorized access.

A new logical grouping can be established, or an existing one changed, by submitting a request through a help desk ticket directed to the Security Team and assigned to the Assessment Team.

Vulnerability Scan Frequency/Schedule

All devices are scanned on a consistent scan schedule and also on a by-request or as-needed basis. The defined scan frequency makes provisions for an assessment at least once per week for servers and sensitive hosts, and once per month using a rolling scan for all other devices on the network.

- All server and sensitive host scans should be scheduled between the 1st and the 15th of each month. This accommodates critical patches released by vendors such as Microsoft.

- All desktop and other scans should be completed between the 16th and the 29th of each month.

- New asset discovery scans should be run daily to identify any new assets and classified automatically into the appropriate logical scan groups.

- All new assets to be included as production for desktops or servers must be assessed and documented with no critical or high vulnerabilities.

- All scans should be allocated at 36 hours to complete with no other scans running.

- The scan cycle should be established when the logical scan group is defined and should be part of the assessment request.

- Ad hoc/individual system scans may be requested via a work request and performed at any time.

- All software images (operating systems) on the network devices (routers, switches, VPN, firewalls, wireless, and DNS/DHCP) are to be reviewed monthly.

Vulnerability Reporting

A flexible reporting schedule that works in tandem with system administration patching cycles has been implemented to manage resources and potential outages. A report will always be generated as proof that an assessment occurred. Automated delivery of the reports will depend on the scan date within the cycle.

Systems are organized into logical groups consisting of a collection of systems that pertain to a specific application, managed by a specific set of administrators, etc. A device may belong to one or more groups. Reporting is done by group so that the devices and vulnerabilities can more easily be distributed to staff. Groups may be added or changed via the corporate ticketing system. Table 18-2 and Table 18-3 are a listing of key reports that are automatically generated and delivered to implement this process:

Table 18-2. *Schedule for Executive- and High-Level Vulnerability Reports*

Status Reports	Frequency	Purpose
Threat Analyzer	Weekly	Provides recommended remediation to maximize resources by mitigation type.
Executive Dashboard	Weekly	Provides executive team members a status of risk mitigation processes established within the organization.
Service-Level Agreement	Monthly	Provides a definitive report to ensure remediation is being implemented in adherence to the SLAs defined in this document.
Regulatory	Quarterly	Executives and auditors are presented with quarterly reports to ensure that compliance initiatives are being adhered to.
Exceptions	Monthly	Provides all team members a listing of exceptions and expiration dates for findings throughout the environment.

Table 18-3. *Schedule for Actionable Reports Delivered to Mitigation and Remediation Stakeholders*

Actionable Reports	Frequency	Purpose
Vulnerability	Weekly	These reports are sorted by asset, vulnerability, or risk and detail findings by Smart Group.
Patch Report	Weekly	This report identifies OS specific patches that can be applied per asset
Delta Reports	Monthly	Delta reports provide "proof" to technical team members that mitigation strategies are affecting the outcome of assessments.

These reports are generated in sequence, per logical scan group, with an allowance for change control windows and system change control freezes (e.g., holiday season). However, actionable device reports are readily available upon completion of a successive scan.

Remediation Management

Vulnerability reports provide system owners and administrators the opportunity to understand the potential risk to which their systems may be exposed, and to take proactive steps to address the identified vulnerabilities. Between each official reporting period, the Security Team, system administrators, vendors, or other sources may identify vulnerabilities. The initiation of this process begins with the dissemination of actionable system reports as generated by the weekly scan cycle or by custom reporting based on requests or new asset deployments. Unplanned reports and alerts are made for issues regarding industry-wide or zero-day vulnerabilities and are treated by risk. For example, out-of-cycle critical vulnerabilities should be reported immediately with a custom assessment and remediated within the guidelines of this document. Table 18-4 outlines the general responsibilities by role:

Table 18-4. *Stakeholders and Their Ownership Responsibilities*

Security Team

The Security Team maintains the vulnerability management solution, generates reports, and monitors the vulnerability posture of the company. The team ensures that systems are scanned for vulnerabilities on a regularly scheduled basis, and that identified vulnerabilities are brought to the attention of the appropriate personnel.	• Disseminate vulnerability reports • Manage reports and vulnerability database • Issue resolution recommendations and guidance • Track the vulnerability resolution progress • Report unmitigated vulnerabilities of significance to executives • Respond to requests for vulnerability reviews

System Owner

System owners work with the system administrators to authorize, prioritize, and schedule changes to their systems or implement acceptable mitigating controls to reduce the risk to an acceptable level. Corrective actions such as patches are considered normal business maintenance. However, if other mitigating controls are used, teams should review and approve the controls as appropriate to address the vulnerability. It is ultimately the system owner's responsibility to accept any unmitigated risk that remains.	• Review vulnerability reports • Assess the degree of risk that the vulnerabilities represent • Review and approve proposed corrective actions or mitigating controls • Schedule changes with the users and the system administrators • Formally accept the unmitigated risk

(continued)

223

Table 18-4. (*continued*)

System Administrator	
System administrators implement the corrective actions authorized by the system owners. They are technical resources that may research and propose various resolutions and mitigating controls.	• Review vulnerability reports • Assess the risk of vulnerabilities to the system • Propose corrective actions or mitigating controls to the system owner(s) • Request vulnerability exceptions where appropriate • Implement changes authorized by the system owner(s)

Exceptions Management

Vulnerabilities may exist in operating systems, applications, web applications, or in the way different components interoperate together. While every effort must be made to correct issues, some vulnerabilities cannot be remediated. Vendors may have appliances that are not patched, services may be exposed for proper application operations, and systems may still be commissioned that are considered end of life by the developer and manufacturer.

In these cases, additional protections may be required to mitigate the vulnerability. Exceptions may also be made so that the vulnerabilities are not identified as items of risk to the system and organization. In rare cases, the vulnerability scanner may falsely identify a vulnerability that can't be corrected by the scan vendor. These types of shortcomings don't accurately reflect the risk of the system and require an exception process. This elaborates itself in the form of multiple exception types:

- **False Positives** arise when the scanner has identified a host as being vulnerable when, in fact, it is not. This can occur because some vulnerabilities can only be identified by software version numbers and some applications will "back patch" or patch the issue without updating version numbers. These findings have subsequently been reported back to the scan vendor, and no improvements can be performed to the automated check.

- **Acceptable Risk** vulnerabilities are those where the vulnerability is real, but compensating controls are in place to mitigate the risk, or the service has been deemed too critical for intervention.

- **Delayed Action** is made up of real vulnerabilities that cannot be mitigated in the time frame specified by the SLA due to business impact (downtime to apply remediation) or because of testing that is required to ensure operations are not affected by the recommended remediation.

All exception requests must present justification for the request and an expiration date. No exception can be permanent, and each must be reviewed and extended using an expiration date to ensure no exceptions are permanently ignored. The request should clearly state the exception type and be recorded using the exception features in the vulnerability management solution.

- **False Positives** identification may be documented through emails or the corporate ticketing system with the security staff. These will be escalated to the solution vendor for solution improvement and then reassessed. If no correction can be made, the exception is logged within the solution.

- **Acceptable Risk** exceptions must be requested through the Information Security Team with an explanation containing:

  - Mitigating controls – what changes, tools, or procedures have been implemented to minimize the risk;

  - Risk acceptance explanation – details as to why this risk is not relevant to the company and systems;

  - Risk analysis – if the vulnerability is indeed compromised, what risk and systems will be affected.

- **Delayed Action** – exceptions require a plan to test the recommended remediation and a date that corrections can be implemented by without impacting the business.

Once an exception has been approved, the vulnerability application will be updated by security personnel to reflect the exception, along with a summary for why it was approved and what controls are now in place, including the exception type. A new vulnerability scan will be performed on the device to document the impact of the exception being posted. Confirmation of the posting will be reported back to the requester via monthly exception reports.

The Security Team reviews all posted exceptions at least quarterly to validate that the exceptions are still appropriate. The staff will remove any exception that is no longer required and alert the appropriate system administrators.

Exclude from Assessments

When implementing a Vulnerability Management Program, take into consideration both the security and compliance goals of the organization. Additionally, as vulnerability management is only one layer of a broader security defense program, the most effective programs integrate and complement other security processes including:

- Patch Management

- Configuration Compliance

- Regulatory Compliance

- Privileged Account Management

- Attack, Malware, and Advanced Persistent Threat Protection

- Network Access Protection

Any assets that are excluded from assessments, for any reason, need to be evaluated for the impact in any of these other initiatives. Any exclusion will impact other security processes, and we must first define the scope of our vulnerability management program before we allow a change to impact the rest of our security solutions.

CHAPTER 19

Regulatory Compliance

A threat actor does not care about the law, compliance, regulations, and security best practices. In fact, they are hopeful that your organization is lax on many of these specifications and frameworks in order to leverage them for malicious intent. While regulatory compliance is designed to provide legally binding guidelines for industries and governments, they do not provide the necessary means to stay secure. Compliance does not equal security. They are best practices that point toward good cyber security hygiene, but implementing them without good processes, people, training, and diligence will leave you susceptible to a breach. Therefore, when reviewing leading regulatory compliance initiatives, consider the following:

- How they apply to your organization based on laws, sensitive information, contracts, industry, and geography.

- What compliance overlaps exist between the regulations and what processes can satisfy multiple requirements.

- Consider adopting the strictest guidelines for your initiatives. The strictest and most comprehensive requirement will ensure coverage for any overlap.

© Morey J. Haber, Brad Hibbert 2018
M.J. Haber and B. Hibbert, *Asset Attack Vectors*,
https://doi.org/10.1007/978-1-4842-3627-7_19

- Scoping is critical and applying the rules to sensitive systems is often not enough to provide good security. Consider the effort and cost of increasing the scope to mitigate risks through any connected system that could affect the legislative required scope. This is typically referred to as zones.

Therefore, keep in mind that any regulatory compliance requirements are the absolute minimum your organization should be doing when protecting your assets. If you are not meeting the minimums or have lapses in the requirements, you are an easy target for a vulnerability or exploit. Table 19-1 summarizes the leading regulatory compliance initiatives and when they may explicitly call for vulnerability management, patch management, or reference third-party prior art.

Table 19-1. Regulatory Compliance Requirements for Vulnerability and Patch Management

Abbreviation	Name	Public Website (URL)	Vulnerability Management	Patch Management
PCI	Payment Card Industry	https://www.pcisecuritystandards.org	PCI DSS Requirement 11.2.2	PCI DSS Requirement 6.2
	Description	The PCI Security Council maintains, develops, and promotes the Payment Card Industry Security Standards. The council provides the guidance needed for implementation of the standards such as assessment and scanning qualifications, self-assessment questionnaires, training and education, and product certification programs.		
HIPAA	Health Insurance Portability and Accountability Act	https://www.hhs.gov/hipaa/index.html	Risk Analysis Requirement 45CFR§164.308 (a)(1)(ii)(A)	Risk Management Requirement 45CFR§164.308 (a)(1)(ii)(B)
	Description	HIPAA (Health Insurance Portability and Accountability Act of 1996) is United States legislation that provides data privacy and security provisions for safeguarding medical information.		

(continued)

Table 19-1. (*continued*)

Abbreviation	Name	Public Website (URL)	Vulnerability Management	Patch Management
SOX	Sarbanes-Oxley Act	https://www.congress.gov/bill/107th-congress/house-bill/3763	Section 404	
	Description	The Sarbanes-Oxley Act of 2002 is legislation passed by the U.S. Congress to protect shareholders and the general public from accounting errors and fraudulent practices in the enterprise, as well as improve the accuracy of corporate disclosures.		
GLBA	Gramm-Leach-Bliley Act	https://www.banking.senate.gov/conf/fint15.pdf	Title V, Subtitle A, Sections 501 (a) & (b)	
	Description	The Gramm-Leach-Bliley Act, also known as the Financial Modernization Act of 1999, is a federal law enacted in the United States to control the ways that financial institutions deal with the private information of individuals.		
NIST*	National Institute of Standards and Technology	https://nvd.nist.gov/	RA-5	SI-2
	Description	NIST is the National Institute of Standards and Technology, a unit of the U.S. Commerce Department. Formerly known as the National Bureau of Standards, NIST promotes and maintains measurement standards.		

(*continued*)

Table 19-1. (*continued*)

Abbreviation	Name	Public Website (URL)	Vulnerability Management	Patch Management
ISO*	ISO	`https://www.iso.org/` `obp/ui/#iso:std:iso-` `iec:27002:ed-2:v1:en`	Section 12.6.1	Sections 12.5.1 and 12.6.1
	Description	ISO is a worldwide federation of national standards bodies from some 100 countries, with one standards body representing each member country.		
ASD	Australian Signals Directorate	`https://www.asd.` `gov.au/infosec/` `mitigationstrategies.htm`	Top 4 - (2) & (3)	
	Description	The Australian Signals Directorate is an intelligence agency in the Australian Government Department of Defense.		

(*continued*)

Table 19-1. (*continued*)

Abbreviation	Name URL	Public Website (URL)	Vulnerability Management	Patch Management
MAS	Monetary Authority of Singapore	`http://www.mas.gov.sg/Regulations-and-Financial-Stability/Regulatory-and-Supervisory-Framework/Risk-Management/Technology-Risk.aspx`	Chapters 9.4 & 10.1	Chapter 9.5
	Description	The Monetary Authority of Singapore is the central bank of Singapore. Their mission is to promote sustained non-inflationary economic growth, and a sound and progressive financial center.		
SWIFT	SWIFT	`https://www.swift.com/myswift/customer-security-programme-csp/security-controls`	Control 2.7A	Control 2.2
	Description	SWIFT is a global member-owned cooperative and the world's leading provider of secure financial messaging services		

(*continued*)

Table 19-1. (*continued*)

Abbreviation	Name	Public Website (URL)	Vulnerability Management	Patch Management
Act 10173	Republic of the Philippines, Data Privacy Act of 2012	https://privacy.gov.ph/ implementing-rules-and- regulations-of-republic- act-no-10173-known-as-the- data-privacy-act-of-2012/	28.d and 28.f	28.d
	Description	The goal of the Philippines Data Privacy Act is to combat the ever-growing threat posed by the theft of personal information by nation-states, terrorist organizations, and independent criminal actors.		
NYDFS	New York State Department of Financial Services	http://www.dfs.ny.gov/ legal/regulations/ adoptions/dfsrf500txt.pdf	Sections 500.05 and 500.09	Section 500.09
	Description	The New York State Department of Financial Services is a department of the New York State government responsible for regulating financial services including those subject to insurance, banking, and financial services.		

(*continued*)

Table 19-1. (*continued*)

Abbreviation	Name	Public Website (URL)	Vulnerability Management	Patch Management
NERC	North American Electric Reliability Corporation	`http://www.nerc.com/Pages/default.aspx`	CIP-010	CIP-007-5
	Description	The North American Electric Reliability Corporation (NERC) is a not-for-profit international regulatory authority whose mission is to assure the reliability and security of the bulk power system in North America. NERC develops and enforces Reliability Standards; annually assesses seasonal and long-term reliability; monitors the bulk power system through system awareness; and educates, trains, and certifies industry personnel.		
FERC	Federal Energy Regulatory Commission	`https://www.ferc.gov`		FERC references NERC, ISO, and security for ICS implementations. They do not provide unique guidance.
	Description	The Federal Energy Regulatory Commission (FERC) is a United States federal agency that regulates the transmission and wholesale sale of electricity, natural gas, and oil transported between states in the wholesale market.		

(*continued*)

Table 19-1. (*continued*)

Abbreviation	Name	Public Website (URL)	Vulnerability Management	Patch Management
HITECH	Health Information Technology for Economic and Clinical Health	`https://www.healthit.gov/policy-researchers-implementers/health-it-legislation-and-regulations`		Technical Safeguards - §164.312 (HIPAA)
	Description	The HITECH Act established the Office of the National Coordinator (ONC) into law and provides the U.S. Department of Health and Human Services with authority to establish programs to improve health care quality, safety, and efficiency through the promotion of health IT, including electronic health records and private and secure electronic health information exchange.		

(*continued*)

Table 19-1. (*continued*)

Abbreviation	Name	Public Website (URL)	Vulnerability Management	Patch Management
URL				
GDPR	European Union Data Protection Regulation	`https://www.eugdpr.org`		GPDR Risk Assessment infers the requirements for vulnerability and patch management to protect data.
	Description	The EU General Data Protection Regulation (GDPR) supersedes the Data Protection Directive 95/46/EC and is designed to harmonize data privacy laws across Europe, to protect and empower all EU citizens' data privacy, and to reshape the way organizations across the region approach data privacy.		
DFARS	Defense Federal Acquisition Regulation	`http://www.dcaa.mil/home/dfars`		DFARS is a regulatory vehicle for procurement and will reference NIST 800-53 and NIST 800-171 in order to be compliant.
	Description	DFARS provides Department of Defense (DoD) specific acquisition regulations that government acquisition officials and those contractors doing business with DoD, must follow in the procurement process for goods and services.		

(*continued*)

Table 19-1. (*continued*)

Abbreviation	Name	Public Website (URL)	Vulnerability Management	Patch Management
URL				
ATT&CK™	Adversarial Tactics, Techniques, and Common Knowledge	`https://attack.mitre.org/wiki/Main_Page`		ATT&CK phases from persistence, privileged escalation, defense evasion, credential access, discovery, lateral movement, execution, collection, exfiltration, and command control can be mapped to vulnerabilities, exploits, and remediation strategies.
	Description	MITRE's Adversarial Tactics, Techniques, and Common Knowledge is a curated knowledge base and model for cyber adversary behavior, reflecting the various phases of an adversary's life cycle and the platforms they are known to target.		

It is important to note, that standards like NIST and ISO are actually not regulatory compliance initiatives but rather regulatory frameworks. Organizations implement them due to contractual requirements; best practices; and they tend to blur the line between frameworks, regulations, contracts, and legal requirements. For the sake of protecting assets, they are covered in this chapter and detailed further in Chapter 20, Risk Management Frameworks. In addition, it is important to note that NIST and ISO are also referenced and form the basis for many other regulations not covered in this book.

239

CHAPTER 20

Risk Management Frameworks

Compliance frameworks provide the link between regulatory mandates and the business practices required to support them. Frameworks provide a model and structure that organizes and categorizes risk and associated internal controls to help organizations monitor and measure the effectiveness of their activities and investments. This goal is typically achieved through a set of control objectives outlined in the framework, which allows the organization to assess the security posture and set goals to improve procedures to protect systems and data. Another significant benefit of leveraging a compliance framework is that it can help an organization prioritize and coordinate activities, not only for a single regulatory mandate but across multiple compliance mandates as well.

It is important to note that throughout the years, information technology professionals have seen an increase in required regulatory mandates that must be supported, and they are also presented with an increasing number of potential frameworks and methodologies for managing information technology risk in a verifiable and measurable way. Living frameworks such as NIST, ISO 27001, CIS, and HITRUST have become widely accepted as best practices for organizations to assess, monitor, and measure the effectiveness of their security and compliance investments. While some frameworks such as the SANS 20 are technically oriented and explicit in the technologies and security controls, others

© Morey J. Haber, Brad Hibbert 2018
M.J. Haber and B. Hibbert, *Asset Attack Vectors*,
https://doi.org/10.1007/978-1-4842-3627-7_20

refer more to best practices and recommended guidelines. Regardless of the approach, the goal of the framework is to provide recommendations and guidance to enable practices and procedures to be established to create business value and minimize risk. While this book will not go into the details of every framework, it is important that security personnel be familiar with the common frameworks they will likely encounter. Table 20-1 outlines the most common frameworks and their use cases. As you read through them, you will see the overlap that is not business vertically dependant.

Leveraging industry standards provides a level of assurance that best practices are followed both by the organization and by business partners to protect systems and data. There is no "one size fits all" when it comes to selecting a security framework, and in most cases, the most appropriate framework may be in place prior to initiating the vulnerability program. When initiating a vulnerability management project, it is important to understand which regulatory mandates the organization must comply with; and which risk management frameworks have already been implemented. In some cases, frameworks such as ISO 27001 can complement the existing ISO framework implementations. In other cases, industry vertical and compliance mandates may play a more important role in the framework selection. For example, COBIT may be better aligned to comply with SOX. ISO 27000 offers breadth and applicability across industries but is more likely to be adopted when a company needs to market ISO certification. NIST SP 800-53 controls were designed specifically for U.S. government agencies, but NIST SP 800-53 also provides information security standards that are applicable across industry verticals and organizations.

Table 20-1. *Common Risk Management Frameworks*

Organization	URL	Framework Name	Security Controls
PCI Security Standards Council	https://www.pcisecuritystandards.org/	Payment Card Industry Data Security Standard (PCI DSS)	12 Requirements organized into six groups of control objectives.
		Description: Initially developed in 2004, the Payment Card Industry Data Security Standard (PCI DSS) is an information security standard outlining 12 security requirements for every organization that accepts credit cards such as Visa, MasterCard, American Express, and others. The PCI Security Standards Council is a global forum for the ongoing development, enhancement, storage, dissemination, and implementation of security standards for account data protection. By adhering to PCI regulations, you can secure critical systems and protect sensitive cardholder data.	
Center for Internet Security (CIS)	https://www.cisecurity.org/controls/	CIS Critical Security Controls	CIS 20 controls
		Description: Originally developed in 2008 and currently on version 6.1, The Center for Internet Security's Critical Security Controls for Effective Cyber Defense (known as the CIS Top 20 Controls) are "a recommended set of actions for cyber defense that provide specific and actionable ways to thwart the most pervasive attacks."	

(continued)

243

Table 20-1. (*continued*)

Organization	URL	Framework Name	Security Controls
Open Web Application Security Project (OWASP)		OWASP Top 10	Top 10 controls
		Description: The Open Web Application Security Project (OWASP) is a not-for-profit worldwide charitable organization focused on improving the security of application software. The OWASP Top 10 Web Application Security Risks provides guidance to developers and security professionals that target the most critical vulnerabilities that are commonly found and exploited in web applications. The OWASP Top 10 is not an exhaustive list of risk elements but provides a solid starting point for organizations looking to strengthen the security posture of their web application environment.		
National Institute of Standards and Technology (NIST)	https://www.nist.gov/	NIST 800 series Framework for Improving Critical Infrastructure Cybersecurity	NIST Special Publication 800-53 NIST Special Publication 800-171
		Description: NIST SP 800-53 outlines a comprehensive strategy combined with various security controls for continuous monitoring designed to enable better risk-based decision making. Another popular set of NIST controls is 800-171. The primary difference between NIST 800-53 and 800-171 is that the latter was developed specifically to protect sensitive data on contractor and other nonfederal information systems.		

(*continued*)

Table 20-1. (*continued*)

Organization	URL	Framework Name	Security Controls
International Organization for Standardization (ISO)	`https://www.iso.org/isoiec-27001-information-security.html`	ISO/IEC 27000 family – Information security management systems	ISO/IEC 27001

Description: ISO provides a family of standards to help organizations secure information assets. Each standard is designed to provide guidance in relation to a specific set of activities focused on a specific set of objectives. For example, building the foundation of a security program is covered in ISO 27001, implementing detailed controls is covered in 27002, and risk management is covered in 27005.

(*continued*)

Table 20-1. (*continued*)

Organization	URL	Framework Name	Security Controls
UK Government's Office of Government Commerce (OGC)	https://www.itlibrary.org/	Information Technology Infrastructure Library (ITIL)	ITIL itself does not provide prescriptive guidance on controls and relies on other frameworks such as ISO for that aspect of security management. ITIL focuses more on the broader activities and relationship with security of service delivery and support.
	Description: (ITIL) is a framework of best practices for delivering IT services. ITIL v3 is comprised of five distinct volumes: ITIL Service Strategy; ITIL Service Design; ITIL Service Transition; ITIL Service Operation; and ITIL Continual Service Improvement.		
FAIR Institute	http://www.fairinstitute.org/	Factor Analysis of Information Risk (FAIR)	
	Description: FAIR is a framework for understanding, analyzing, and measuring information risk. Basic FAIR provides a framework comprised of 10 steps in 4 stages designed to quantify and communicate risk consistently across the organization		

(*continued*)

Table 20-1. (*continued*)

Organization	URL	Framework Name	Security Controls
Software Engineering Institute, Carnegie Mellon	`http://www.cert.org/`	OCTAVE	
	Description: OCTAVE was developed by Carnegie Mellon University's computer emergency response team (more commonly known as CERT.) This security framework offers a strategic approach to information security.		
Information Systems Audit and Control Association (ISACA)	`http://www.isaca.org/cobit/` `pages/default.aspx`	COBIT	COBIT5 Governance and Management Practices
	Description: COBIT is a management and governance framework that defines and organizes implementable controls that are organized into IT-related processes.		

(*continued*)

CHAPTER 21

Making It All Work

The evolution of network computing environments – including the increased use of mobile, cloud, and virtual infrastructure – has created a continuous stream of new attack vectors for adversaries to prey on. This is the ever expanding security perimeter outside of your organization including privileges and vulnerabilities. Regardless of the tactics used, most breaches comprise some exploitation of software vulnerabilities, system configuration settings, or poor privileged hygiene.

However, despite widespread deployment of vulnerability technologies, many security professionals still struggle with how to best protect their organizations, achieve compliance, and communicate risk enterprise-wide. In fact, most vulnerability management solutions do little to help security leaders put vulnerability and risk information in the context of business.

Saddled with volumes of rigid data and static reports, the security team is left to manually discern real threats and determine how to act upon them – leaving organizations ill-equipped to defend themselves against even novice attackers. A harsh reality, underscored by Verizon's 2017 Data Breach Report that found "99.9% of exploited vulnerabilities were compromised more than a year after the CVE was published." Security professionals deserve more from their vulnerability management solutions. That's why delivering vulnerability data in the proper context is so important.

© Morey J. Haber, Brad Hibbert 2018
M.J. Haber and B. Hibbert, *Asset Attack Vectors*,
https://doi.org/10.1007/978-1-4842-3627-7_21

Know What's On Your Network

In today's digital economy, businesses have to move quickly to respond to the needs of their customers. This often involves frequent changes to networked computing environments like adding new systems and applications, as well as a constantly shifting user populations. And as such, the use of technologies like Web, mobile, cloud, and virtualized platforms have become an essential part of business strategy to stay ahead of the competition. Within this ever-changing landscape, do you know what's connected to your network?

With a vulnerability management solution, you have the power to effectively discover an unlimited number of network-based assets. If it has an IP address, then you can find it, catalog it, and audit it. In fact, every solution on the market can discover assets and perform network-based vulnerability assessments. After all, you can't protect what you can't see.

All deployments must zero-gap coverage for any asset, satisfy diverse IT environments by delivering a comprehensive analysis of all assets including Web, mobile, cloud, and virtual platforms. In addition to network-based scans, deployments should consider agent-based scanning, ensuring that all your assets are protected, whether they are connected to your network or not.

Beyond just locating all of your known and previously unknown (new) assets, across your entire network, consider the following "key takeaway perspectives" you need to make smarter security decisions, including:

- **Asset Profiling** – collect user and device information including IP, DNS, OS, Mac address, ports, services, software, processes, hardware, event logs, and more;

- **Asset Grouping** – logically group, assess, and report on assets according to IP range, naming convention, operating system, domain, applications, business function, Active Directory, and more;

- **Asset Context Awareness** – understand grouped values and risk based on collateral damage potential or target distribution, as well as confidentiality, integrity, and availability requirements.

This includes a vulnerability management solution's capabilities (Figure 21-1) tool that can perform:

- Enumeration of hardware and software regardless of OS

- Enumeration services and service accounts

- Identifying open ports, running processes. and shares

- Enumeration of local and domain users, privileges, password age, last login date, etc. used to identify privileged risks

5 ASSETS HAVE BEEN FOUND

Asset	Vulnerabilities	Ports	Shares	Services	Software	User Accounts	Attacks
192.168.001.216	19	1	0	25	390	54	0
enterprise	18	10	0	0	0	125	0
GEMINI	46	14	5	177	13	23	0
PROMETHEUS	8	9	0	0	0	0	0
RELIANT	102	15	3	171	30	24	0

Figure 21-1. *Example of enumerated data via a discovery scan or vulnerability assessment*

Automate Credentialed Scans

Authenticated vulnerability scanning is a method that is more accurate and provides greater insight than unauthenticated scans. But authenticated scans require the use of privileged credentials, which can often be continuously and anonymously changed for their protection. Complicating matters further is the fact that regular scans require automation. How can organizations both protect privileged credentials while making them automatically available for vulnerability scanning?

To address this challenge, vulnerability management solutions should integrate into password safes, password vaults, and/or password managers to automate the use of continuously rotated privileged credentials, for authenticated vulnerability scans (Figure 21-2). This prevents stale or weak passwords themselves from being another attack vector that could compromise an environment.

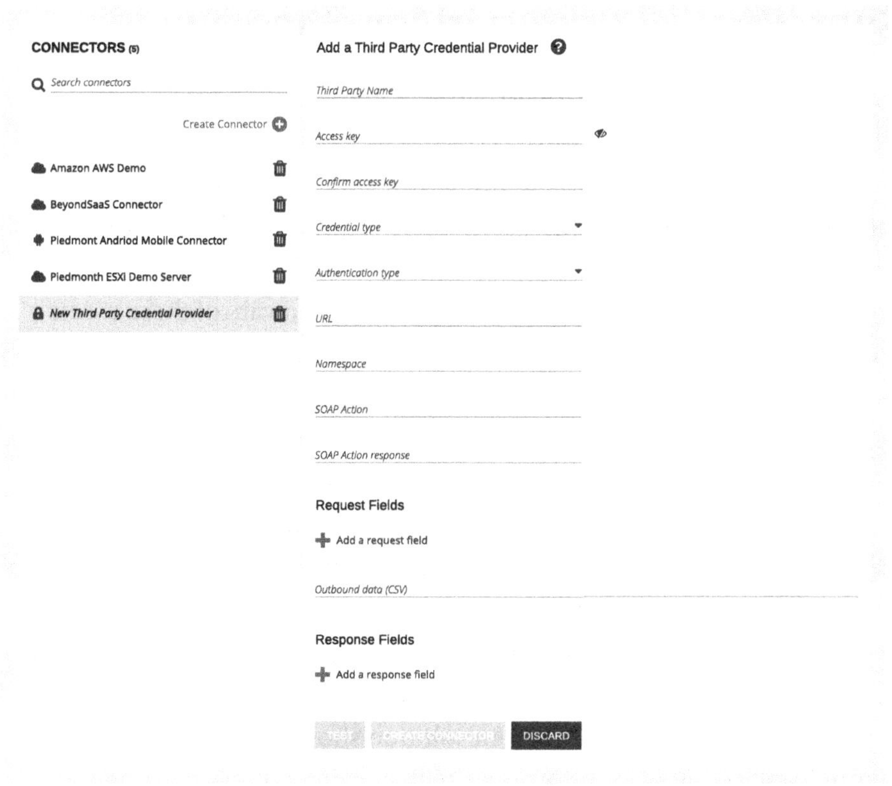

CONNECTORS (5)

Q Search connectors

Create Connector ⊕

☁ Amazon AWS Demo   🗑

☁ BeyondSaaS Connector   🗑

📱 Piedmont Andriod Mobile Connector   🗑

☁ Piedmonth ESXi Demo Server   🗑

🔒 New Third Party Credential Provider   🗑

Add a Third Party Credential Provider ❓

Third Party Name

Access key   👁

Confirm access key

Credential type   ▾

Authentication type   ▾

URL

Namespace

SOAP Action

SOAP Action response

Request Fields

➕ Add a request field

Outbound data (CSV)

Response Fields

➕ Add a response field

[TEST] [CREATE CONNECTOR] [DISCARD]

Figure 21-2. *Vulnerability management integration for retrieval of credentials*

Spot What's Lurking in the Shadows

Fueled by the ongoing consumerization of information technologies, "shadow IT" is a growing security concern for organizations of all shapes and sizes. Unauthorized and oftentimes unsupported hardware or software are brought into organizations, by right-minded employees who are simply trying to find better ways to do their jobs. However, since information technology professionals are likely unaware of these assets they certainly didn't have a chance to scrutinize them. Mobile devices such as smartphones and tablets as well as cloud-based file sharing services like DropBox are just a few examples of common shadow IT technologies that can pose a significant security and compliance risk to organizations.

Whether you're a fan of bring your own technology (BYOT) or not, this transformational shift in employee behavior is likely here to stay. And since you can't stop the rising waters from seeping into your organization, you need better capabilities to spot high-risk assets immediately, so that they can be brought up to code or quarantined as quickly as possible.

Your vulnerability management solution should allow organizations to automatically create groups of assets with commonalities, flag unknown applications, and detect known threats. This added context makes you smarter about where unknown dangers might be hiding, with the ability to:

- Recognize systems, for example, with open ports including 1521 or 1433, that can then be categorized as "database servers";

- Alert security staff and assign tickets to high-risk vulnerabilities, unknown ports in production systems, unauthorized software like Team Viewer, VNC, P2P clients, and more;

- Create risk indicators that generate alerts if detected, including systems with unauthorized software installed, open exploitable ports like 6667 and active processes such as conficker.exe or malware01.exe.

Figure 21-3 illustrates this logical grouping in a leading vulnerability management solution to demonstrate that groups can be used to categorize assets.

ASSETS

Last Updated	Asset	Operating System	Workgroup	Solution	Asset Risk
24 Aug 2017 04:49 p.m.	192.168.1.23	Windows Server 2012 R2 (x64)	Default		2.28
18 Aug 2017 02:36 p.m.	192.168.1.216	Windows Server 2012 R2 (x64)	Default		3.70
12 Aug 2017 01:14 p.m.	GEMINI	Linux	Default		3.09
06 Aug 2017 11:10 a.m.	PROMETHEUS	Windows Server 2012 R2 (x64)	Default		2.28
21 Jul 2017 09:57 a.m.	RELIANT	Windows Server 2012 R2 (x64)	Default		3.70
17 Jul 2017 01:31 p.m.	SCOOBY	Windows Server 2012 R2 (x64)	Default		3.09

Figure 21-3. *Logical grouping of assets by discovered traits – in this case, virtualized workstations*

See Your Data in High Definition

Most vulnerability management solutions generate vast amounts of data, reported across hundreds of pages, listing found vulnerabilities along with their associated criticalities (high, medium, low), CVE identifiers, CVSS characteristics, and recommendations for corrective actions. While these reports provide valuable security data, they lack the additional context to prioritize which assets or vulnerabilities to focus on – leaving organizations unable to identify the greatest threats amidst the sea of data they have collected.

Because you will never be able to fix all of your growing number of vulnerabilities, you must be smarter about what to fix first, second, and third, as well as last. Make sure you are capable of providing results-driven reporting that puts risk into focus by enabling you to prioritize vulnerabilities based on attributes such as whether or not a known exploit exists, can it be exploited remotely and by someone without privilege, is there active malware using it, and how its severity-level changes after other weaknesses have been remediated. This is broadly classified as Threat Intelligence.

To that end, reports, dashboards, and user interface should be able to provide SLA, PCI, ISO, HIPAA, etc., compliance reports, and define the business context of your assets. Then the solution needs to deliver targeted, relevant, and actionable vulnerability intelligence in a wide variety of formats (Figure 21-4) to the proper owners, including:

- Asset inventories, risk trends, deltas, and logical groups

- Risk matrices, severity scores, and trends

- Attack severity, impact, and targets

- Scan job histories and metrics

- Configuration assessment reports (optional)

- Virtual asset vulnerabilities, trends, and deltas

- Database vulnerabilities and severity scores

- Vulnerabilities by CVSS, OS, severity, and type

- Patch-management reports for teams to remediate assets based on findings

- Vulnerability impact dashboards and scorecards

- Privilege and identity management reports to support other security initiatives

- Vulnerability SLA reports

- Regulatory compliance reports per your business regulations

- Web application vulnerabilities, trends, and delta or change reports

- Remediation reports

- Zero-day vulnerabilities, trends, and exclusion (exception) reports

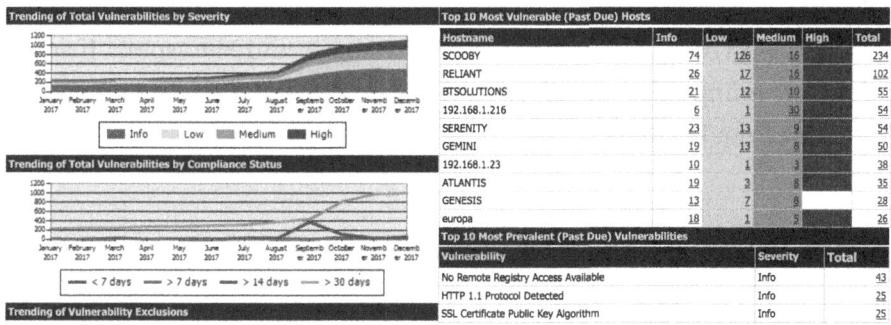

Trending of Total Vulnerabilities by Severity

Info   Low   Medium   High

Trending of Total Vulnerabilities by Compliance Status

< 7 days   > 7 days   > 14 days   > 30 days

Trending of Vulnerability Exclusions

Top 10 Most Vulnerable (Past Due) Hosts

Hostname	Info	Low	Medium	High	Total
SCOOBY	74	126	16		234
RELIANT	26	17	15		102
BTSOLUTIONS	21	12	10		55
192.168.1.216	6	1	30		54
SERENITY	23	13	9		54
GEMINI	19	13	8		50
192.168.1.23	10	1	3		38
ATLANTIS	19	3	8		35
GENESIS	13	7	8		28
europa	18	1	5		26

Top 10 Most Prevalent (Past Due) Vulnerabilities

Vulnerability	Severity	Total
No Remote Registry Access Available	Info	43
HTTP 1.1 Protocol Detected	Info	25
SSL Certificate Public Key Algorithm	Info	25

Figure 21-4. *Assets prioritized by the number of critical vulnerabilities*

Find Which Threats Are Soft Targets

As previously mentioned, vulnerability management solutions are notorious for generating large volumes of data. Within this data set, it is not uncommon to find hundreds of high-severity vulnerabilities. However, since organizations undoubtedly have limited resources to address these weaknesses, they can't possibly fix them all immediately or even within a short-maintenance time frame. Knowing not only the severity (CVSS) of a vulnerability but also how easily it could be exploited is a key factor that will help organizations quickly prioritize vulnerabilities and stay ahead of their adversaries.

Beyond what preconditions are required to exploit a vulnerability, or what impact a successful attack may have, organizations should also understand which vulnerabilities have published exploits and which do not. And while that doesn't mean vulnerabilities with no publicly available exploits are not potentially dangerous, it does allow security operations to classify which assets may be easier targets and priotize them accordingly.

It is extremely helpful if your vulnerability management solution can correlate malware and exploit research together with several third-party exploit databases and highlights which vulnerabilities have readily available exploits, and in turn, can be easily attacked. This includes known malware that may be present in databases like VirusTotal and also exploit tools like CANVAS, Core Impact, Exploit Database, and Metasploit. If any of these are found own your crown jewel assets, you castle is at a much higher risk from invaders.

Mind Your Vulnerability Gaps

The increasing popularity of both cloud-based applications and virtual machines pose some unique challenges for traditional network-based vulnerability management solutions. Assets that are mostly online are typically not too difficult to find and audit. However, what about those devices and applications that don't connect to your network or do so randomly or infrequently? Virtual systems may or may not be running during network-based scans, and cloud-based applications are literally out of your control. You may also have a number of connected systems that have been hardened – limiting what you can see from the outside looking in. How can you cover these vulnerability gaps?

To ensure that all of your assets are accounted for, use agents when appropriate. If it has a risk surface that can lead to lateral movement and a breach, it needs to be assessed; somehow.

Once viewed as problematic, agent-based capabilities are a reliable way in a diverse environment to solve problems in modern-day network environments. Deploying agents for vulnerability assessments allows the organization to close their vulnerability gaps with:

- Full authenticated scans without the need to provide credentials

- Faster vulnerability assessments

- The ability to find and audit transient virtual platforms

- Support for cloud environments where active scanning is forbidden

- Comprehensive risk intelligence from systems protected via hardening, firewalls, IPS, etc.

- Seamless centralized management of all local scan data

- More frequent or continuous assessments

Unify Vulnerability and Privilege Intelligence

Large-scale information breaches often begin with an attacker exploiting a single external vulnerability on a low-level system and then capitalizing on privileges to gain access to critical systems and data. Such was the case with Adobe's well-publicized breach when a path from the Internet to a Cold Fusion server was opened without the company's knowledge. Unfortunately for Adobe, that server had a low-priority vulnerability that was exploited, and the breach was publicized with devastating results.

Businesses need a way to unify their vulnerability and privilege risk intelligence, so that IT and Security Ops can make least privilege and security decisions based on their collective information, working together, and not have to settle for using fragmented pieces or parts.

By centralizing and correlating privilege, access, and vulnerability information, the BeyondInsight platform provides IT and security staff with a clearer, more-informed picture of enterprise risk.

Threat Analytics

It's no secret that IT and security teams are overwhelmed with privilege, vulnerability, and threat information. And with limited ability to associate these diverse data sets with one another, organizations are often blind to advanced persistent threats (APTs) cloaked in isolation. An application is launched for the first time. An administrator logs in at 2 am. A server has unpatched vulnerabilities. Seen individually, these events may be written off as low-risk occurrences. However, when looked at together, these seemingly innocuous incidents spell big trouble.

Using analytics and vulnerability data can help empower IT and security professionals to identify data breach threats typically missed by other security solutions. Like a good detective, analytics is masterful at gathering disparate clues, making connections, and exposing would-be cyber criminals. How? Analytic solutions pinpoint specific, high-risk users and assets by correlating low-level privilege, vulnerability, malware, and threat data from a variety of sources including vulnerability management data.

To put the malware pandemic in proper context, Verizon counted the number of malware events across 10,000 organizations during 2014 and tallied a staggering 170 million of total episodes, or roughly five malicious code incidents every second – putting it on par with the number of babies born worldwide. And whether or not you think anti-virus (AV) is dead, one thing is for certain: trying to defend this onslaught of malware with a single AV solution is like bringing a knife to a gunfight.

Streamline Your Patch Process

While cataloging all your assets and detecting their associated vulnerabilities is an important first step, security experts unanimously agree that it's not good enough to just identify weaknesses. Organizations need simpler and more automated ways to remediate them. And though most vulnerability management solutions provide guidance on how to mitigate vulnerabilities, they require you to manually download, install, and verify corrective software patches, which can be a difficult and lengthy process – all the while leaving your systems at risk of attack.

Vulnerability management integration with Microsoft System Configuration Manager (SCCM) Windows Server Update Service (WSUS), Ivanti Shavlik, Tanium, BigFix, etc., lets administrators correlate patches and deployments from a single pane of glass, allowing organizations to gain visibility into the risks associated with missing patches while continuing to leverage their existing patch infrastructure. Therefore, integration into patch management can take the pain out of patching vulnerabilities by:

- Streamlining the entire process from discovery and assessment to patch deployment, verification, and context-aware reporting for all machines across Microsoft and third-party applications.

- Mapping discovered vulnerabilities to available patches and utilizing the advanced targeting and categorization of assets to better prioritize patch activities.

- Automatically downloading missing security updates based on discovered vulnerabilities and deploying those missing patches or service packs throughout your network at the end of your scans.

The goal for all organizations is to close the loop on vulnerabilities and provide seamless patching from a single console by prioritizing remediation activity quickly, fixing weaknesses for any solution including custom applications using instant or scheduled patching, and seeing the big picture with end-to-end reporting on the entire patch-management life cycle. Figure 21-5 illustrates how a vulnerability management solution can be integrated with a patch-management solution for a streamlined workflow.

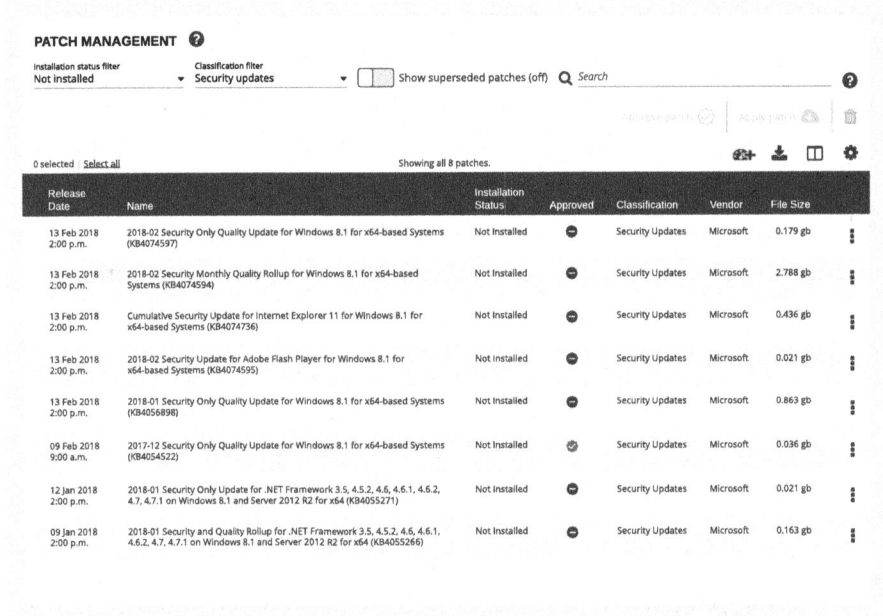

***Figure 21-5.** Vulnerability and patch-management integration for workload prioritization and simplification*

Share and Collaborate

While the terminology may vary, for nearly two decades the basic approach to vulnerability management has remained the same – discover assets, audit them for vulnerabilities, prioritize and patch them, and report on progress. While valuable in limiting an attack surface, this find, fix, automate and repeat approach does little to give organizations visibility into new and emerging threats. Nor does it help escalate security events to other defenses or other systems within your organization.

An enterprise end-to-end solution can extend your vulnerability management program by sharing real-time asset intelligence with other security infrastructure such as SIEM, Privilege, Firewall, GRC, and more. This occurs by empowering a network of solutions that cooperate to both solve new challenges and resolve existing ones in new ways. The goal is to help organizations with greater situational awareness so they can make smarter, more well-informed security decisions. Consider the following integrations for ingesting and exporting vulnerability and risk data that may help your environment:

- **Security Information Event Management (SIEM)** – Adding real-time vulnerability intelligence to SIEM solutions, like HP ArcSight, IBM QRadar, LogRhythm, McAfee, Splunk, and more, arms organizations with superior targeted attack and breach detection, as well as broader compliance visibility.

- **Privilege Access Management (PAM)** – Combining asset intelligence with Privileged Access Managment (PAM) products empowers organizations to make privilege-access decisions based on an application's known vulnerabilities, their age, potential risk, and compliance impact.

- **Next-Gen Firewall (NGFW)** – Correlating network traffic from next-generation firewalls, with detailed vulnerability, malware, and attack data – as well as user and application event information – gives businesses a holistic and more informed view of critical assets risks.

- **Network Management Systems (NMS) & Ticketing** – Communicating bidirectionally with NMS and ticketing systems, such as ServiceNow. BMC Remedy, HP Openview, Microsoft SCCM, and Solar Winds, enables organizations to escalate security and compliance events into their current IT workflows and then automatically run scan jobs to verify results and report on them.

- **Cloud** – Discovering and classifying Microsoft Azure, Google Cloud, and Amazon AWS assets, and auditing their associated vulnerabilities, gives organizations a clear picture of their risk and compliance profiles in the cloud.

- **Governance, Risk, and Compliance (GRC)** – Inserting security configuration assessment (SCA) data into GRC solutions, like Agiliance, Control Case, LockPath, Modulo, and RSA Archer, lets change managers, IT admins, auditors, and security personal reliably track and validate how configuration changes affect their compliance with regulatory standards.

- **Business Management** – Establishing two-way communications with business management solutions allows companies to import asset profiles, launch vulnerability scans, and generate incident tickets (based on data) – staying up to date with the latest asset profile and risk information from an executive perspective.

Figure 21-6 illustrates how all of these different solutions can be integrated into your vulnerability management program in a subway map.

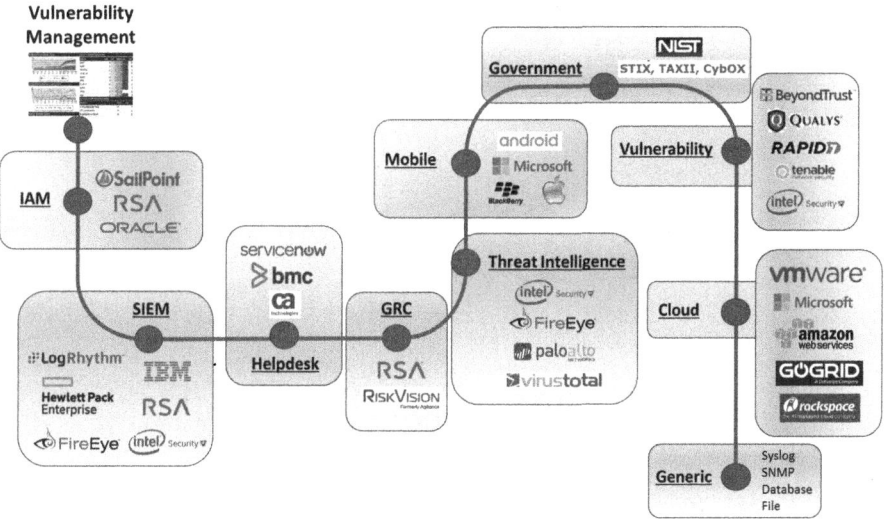

Figure 21-6. *Third-party integration subway map*

CHAPTER 22

Tales from the Trenches

Over the last few decades, I (Morey – and not John Titor as some readers may believe) have experienced a plethora of use cases and clients that inherently did not understand the risks to their assets and processes within their own organizations. In that time, I have documented my favorite ones and included them in this book as lessons learned: tales from the trenches. They may sound personal (written in the first person) and even a little loose, but they make good stories we all can learn from and how not to make the same mistakes. These short stories are from real clients and sales teams that failed miserably managing information technology security, vulnerabilities, processes, and sales cycles. Hopefully, the results become a reference point for all of us – what not to do when trying to protect our precious resources.

A Lost Enterprise Client

As a product manager for a leading vulnerability management solution, I thought I had seen every type of client until a recent trip at the end of 2010. A potential new client, a Fortune 100 company, was using a point and shot vulnerability assessment solution for the past six years. They needed to grow into an enterprise solution that covered all aspects of the business

© Morey J. Haber, Brad Hibbert 2018
M.J. Haber and B. Hibbert, *Asset Attack Vectors*,
https://doi.org/10.1007/978-1-4842-3627-7_22

and embarked on an RFI to gather criteria. This is where it all began; the security department wrote the RFI as a one-page document without a budget, management approval, and without the knowledge of legal and procurement. That was our first tip something was wrong. The RFI arrived with no cover letter and not even formatted on company letterhead. There was no document control number or even a disclaimer. My first instinct was to delete the email and move on. I should have followed my business instinct. But, at the assurances of my enterprise account manager, I answered the questions and began the pilot.

With any enterprise pilot, having hardware and solution prerequisites in place is critical for success. If the client cannot provide a basic lab environment with minimum hardware and software, you are doomed from the moment you put your foot in the door. A lesson every systems engineer learns the hard way at least once. Well, the Friday before we went onsite, the client still had no hardware for our pilot but assured us everything would be great Tuesday morning when we arrived. Flights are booked, the weather was holding, and we took the trip.

As a backup plan to loading the solution, I learned another lesson a few years ago. Have a plan B. In this case, I had a virtual machine with all of our solutions loaded, with demo licenses keys, and an evaluation version of the operating system and database. If the client did not have the hardware and software I needed, surely, I can find a workstation with enough RAM and CPU to run VMware Player and my plan B.

So, we arrived onsite that Tuesday morning and of course, security has no knowledge of our visit. In addition, the salesperson does not even have the correct building, so once we get in, we had to fumble around the campus to find the right entrance. Did I mention it was 20°F outside?

In either case, we get there, meet our contact, and are directed to the lab. The newest server they have is from 2001 in the lab. It is running tons of other software, takes forever to boot, and is not a candidate for an enterprise pilot with only one hard disk and no available resources. The box is maxed out.

So, we hunt for another desktop and implement plan B. We find a desktop from about 2003 with 6GB of RAM and Windows XP x64-bit. Surely this should work, but no. Without the CPU supporting VT technology, VMPlayer cannot run a VM an x64-bit OS with 8GB of RAM. Strike Two. We identify a newer desktop with much less RAM, but it meets the other requirements. Three hours later, we are uncompressing an 80GB VM on an underpowered VM.

Now, I pull the salesperson aside and tell him the bad news. He, of course, does not care and tells me to make it work. I was a systems engineer before I was the product manager, then vice president, and CTO; and I knew better even back then. But what should I do? Punt?

Well, midway through the day, I got the VM running and did some initial scans. Everything ran very slowly and made the product look awful. I am not sure what is worse: having a buggy solution, or a solution that shows poorly because of the operational environment.

Now, I must add one piece regarding personnel throughout this process. During the ordeal of finding a system, we got passed through three different individuals that acted as our escorts. No one would take ownership of our presence. Is that another red flag or what?

Anyway, we finished doing some scans, ran some reports, and left for the day. I thought for good. We never did a demo for management. We never wrapped up the pilot and never asked what was important. There were no sales questions and no follow-up plan. Doomed from the start, and I was a sucker for listening to the account manager.

So, it is now the end of the year. Sales wants every dollar in. The account manager informs me that they are really serious now and need to go back onsite to close the deal. My "Spidey" sense kicked in again and said this is nuts. Yup, nuts. But, as a good PM, I listened and went.

We arrived onsite with snow and foul weather. We were escorted to a conference room and spent about two hours with one individual demoing the solution. Then they left. We were left alone for lunch and almost three more hours before they return. We wrapped up the lesson in less than an hour. We never met the executives in charge of the project, and they wouldn't give us any answers on procurement. This was our second visit, and the account manager was certain we could close this deal. He was wrong. We left, and I battled bad weather flying to my next city for a speaking engagement. This was doomed from day one. The client went dark, and we never found out what they purchased, if anything.

Lessons learned:

- Make sure any pilot for a company this size is funded and approved.

- If paperwork is incomplete, find out why.

- Make sure all prerequisites for a pilot are met before arrival.

- Always have a Plan B, especially for travel. This is kind of like the rules from Zombie Land.

- Make sure you are speaking to the right individuals in the company, especially procurement and management.

- Trust your instinct and never let a salesperson talk you into a sure win.

Just a Win

Once in a while, you win a client that will do anything for you. It is almost like having a best friend for life. If you solve a problem for them, one that makes a difference, nothing will ever jade them. In about 2004, I assisted a client with the rollout of our endpoint solution. It was a raw product back then. Barely out of the 1.0 release. The management console was honestly very immature and the deployment tricky as heck. But, we had a paying client, and the boss wanted this thing rolled out and operational.

The one thing about this client, compared to so many others, is that they would bend over backwards to get something done and working. Hardware, no issues. The right security profiles on workstations, "No problem."

So early one morning, we began deploying agents and had to stop almost immediately. All of the agents being deployed were creating a message storm of events. No idea why. As I mentioned, the management console was a wet noodle, and all we could do is watch logs scroll by. It was rather ugly.

So, after troubleshooting some to settle the noise down, we determined that all of the deployed agents were spamming messages about three different IP addresses on the network. What was odd was that the message was the same in every event.

Our liaison isolated the IP addresses to medical equipment in a corresponding building. Our next step was a short visit to see what they were and what they were doing. After arriving we noticed that all three pieces were identical GE pieces of medical diagnostic equipment and that they had Windows XP with no service packs, firewall, or anti-virus running on them.

All three of these systems were infected by a worm. They were scanning the network for other devices to infect and when they attempted to infect a machine with our endpoint solution on it, it generated an alert. That is what we were seeing.

Critical pieces of medical equipment in a health care-providing facility were infected and trying to infect other devices on the network. Can you imagine the CISO's face when he saw this?

We promptly disconnected each piece of medical equipment from the network, configured them to run in stand-alone mode (put the results on a floppy versus communicating them to a PACS system on the network), and observed the message storm completely drop to zero.

This is one find and in one place were the technology worked so well, saved the client an embarrassing problem, and made the decision makers and stakeholders of our solution look like kings. We won a client for life, made a huge difference in their network, and potentially saved someone's life. It does not get much better than that.

Lessons Learned:

- It only takes one event to win or lose a client. A big win will keep them for life.

- No matter how wet the code is, do not dismiss errors and problems quickly. It may just be working correctly.

- When your solution solves a real problem, make sure everyone knows. If you do not, others cannot learn from your win.

Just Too Much to Manage

I hear all the buzz about application whitelisting, and application blacklisting. Philosophies on how to best protect applications and control what executes. Now before companies began building these massive MD5 hash libraries to support these initiatives, clients have to register applications one at a time with their host based firewalls and application contol solutions. When a new version came out, and when a new version was patched, the IT department had to register the version for it to work and let it communicate on the wire.

So, in visiting a client in NYC only a few years ago, they told us that across the several thousand assets they had, they had three versions of Microsoft office in their environment. Some versions were professional, some were basic, and some were business based on the time of acquisition and user needs. All of these versions had various service packs and security patches loaded. At the end of the meeting, we estimated over 100 different versions of files for MS Office that would need to be managed by the host-based firewall since the client had no patch management or standardization in process.

Now, add to that all the third-party applications, and custom applications they developed (and there were a few), they needed to manage a few thousand MD5 hashes for all the desktops, and the list kept growing. Admittedly, they knew this was nuts and wanted a better solution. We discussed the technology my company had to offer, but they wanted to still do everything with hash control. They just wanted a better way to manage them versus their current tools and could not accept a better, newer technology that did not require management at this granular level.

Needless to say, they stayed with the current technology they had and added more people to manage the security of these devices.

Lesson Learned:

- If you cannot convey a better technology that the client will accept, the ROI does not matter.

- The client must be willing to change their opinion on what they are using. Otherwise, they will just buy a bigger version of what they already have.

- Throwing people at a problem rarely works. It works best for labor-intensive applications.

- Change is good, but the client has to be willing to change. Sometimes they are just looking to justify continuing what they currently do.

Obsolete

An overseas visit was requested by an enterprise client to review odd vulnerability data and a worldwide architectural deployment. Upon arriving at the client, I expected things to be in pretty good shape, but we did have a few vulnerabilities that required global exceptions. After cleaning up the data, we began looking at the highest-risk assets and low-hanging fruit for remediation. This led to some startling findings.

The first was an obsolete system running Windows NT 4.0. This server was critical for business operations and client fulfillment. It was also deemed end of life by Microsoft several years earlier. After determining who owned the system, why it was never updated, and even decommissioned, it was identified that the hardware was provided by a third-party contract and the owner had no obligation to update it or provide any security. If the device was compromised, it could bring operations to a dead halt. The only mitigation was to install inline security devices and configure heavy ACLs around access and configuration to the device. The server could not be updated or replaced, and the contract provided no provisions for any disputes over the equipment outside of an SLA to repair. There where no security provisions.

The second finding involved domain controllers. The scanner reported Anonymous Share Access on several mount points on their domain controllers. The share name was a little nonstandard, so we decided to investigate. After connecting from a lab workstation that was not on the domain, we saw the user directories for every account in Active Directory. There was no security on any folder, and we could browse any folder, including the CFO. So, what was a good security professional to do? We copied a couple of financial documents with sensitive information and sent it to the CSO. That caused a ripple effect that I never heard the full extent of, but I did find out the share was placed there in lieu of a back agent in order to back up all user data. The lack of security was so that the remote connection could read all the directories. In doing so, it left everything wide open for any user to browse, copy, read, and even delete files if they wanted to. The share was promptly removed and another process put in place instead.

Lessons Learned:

- Vulnerability exceptions are acceptable in any business as long as proper mitigation and risk acceptance procedures are in place.

- When negotiating contracts with third-party vendors for services and equipment, make sure security and maintenance are a part of the contract.

- Verify that other processes and services do not jeopardize security.

- Something like backup procedures needs to be just as secure as any other process. Remember the data in a backup could represent all of the company and not just one finite element.

Complex Is Best

Have you ever seen a complex architecture that just looks like overkill? Sometimes it is needed and sometimes absolutely required based on all the use cases. One enterprise client had one of the most nightmarish environments I have ever seen. Multiple sites, low, unreliable bandwidth, and frequent problems at each site with workstations and servers were just some of the problems I found. To top it off, the datacenter at each location is limited to one rack and adding servers and appliances is not an option. So, we were left deploying a software solution that shared resources with another server.

So back in headquarters, we set up a standard management server and connected all of the scanners. After a few days of test scanning, we found the results streaming back to the server over poor satellite links was choking the bandwidth and causing business interruptions to other applications. So, our first step was to schedule the scan job off hours. The second step was to schedule the data to only upload in a very small window in the middle of the night. Then scans could run, not cause runtime issues due to a restricted infrastructure, and the data upload when other operations are dormant. After all was said and done, this complex architecture had multiple scan windows scattered throughout a month and rolling data upload windows scheduled back to back for all locations. A whiteboard carried the initial calendar and schedule that was implemented, and a complex architecture was reigned in and made the difference. The client was happy, the architecture worked, and the environment benefited from aggressive patch verification and PCI compliance.

Lessons Learned:

- Do not be scared of complex architectures. Sometimes they are necessary to meet the business requirements. Just make sure they are necessary and not overkill.

- Flexibility. Using tools that are flexible for a deployment, whether it be software or appliances, or has settings to manage data flow and jobs at a granular level is important to meet unique business requirements.

- Planning. Project Management is key to a complex rollout. Planning, scheduling, and documentation can make the difference and make sure all responsible parties are on the same page.

Forfeit the Game

In watching high school sports with my kids, I have seen a few games that were forfeited because the other team did not show or had too few players. This only happened a few times, but in the business world, it has happened too many times. One large successful deal my team won was because we were the only player willing to play. The requirements were straightforward, and the mission was to show up onsite and ready to install the pilot. All of my competitors sent software and instructions, or appliances, and offered webinars to get things started. None offered personnel to come onsite. And, why? I honestly did not blame them, but in order to play, they needed to show up and participate. This was a customer requirement and a statement they made that would help determine the winner. So, why did no one show up? Because the pilot was just below the Arctic border in the middle of December. That is where the customer was, and that was where I needed to be. So, four connections later and a flight that lands only every other day, I made it to my destination.

As with any trip, the first step on landing in absolutely freezing weather is to bundle up and dress warmly. That worked. The next step was to find my rental car. Well, the same person that helped me off the plane rented me a car. This was a really small town. In fact, the waitress at the hotel restaurant told me men outnumber women four out of five to one in the town, and she could not wait to leave: for anywhere but there. Anyways, I got to my rental, and it had a cracked windshield. In fact, all the windshields on the rental cars were cracked. I went back to my deboarding agent and rental car staff member and queried why? By this time, I was already freezing. The agent informed me that all the roads are dirt and rock and that they kick up stones and break the windshields frequently. They are left this way, so should I still care? The cars have traction regardless of ice and snow build-up. I knew this was going to be a fun trip. In order to play, you need to show up.

So, I proceeded to my hotel and parked. I went to check in and was asked if I plugged in my car. Now, I live in the sunshine state of Florida and have only heard of plugging in my car if it was an electric or hybrid. So of course, I said "What?" The polite attendant told me that you need to plug in the engine heater overnight to keep the engine oil warm or the car will not start in the morning. No wonder my competitors did not show up. So, I brazed the cold again and plugged in the car into the outlet on the outside of the building.

It was now time for dinner and sleep.

The next day I arrived at the client, did the installation, and proceeded with a very normal pilot. After all was said and done, we won the business and I froze every moment I was up there. I flew back the next day, 16 hours in transit, and had a purchase order on the salesperson's desk within the next few weeks. The client did not even try the other solutions. They wanted personal attention in the Arctic, and after the client had lived there so many years, he had the authority to bring someone there to help make his decision. That made all the difference in the world.

Lessons Learned:

- If a client wants an onsite, saying no may lose the business. You need to know if you push back, will it hurt you.

- If you are going to engage a client, a half-assed effort will fail. You either give it your all or not at all. You will not win business on a whim, or half energized approach.

- Regardless of the place or weather make the trip. Just because it is too cold or too hot, it should not stop your trip.

- Being personal and meeting your client face to face builds relationships. Sometimes this is absolutely required to close the sale.

Listening Skills

You may have a client for years. They may have your product and solutions fully deployed and in everyday business. but if they want to get rid of you, they will. As a fact, every vendor can be replaced, and no vendor is so entrenched that they cannot be removed. So, let's start with listening skills. A client environment was partially deployed with the solution and was hitting technology problems with regard to scalability and reliability. An executive meeting between the vice president of product management and vice president of enterprise sales was scheduled to review the issues one at a time with executives and key team members. A one-hour meeting turned into almost four hours, and every item was documented and commitments made to as many of them as possible. We listened to their problems, commitment to resolve the problems, and presented a plan to fix everything possible. Now they never told us we would be thrown out, but we knew that would happen.

Now over the course of the next six months, we had several maintenance releases, and we called the client each time and told them what we fixed, and what we added to solve his problems. Fixing his problems and delivering them was about 90% of the answer. The other 10% was showing him what we did and confirming it was the right fix. This gave us a deeper trust in the client and listening paid off.

Lessons Learned:

- Addressing your client's issues is important. You need to step back, listen, and document what they need and figure out how to deliver.

- Listening without delivering will only set you up as one of those vendors that do get removed.

- Showing your client the progress you made is just as important. It shows you listened, cared, and were willing to work with them.

- Never underestimate a client's ability to remove a vendor from operations.

Contractors

Shortly after 9-11, my presence was requested at a secure facility in South Florida. With security being the most paramount concern in everyone's mind, I hightailed it down the Florida Turnpike to my destination. Needless to say, the police officer that pulled me over for doing 90 did not share my enthusiasm for security. After a nice hefty fine, I arrived onsite and began my work. I was delegated to work with a contractor that was completely unfamiliar with my tools and had an open source product he preferred better. He loaded it and showed me all the capabilities he liked and wanted. Needless to say, he was trying to convince me what he wanted was better than what the client had paid for and wanted installed. After his brief demo, we began installation and usage of the solution the client wanted. Now this facility was so secure, I was not allowed to touch the keyboard. The contractor needed to do all the typing, and simple things like passwords just did not seem to work. He blamed my tool and again reinforced why his was better. Did I say this was a secure government facility? In either case, after troubleshooting for more than a day, I finally had him re-enter credentials, and things started to work. We had barely enough time to finish the setup before we did a demo for the officers in charge of the facility. The demo went fine, and we were fully installed, operational, and the contractor was trained.

Before I left, I had a debriefing with a senior official at the facility. We discussed the delays, and I mentioned the open source software the contractor loaded. He was completely lost in the conversation and stated that this was a secure facility, and no one should ever load unapproved software on the network. He promptly called the contractor in and confronted him with the accusation. He attempted to do the installation and pleaded his case. I was asked to leave and not to worry about anything else.

I gathered my things, turned in my bathroom hall pass, and saw the contractor leaving too. I said goodbye and found out through a rather awkward conversation that he was terminated for installing unauthorized software. I have never heard from either of them again.

Lessons Learned:

- A contractor never has the final say and must follow the rules of the company. They may have other restrictions as well that go above and beyond direct employees.

- Change control, highly secure environments, and proper procedures can get anyone fired if they are intentionally violated.

- If something is not working as expected, check your passwords. Fat fingers can cause many of the problems.

- If you intentionally sabotage a project, it will bite back. This is a simple lesson: what goes around, comes around.

- Nothing said behind closed doors is truly ever behind closed doors.

The Rogue Device

Before Hurricane Katrina hit the Mississippi area, there were a plethora of casino barges on the Gulf Coast and river. One of these clients had a datacenter located nearby and a major corporate office. After a fairly extensive pilot, and evaluation of casino devices, servers, and workstations, we proved a scan would not disrupt operations or devices like slot machines and cash changes that were connected to the network of the casino floor. After a routine scan one day, we started noticing what appeared to be rogue IP addresses. They were in the normal IP range but had no reverse DNS look-up, and the operating system was reported as a Turtle Beach MP3 Player. That in and of itself was very odd. After some rather complex tracking of the IP address, since the entire casino floor was a flat subnet, we found network-based MP3 players plugged into the casino network by two employees sharing large quantities of music and using the backbone to copy gigabytes at a time.

The devices were promptly confiscated and the owners identified. This was a quick identification of rogue devices and illegal activity, but we truly got lucky in finding them and emphaized the power of a good discovery.

Lessons Learned:

- Having rogue devices can represent a risk to the business that is unacceptable.

- Users having physical access to the network need to be controlled and locked down when appropriate.

- Illegal contents on the network, like MP3 files, can make the company liable for the contents.

- Identifying rogue devices is critical for sensitive networks.

- Using cameras and other security devices in critical wire closets will booster your security profile and prevent tampering.

The Big Fish

Some salespeople go after the biggest fish. The biggest enterprise client, the biggest partner, or the biggest OEM deal. Winning that business, getting a fat commission check, make you feel that the effort was worth it, but to a small business, it can be incredibly destructive. The needs of the biggest client can easily consume the resources of a small business and ultimately make the entire deal a losing proposition. Consider winning a deal with the big three server and desktop vendors for a piece of software that they will all embed. The cost to localize the product, provide technical support and training, and service the client can easily bury a business. The cost of business for the biggest fish must consider adding resources, the pains of growth, and what it will take to service them without making them your only client.

Now, consider you are the small fish and went after the biggest fish in the world. Well, we did. And we won it. Seven years later we have learned a ton. Here are some of biggest lessons learned:

- Stick to the contract. If you give too many free services away, it may be your undoing to keep the client happy.

- Define roles and responsibilities clearly, so there are no missed steps.

- Any service-level agreements must be achievable. Do not agree to them just to win the deal.

- Providing services that have never been done by you before must be estimated and gauged for viability. The worst scenario is the service is completely unobtainable in the time allotted.

- As my boss always states, crawl, walk, run. Do not expect to manage the biggest client from day one running.

Rootkits Anyone?

My enterprise account manager received a panic call from a prospect on a Friday afternoon requesting our presence first thing the following week. Based on that call, we determined the client was in real hot water due to a recent malware infestation. The scope of which we did not know. So, we booked flights and made arrangements to be there promptly and early on Monday morning. The early bird gets the worm, right?

As our meeting started, we learned the domain controllers throughout the organization had been infected with a rootkit. This was shortly after the big news storm about Sony installing rootkits on PCs using audio CDs. Well, the client did the right thing and did not bother to clean these machines. They started the painful process of creating a new domain and reinstalling all of the domain controllers one at a time and migrating users over. A process that took months to complete.

So, why the sudden urgency to have us onsite? Well, with the news about Sony, the executive team decided they wanted some sort of protection capabilities, so this type of exploit would never happen again. Can you image reinstalling everything from scratch? Drivers, software, users, policies, settings, and even restoring user data after it has been scanned? This was well before widespread DevOps and virtualization. The cost and time were enormous, and they did not want to repeat the mistake since they never determined how the machines were infected in the first place.

My account manager and I presented a textbook case for our solution, and I can proudly say that even after eight years of loyalty, they have never had a problem even close to this again.

Lessons Learned:

- A prospect in need can be an easy win. Just be honest and solve their problems with real results. They will stay loyal and reference over and over again.

- When you have an infection with the magnitude of rootkits on domain controllers, there is no safe or guaranteed way to remove the malware and be certain you are in the clear. A complete reload is the only proper course of action.

- If you follow the lead of your prospect, including their urgency, it shows your ability to empathize with their issues and provide solutions. If you dismiss their urgency and claim they are just crying wolf, they will not trust that you understand their problems.

- No one ever wants to wait for a fix to a problem. People want the pain to go away immediately.

Not the Only One

At one time to create leads, my company offered our endpoint protection product for free to end users. One of those downloads was from a CFO for a very unique vertical that had sensitive data from many, many clients. This is way before GDPR. He was running the product on his corporate machine when Conficker broke out. We received one of those desperate calls for help, and we immediately reacted with an onsite visit and a solution to meet their needs. During our fact-finding mission, we discovered every server in the environment was compromised, since nothing was being patched, and that the majority of desktops had also been compromised except for the CFO's machine. He suspected a problem when the agent repeatedly showed Conficker Alerts from critical servers in his environment. Our solution was protecting him from exploitation, but for the rest of the systems, it was too late.

So, we received a purchase order for the entire environment in very short order and began a rollout of key assets as the IT department began patching and disinfecting all of the systems, one at a time.

Lessons Learned:

- Endpoint protection is only truly effective if everyone is covered. Missing any systems leaves them open to threats.

- If your solutions are sending critical alerts, you need to investigate them. Dismissing them as false positives or noise will make you complacent to real threats.

- If the CFO never used our free version, they would never have considered us a viable vendor to solve the problem. Never underestimate the power of trial and free versions of your product.

My Favorite Story

This client story has to be my favorite since it is the most outrageous. An enterprise client with a vast quantity of kiosks deployed worldwide chose to use a competing HIPS product for protection. The solution was behavioral based and had a runtime mode and a learning mode. Since the product was deployed, it was left in learning mode building a profile of "acceptable" behavior. This was in the early years of machine learning technology. This process had been going on for months. Well, in that time period, a massive worm wreaked havoc on many major corporations for millions of dollars in damages. This client was no exception.

So, the first reaction of the client was to put the kiosks' HIPs product into protection runtime mode to stop the threat. Unfortunately, they were too late, and all of the kiosks were infected. So, they left the agent in runtime mode and began patching and disinfecting the systems. After a few thousand machines, they found that the kiosks became re-infected with the worm.

In simple terms, the machine learning-based HIPS product "observed" that the behavior of the worm and profiled it as acceptable communication for the device. When they tried to patch the system and remove the worm, the HIPS product rolled off the patch since it was never "learned" as an acceptable change and reintroduced the files and runtime of the worm, since it was acceptable. The HIPS product kept re-infecting the systems!

At this time, the client was clearly getting frustrated to the point of legal action. Their business was interrupted and operations actually ground to a halt. Thank goodness this was not my product. They placed the system back in learning mode, patched the system, and retrained the system that the new behavior was truly the correct one. They needed to correct every system before they could proceed and when they finally finished went back to runtime protection mode. For some unknown reason, the new profile did not take, and every machine was rolled back to the infected state once again. Needless to say, the solution was uninstalled and never used again.

Lessons Learned:

- Machine learning can learn bad behavior.

- Automated actions can be just as bad as the original threat.

How Many Class B Networks?

While working as a systems engineer, my account manager and I did some heavy lifting in Canada. We had an early prototype of our appliance and sent it to a trusted client for his opinion, and possible upsell opportunity over software alone. A few weeks earlier, he received the appliance, configured it, and began scanning his desktop environment. Previously, they only scanned servers. A few days before the visit, we had a debriefing, and it was ugly. Scans he started weeks early were still running, and he had no results or reports from anything he had tried. The user was very familiar with our software solutions so we could surmise that there was a major problem with the new appliance. He was only trying to run a scan of one floor of his building, and only 100 devices are active per floor. The network itself was a little older too, only 10Mbps half-duplex. This should not have made too much of a difference.

We arrived onsite (I always love Canadian customs after frequent trips back and forth over the border) and began to work. We reviewed the scan settings, jobs, and finally address groups. Immediately, we identified the problem. Each floor above his office building only had 100 active devices, but each floor was segmented into its own Class B network. The scanner was trying to reach all 65k+ devices to determine which 100 were active. And what was worse is each of these devices randomly scattered throughout the range, and no one had a list of the addresses or names to build a concise list for scanning. So, the only choice was to try and scan everything. There was nothing wrong with the appliances, but it was determined with the settings required, it would take 30+ days to find the devices and let the scanner timeout on all the other addresses. It would be faster to visit each device using SneakerNet and write down the IP address rather than trying to scan for them using an address group and scan range. Why in the world the network engineers configured this building this way is beyond my comprehension. Needless to say, they created a management nightmare that normal tools could never accommodate.

In the end, we did a manual inventory and built new address groups. The appliance worked flawlessly after that and ever since.

Lessons Learned:

- Blindly scanning large address ranges takes time. It can take lots of time if you are scanning with all ports and regardless of an ICMP response. You need to wait for everything to timeout before you can proceed to the next address. Even just relying on ping sweeps to determine active devices can take a long time.

- Always check your scan settings and address groups. Long scan times can be due to incorrect options or misconfigured address groups.

- Slow networks restrict the number of targets you can scan simultaneously and increase you scan time as well.

- When scanning a distinct list of targets, you can never identify rogue devices.

The Blog from Hell

One of the new initiatives by the company was to start a blog. We identified who the writers would be and hired a consultant to teach us how to write good blog articles and set up a regimented schedule for delivery. At first, I thought writing a blog would be simple. Little did I know. The consultant recommended using hyperlinks when possible, including things like Top N recommendations, and to be controversial in order to simulate conversation. To that end, each writer submitted a sample, and the consultant critiqued it and added his own spin much like an editor and to even a greater extent, a ghostwriter. This appeared to be great approach at first, but the consultant was an expert blog writer, not an expert in security.

One of my first "sample" blogs discussed penetration testing and discussed the legality of it. Our consultant and not-so-expert security ghostwriter changed the first sentence to say, "I think penetration testing should be illegal." Without sending the blog around for approval, it was posted and caused an absolute uproar for our new site within the community. For a few days, I received a wide variety of phone calls and outrageous statements about how ludicrous this comment was. And they were right. I ended up pulling the blog since it was altered, and writing a new one that stated, "what I really meant to say..."

The consultant quit out of embarrassment, and we now have a review procedure for all blog postings to make sure this never happens again. And, no more ghostwriters.

Lessons Learned:

- Before publishing anything public, have someone else check your work.

- If you use a ghostwriter, make sure they have enough expertise in your field to write about the topic. For me personally, I have never used one again, and everything is original.

- Consultants know that piece of the puzzle very well; do not assume they know the rest of your business well enough to be an expert.

- When something gets published to the Web, it is there forever. Even if you remove the page. Someone probably indexed it, made a cached copy, or copied it, and it can never be completely erased. Someone can find it if he or she wants to. Including my unapproved blog post.

Nice Portal, Baby

In a former life (previous job) my company had developed a brand-new portal technology. This was way before Microsoft SharePoint was even a product. We went on an aggressive marketing campaign for the product, and it started to get a really good reception for analysts and press.

For a tradeshow in Vegas, around the late 1990s, we had several thousand t-shirts made with the logo "Nice Portal, Baby." Marketing thought this was brilliant and a great tagline to advertise the new release. Little did they know the choice of words was actually inflammatory in British English. The word "Portal" also means "Vagina" in the British dictionary. I will leave it to you to do the word substitution and see what the t-shirt really meant to our overseas guests.

Needless to say, we never gave out one t-shirt and threw out almost every single one. Their brilliant idea was not so politically correct after all. By the way, some of us snagged a few as souvenirs after all the laughing and explaining was over to management.

Lessons Learned:

- When doing outboard marketing, consider your choice of words carefully. Definitions in other languages or even dialects can mean different things.

- A pun on words can be misunderstood; vet out all the possible variations before releasing.

- Know your audience. If the clients were only American, this would never have been a problem.

- Mistakes like this are costly. Like other examples in this book, try to have someone else check your work.

Online Banking

During the .com bubble, my sales manager and I engaged in a bank that performed all transactions online. They had no brick-and-mortar locations and offered higher interest rates on savings accounts compared to everyone else since their only overhead was the corporate office, mail room, and data center. The business model sounded great, and many physical security problems were a moot point since no physical locations ever existed. Depositing checks was done through the mail and getting cash was through any participating ATM.

Early in the sales cycle, we identified that vulnerability assessment was key since all of their work was done through information technology. There were no manual procedures since the primary presence was through the Web. This was our business, so this seemed like a natural fit.

Now at this time, PCI DSS did not exist. The client was only concerned with things like worms and rightfully so. This was the biggest threat at the time. When we did an initial scan of the environment, we found all of the modern systems of the time (Windows 2000) and problems across the board ranging from null session, blank and default passwords, and anonymous shares. The client did not care since these were all behind the firewall and only the forward-facing web servers, the front doors to the bank, were a concern for threats.

Well, after our pilot, the primary contact went dark. His boss went dark. We could not find anyone willing to speak with us regarding the pilot or if they wanted to license the solution. We later learned both individuals left the Internet bank for unspecified reasons. Based on the feedback we did receive from the new security officer months later, was that both individuals participated in illegal activities and were terminated. What they were, we never found out. It was a closed, lost opportunity. My sales manager and I think they used our data to rob the bank, based on the buzz in the community. We never found out for certain.

Lessons Learned:

- Vulnerability assessment data is very sensitive information and if in the wrong hands, can be used against an organization in the worst ways possible.

- Even the most trivial of critical threats can be a real risk to the business. If you do not understand why they are critical, research the problem. Do not dismiss them based on other mitigation strategies like a firewall.

- When a client goes dark and does not communicate anymore, you have a problem. It is generally never good.

- Bank robbers will go after the money any way possible. Brick and mortar or electronic. In today's world, a cyber attack is preferred if it can go on undetected for long periods of time.

Lies

One of my competitors just lies. You may have vendors or competitors that do too. They hand out competitive analysis documents of their products versus ours, and they are now dated and years old. In fact, when they were published, they were grossly inaccurate and aged rapidly as the solution was actively being developed.

The problem with these documents is the unwarranted defensive it places us vendors when a potential client receives them during a sales cycles. A salesperson's initial response is to formulate a rebuttal to each statement. It is our belief that once you do that, you have already lost because you are explaining yourself and playing directly into the competitor's game, regardless of how accurate the document is.

After trial and error, the only way to respond is the high road. The highest road possible. You do not answer the document. You explain that you have seen this before and this is standard tactic to win the mindset of clients and that it is dated and inaccurate, even when it was released. You basically play against the credibility of the competitor and make them question every fact they state that they do better.

Here is a simple example. The competitor stated that they do not need remote registry access in order to perform a credentialed scan. Lie. There is no way to inspect a remote registry on a windows host without the remote registry service turned on (This was before WMI remote enablement). They stated to the prospect that we needed it, and they did not. Hence, their scans were more secure. The truth was because our prerequisites document stated it as a requirement and theirs did not. So, in lieu of coming clean on the oversight in their documentation, they spun it into a competitive advantage that was laden with errors.

So, when we took the high road in explaining the quality and accuracy of statements such as this, we built a strong relationship and replaced their fear, uncertainty, and doubt (FUD) with our own, based on facts. Ultimately, we won the deal.

Lessons Learned:

- If you lie to the client, you will get caught.

- If you misstate features and requirements, you will get caught and have to explain it later. If it is after the sales cycle is complete, you may destroy your credibility. If it is before, you can easily lose the deal.

- If you choose to build competitive comparison sheets, be prepared to dedicate resources regularly to keep them up to date. Even after a few months, a single release can change the facts and make the document, and its claims, inaccurate.

- If presented with a competitive document, never answer it line by line. It is not an RFP. Take the high road and explain why this approach is flawed. This can be based on business, technical, or even product. Never let an organization compare apples to orange in these scenarios.

Speaking of Comparisons

A regular mistake my sales team makes is requesting comparison documentation and feature tables not with competing products but with their own. This is not to say that comparing your own products is bad, but there is a time and place for this type of documentation and a place when you should never do so.

First, consider a table on a website comparing a free version, to a professional version, and ultimately the enterprise version. This allows you to upsell features and functions of the same product, using different releases, to larger or more experienced clients. This in general works well when you can justify the cost difference between features and functions.

Second, this does not work well when comparing two different products in your portfolio that have overlapping functionality. You have actually turned your own sales cycle into a competition between two products you are trying to sell, one with more or less functionality than the other but in a completely different family.

Consider two products that can do web application vulnerability assessment. One only does web app scanning really well, and the other only does basics with additional scanning functionality for operating systems, applications, and databases. If you compare the two, you highlight the shortcomings of one product (why doesn't it do that) and enforce that your technology is not integrated and lacks a common vision to solve a problem. Why else would you have two different products that do the same thing?

Comparisons are a great way to upsell your technology but a poor way to compare your own family of products. When you have this situation yourself, stick with one product and lead with it. Giving comparisons will just confuse the sales cycle and make you compete against yourself.

Lessons Learned:

- Use comparison documentation correctly to upsell your own products. Not to compare them side by side, literally.

- Avoid pitching two of your own products to clients to solve the same problem. You end up just competing against yourself and confusing the client.

- If you have to explain the differences between two (or more) products that do the same thing or have overlapping features, your strategy for them as solutions is flawed.

Getting Your Facts Straight

Early in my career, I had a salesperson who would embellish facts in order to make the sales cycle slant in our favor. They were not blatant lies but light exaggerations of facts in order to make us look more favorable. This always created problems, especially when both of us would present to a prospect in the same meeting.

This problem led to the angriest I have ever gotten at work and happened after one of these meetings. My salesperson embellished a statistic for an SLA, and when I presented later, I inadvertently contradicted him. He accelerated the time frame (of course), and I stated our contractual requirements.

The client did not appear to notice the difference (we won the business), but the car ride afterward was a bloodbath of angry words and accusations.

After the fighting and yelling was over, we agreed on one simple principle: to listen to the other person's presentation, regardless of who goes first and use their statistics in the rest of the conversations with the prospect. This was incredibly important since sometimes I would go first and present a fact and he would contradict and vice versa. So, getting our facts straight from beginning to end of a pitch was incredibly important.

Lessons Learned:

- Listen to presentations from your peers before you go on to the same audience. Use their facts, emphasize their message, and stay consistent.

- If a peer lies or embellishes a fact, never contradict them in front of a client. Always do it later, in private. You might be surprised that you are actually wrong.

- Yelling at a peer never solves any problem. Keep your cool. This may be obvious, but I have seen it happen too many times, especially to subordinates.

- If you embellish a fact, be prepared to back it up. SLAs can easily be jaded based on collected data, but other facts are not so manipulatable.

Conformal Coating

When I first started in information technology, long before John Titor's visit, I owned a consulting company, and I did third-party consulting work for various doctors, lawyers, and small manufacturers. This was in the OS/2 and Windows 3.1 for Workgroup days and early Windows 3.1 NT Server.

One of my clients was using Intel 386 computers (clones) in a manufacturing floor, and they had become internally encrusted with dust and oils. I learned through a BBS (before the Internet and even basic services from AOL and Prodigy) that most motherboards were conformal coated after manufacturing to protect against moisture and dust. In fact, the spec for them was quite durable, and they could even get wet and safely reassembled if no power was applied.

So, using a standard electronic degreaser, a bathtub, and gentle soap, I took disassembled computers (no hard disks or mechanical components of the system) and proceeded to give them a bath.

Now the client was okay with this because they tried putting new ISA cards in the system and jammed the slots with grease when inserting them. Obviously, they did not work and had no other way of cleaning them except for buying new machines. This approach was a last-ditch effort versus new computers.

So, after a cold bath and several days of drying in the hot Florida sun, the machines were reassembled and worked perfectly. In fact, they worked perfectly until we upgraded to new hardware and Windows 95.

Lessons Learned:

- Just because electronics get wet does not necessarily does not necessarily mean they are broken. Keep them fully powered off and remove the battery if applicable.

Electricity on a powered-on device will most likely burn it out, not the water itself. Then, let them dry out fully, soak them in rice if possible, and if no water seepage occurs in a screen or liquid sensitive area (speakers or sensors), it should work. Most modern circuits are conformal coated today and will protect them against these hazards.

- Research a problem thoroughly before you take action. Soap and water was the last thing I thought of ever using on a motherboard.

- Today, the Internet is the best place for this information. When this event occurred, I relied on BBS's and chat rooms. Modern-day help Forums and private knowledge bases that require a company login can be just as helpful. If all else fails, place the device in a bath of uncooked rice. Some of you probably already know this trick.

Dependencies

One of the biggest "gotchas" for any pilot is system hardware and software dependencies and prerequisites. Most vendors publish an extensive list of what a host system or VM should have in order to support the solution. The problem is that most clients never review the list and provide hardware that is grossly underpowered for the task.

Some manufacturers have resorted to automatic checkers to verify the requirements prior to installation, and others will enter a pilot with appliances that are fully preconfigured in order to avoid these problems, delays, and potentially poor user experiences.

So, this is where our story begins. The current documented requirements recommend a minimum of 4GB of RAM and specifics for the configuration including an installation of MS SQL.

Well, the prospect wanted to engage in a software pilot and decided to install the solution in a VM with only 1GB of RAM and SQL Express. They did not have any spare hardware, and their virtual hosting environment could not support any additional resources.

Of course, the pilot was a disaster. The solution was sluggish, features just did not work, and the user experience was awful. The prospect was still very interested in the solution, acknowledged the shortcomings in their environment, and requested we send a physical appliance. A few weeks later a box arrived in the office.

After setting up the system and doing initial testing, it was clear that we had additional problems. Even though we used an appliance, other environmental dependencies were not met, and certain other features just did not work. This included very old versions of Internet Explorer still in use that tried to access the management console on the appliance and existing installations of WSUS.

Needless to stay, the appliance did better, but we only overcame about half the problems. The client, nor the sales team, bothered to finish reading the prerequisites list and verifying all the requirements for host prerequisites to client dependencies.

Well, the client begrudgingly upgraded a few hosts and began to use the pilot solution with limited success. At this time, they were becoming bitter from all of the back and forth and just wanted a solution that plugged in and worked. None of which was true yet. Every problem from requiring Internet access to license the solution to spam filters blocking license keys was experienced with this client and proved that a prerequisites checklist alone is not enough.

So, after months of working with this client, they did not make a decision to commit to our solution or more importantly anyone else's because none will work out of the box in their environment.

Lessons Learned:

- Before any pilot or post sales installation, always verify the prerequisites.

- If you encounter basic problems like Internet access, your competitors will probably have the same issues.

- Even if your organization has simplified the installation using a VM, software-based checkers, or even an appliance, other dependencies can cause issues. It is important to complete the prerequisites checklist and if new issues arise, fully document them for future clients.

- If a client insists on using older and outdated versions and technology, make sure you can support them, especially for the length of the contract. They will resist upgrades and potentially could make you support older versions that can drain support and QA resources. For example, do you still support Windows 2008 or even Windows 2003?

Odds and Ends

The remainder of these stories are just funny and a touch scary in themselves. Hopefully, you cannot relate to any of them when trying to protect your assets:

- A Fortune 100 Client explained their vulnerability assessment procedures to me. They only scan servers with null session, and no credentials, to look for systems susceptible to worms or bots. They do not scan servers with credentials or workstations since their anti-virus solution will stop any problems before they spread. Only their PCI environment gets a credentialed scan because it has too. I wonder today if that is still their security policy. I surely hope not.

- One client during a presales pilot asked me what I thought of Microsoft. I gave him my normal pitch on how well, and how seriously, they handle vulnerabilities and security threats. He stopped me mid-sentence and said no, that is not what I am looking for. He wanted to know if I liked them because he had a job offer to go work for them and he was a considering a job switch. Mental note, he is my point of contact for the pilot. Would I win this business?

- A systems engineer I know tells me he only hears from vendors when their contract is up for renewal. I asked him if we do a good job keeping him informed as well. He honestly answers that he does not know. Why? Because all of the vendor emails he receives, not from an individual, but rather a list server, is automatically classified as Junk. He never reads them.

- A user decided to exclude a vulnerability from his report since the application related to the vulnerability was not installed on his system. While this sounds like a simple false positive, the vulnerability is also present in the runtime libraries distributed by third-party vendors. In lieu of determining the third-party application using the runtime, and determining whether the system was really vulnerable, an exception was made for almost every Windows server in their environment.

- An enterprise client chooses an anti-virus solution that has frequent false negatives and endpoint malware infestations because it was easy for the information technology department to deploy and use. They considered the risk acceptable since it had no operational runtime challenges.

- A prospect in the middle of nowhere would not use Internet Explorer on any of his Windows machines since it caused so many malware infestations in his environment. Instead, they choose to use Firefox for everything and would not use our management console since it was Internet Explorer (at that time) dependent. At the time of our demo, they launched their VPN client through IE since it did not work with the version of Firefox they chose to deploy.

- One of my first consulting jobs was helping a company design rides for amusement parks. I received a call on a Saturday afternoon that AutoCAD was crashing and corrupting critical design files. I made a trip out to their facility and witnessed the problem firsthand. I ran the MS-DOS command for memory and found that almost all of the 640kb was being used by some odd program I had never heard of. I ran a dir /s to find it, and it was in the AutoCAD subdirectory. I deleted it, rebooted, and let emm38.sys optimize the base memory again. I asked where they got AutoCAD from, and it was on a dozen floppies from a street vendor in Taiwan. They had a bootleg version, with a virus, that had other intentions for their work. My first experience with viruses embedded in commercial software. This was about 1994 on an Intel 386 computer with MS-DOS 5.5.

- When the email says "I Love You" from a peer at work, do not open the attachment. Lessons learned from the trenches. If you do not know what this is, Google "Love Letter Virus" and "Melissa Virus." Some users that are new to security apparently do not know what this is or what the movie *War Games* was about.

- Handing out condoms at a trade show to highlight your new *protection* capabilities is a bad idea. This is still far worse than handing out cheap old pens that do not write. If you think I am kidding, this happened at Networld Interop in the late 1990s and is a story my peers and I regularly reference when marketing goes wild. If you plan to give out swag, know your audience and what you are giving them.

- Just because their name is Anonymous does not mean you should try and piss them off. Organizations have boasted and lost. Know your enemy before you decide and attack. Offensive cyber security is still a very risky venture, even today.

CHAPTER 23

Final Recommendations

As a bad cliché, it is easier to state that we need a vulnerability management program versus actually implementing one. Regulations, compliance, and security best practices all dictate that we need a procedure, but implementing one as an efficient process is a completely different problem. In order to make that a reality, several key takeaways must be instilled within the organization. Without them, your protection of assets and defending against threats will fail. Each of these must be in place in order to succeed:

- Executive Sponsorship – The executive leadership must be fully on board with the implementation of a vulnerability management program and the risks and benefits it will provide. Any severe pushback due to complacency, ignorance, or other political motives will jeopardize the entire program. While the cost of the program will always be a concern, the executive team must conclude the cost will outweigh the risks of poor implementation or not having a vulnerability management program at all. This includes understanding and prioritizing when a

M.J. Haber and B. Hibbert, *Asset Attack Vectors*,
https://doi.org/10.1007/978-1-4842-3627-7_23

risk is acceptable or when it is a major liability to the business. In general, this is the responsibility of a CISO to educate team members without crying, "the sky is falling" every week.

- Procedures and Policy – A vulnerability management program needs to be designed with guidelines and service-level agreements including clear lines of ownership. Executing an assessment without performing actions on the results in a timely and predictable manner will result in a failed program. This workflow should be documented, reviewed periodically, and followed to ensure remediation and mitigation strategies are effective.

- Competition – Healthy competition on who can patch all of their systems first or deploy a new technology better stirs the intellect and spirit. If your organization can afford prizes at the end, team members have bragging rights and a goal. Competition does not need to be like a sport but the most successful vulnerability management programs actually treat them like one. Whether you have a formal competition in your plan is not relevant, but as soon as one department, group, or systems are compared to another, you have already begun down this path.

- Measurements and Consequences – One of the nastiest pitfalls of a bad vulnerability management implementation is complacency, and no one is accountable for a situation. If a problem exists that is not remediated or mitigated in a timely fashion (typically a Service-Level Agreement SLA), something must happen. If teams slack off and risk your security, someone has to own the problem and be held accountable. In addition to procedures and policies, define measurements across the organization and consequences if they are not followed. This can be another form of competition.

- Education and Notification – The threats are all around us and happening every day, even to our competitors. It is a natural human trait to slack off once in a while too. That alone should not stop teams from being trained and from threat being communicated to all stakeholders. There is a risk by not telling teams to not click on a link or open an email that says "I have a package for you in the mail room." Teams need to be notified of a potential risk in a timely manner.

- Basic Hygiene – If you do the basics down – from vulnerability assessments, patch management, and privilege access delegation, you will find flaws in your organization more quickly and be able to maintain them better, so a simple problem does not become a massive liability for the organization. Basic cyber secure hygiene will help you with these problems including the basics like good DNS, AD structures, and even reliable NTP.

CHAPTER 24

Conclusion

Your vulnerability management solution should be designed from the ground up to provide organizations with context-aware vulnerability assessment and risk analysis. All architectures should empower organizations to:

1. **Know what's on Their Network** through a comprehensive analysis of all IP-based assets including web, mobile, cloud, and virtual platforms.

2. **Spot what's Lurking in the Shadows** by quickly recognizing unknown dangers hiding in BYOT devices, unauthorized applications, and unknown ports.

3. **See Their Data in Hi-Definition** with over customizable security views, and audit and compliance reports.

4. **Find Soft Targets** by correlating exploits against Metasploit, Exploit-Database, Canvas, and Core Impact.

5. **Cover Their Vulnerability Gaps** with deep insight into virtual, hardened, and cloud-based environments.

© Morey J. Haber, Brad Hibbert 2018
M.J. Haber and B. Hibbert, *Asset Attack Vectors*,
https://doi.org/10.1007/978-1-4842-3627-7_24

6. **Unify Vulnerability and Threat Intelligence** for a clearer, more-informed picture of enterprise risk.

7. **See Hidden Threats with Analytics** by correlating low-level privilege, vulnerability, and threat data.

8. **Accelerate Patching** via automated remediation of Microsoft, JAVA, Adobe vulnerabilities, and more using third-party integrations.

9. **Share** vulnerability intelligence and **Collaborate** with other IT systems to achieve greater security awareness.

10. **Automate Credentialed Scans** with continually rotated privileged credentials.

Therefore, in order to protect assets and build a solid defense, put the data in the proper context. People like you and me, who are responsible for measuring and mitigating risk within their organizations, can't afford to fail. If you have any doubts, look at how your organization measures up to the strategies and recommendations in this book. If you are starting anew, you have just been imparted with twenty years of experience to build your program from the ground up, right from the start. Good luck, and don't get hacked from a missing patch or poor security configuration.

APPENDIX A

Sample Request for Proposal (RFP)

The decision to change, replace, augment, or start a new vulnerability management program is a tautening task. To simplify this process, we have created a sample Request for Proposal (RFP) that can be modified for any business ({Company Name}) to solicit any vendor ({Vendor Name}). The requirements listed are generic as well as the legal terminology and requirements for vendor selection and features. This should allow you to customize the text to meet your individual business requirements or provide insight on how to make a formal submission process fit within your organization. To that end, it starts with an invitation to the short list of vendors you believe can meet your objectives. It concludes with all the most popular technical questions, licensing, support, and pricing seen throughout the industry. Appendix B contains a sample RFP spreadsheet that can be used to supplement this chapter or as a Request for Information (RFI) to shortlist the vendors for this process.

Invitation

{Company Name} respectfully invites {Vendor} to submit a response based on the information contained in this Request for Proposal ("RFP").

© Morey J. Haber, Brad Hibbert 2018
M.J. Haber and B. Hibbert, *Asset Attack Vectors*,
https://doi.org/10.1007/978-1-4842-3627-7

Overview

{Company Name}'s goals with this RFP are to identify and award business to a vendor that can provide us with a Vulnerability Management solution that meets our business and technical requirements.

The vision for this project is to ensure {Company Name} knows what systems are on our network, within our cloud environments, the criticality of those systems, their vulnerabilities, the risks each vulnerability presents, and ensure the organization has the processes and technologies to prioritize and remediate the risks.

This effort will build on {Company Name}'s existing mature Windows and Linux patching processes and potentially replace or augment our current vulnerability scanning technology. Our current approach has the current flaws:

- Relies on excessive manual steps

- Has a high false positive rate

- Is labor intensive for the team who manages the scanning tool and its workflow

- Is difficult for system owners who are responsible for resolving vulnerabilities to manage

- Produces reports that don't reflect real-world patching efforts.

We seek to identify and implement a tool that matches well with our defined process, a cycle that addresses the following:

- Asset Identification

- Vulnerability Assessment

- Asset Vulnerability Management

- Prioritization and Threat Intelligence

- Automated Communication

- Reliable Remediation or Mitigation Verification

Furthermore, we expect the product to integrate with other systems and processes where appropriate, most notably:

- {Insert critical systems integration vendor and use case}.

{Company Name} intends to scan:

- Number of Public IP Addresses

- Number of Private IP Addresses

- Number of Public Web Applications

- Number of Private Web Applications

- Approximate Number of Desktops, Servers, Mobile, Network Devices, and IoT in scope for assessments

These are located in the following locations:

- {List geographic requirements}

- {List number of isolated or air gapped zones}

About {Company Name}
{Company Name} is a {Company About Use Boilerplate}
{Company Contact Information}
{Critical dates for RFP response}
{Expected RFP award date}

RFP Response Process

Please *immediately* email the {Company Name} Primary Contact to confirm receipt of this RFP.

If you intend to respond to this RFP, you must notify the {Company Name} Primary Contact by email before the {Insert Date}. This email must contain:

- An indication that you intend to respond to this RFP, specifically citing the name of the RFP as it appears on the title page; and

- The name, address, email, and telephone number of your company's {Company Name} Primary Contact for this RFP.

- If you do not intend to respond to this RFP, please indicate that you are declining the opportunity to respond and confirm that you have destroyed all electronic and printed copies of this RFP by the date and time {Insert date}.

- Direct any inquiries regarding this RFP to {Company Name} Primary Contact. Other {Company Name} departments may provide input during the RFP process. However, only the above-referenced individual may be contacted concerning this RFP unless authorized in writing by the {Company Name} Primary Contact or the {Company Name} Finance Department.

- Responses are due by {Insert Date}. It is {Vendor Name}'s responsibility to ensure copies of the response are sent and received by {Company Name} on or before the required deadline. All responses must be sent to the {Company Name} Primary Contact.

- {Company Name}'s intent is to issue a decision regarding preferred vendor(s) for the next round of consideration based on the RFP response by {Insert Date}. However, {Company Name} may elect not to issue a decision by that date. Similarly, {Company Name} may opt not to issue a decision at any time.

- {Company Name} may conduct a proof of performance to confirm the proposed solution will meet {Company Name}'s needs.

RFP Response Format

Two copies of the response should be sent. One should be a PDF document and the other a Microsoft Word document.

RFP Response Contents

Responses shall be prepared in a simple and straightforward manner, and in the format outlined below. Each response must include:

- **Signatory** - An authorized signatory addressed to the {Company Name} Primary Contact stating that the response is a best effort and contains a valid-through date.

- **Executive Summary** - An overview of the proposed solution, including summary cost information.

- **Detailed Response** - A detailed written response to the requirements and questions. Each question needs to be answered, and responses must be placed directly below each question.

Missing Answers

Missing answers will be assumed to indicate "not available" or "not supported by your product or proposed solution." Where your response must be provided in narrative form, make it clear and concise. The use of "canned" marketing or public relations materials may impede or confuse the analysis of competitive responses and is discouraged.

Terms and Conditions

Confidentiality and Non-Disclosure Agreement

The material contained in this document is proprietary to {Company Name}. No rights in this material are transferred to any other organization. Except as needed to respond to this RFP effectively, this material may not be disclosed, duplicated, or otherwise revealed, in whole or in part, without the written consent of {Company Name} and is subject to the terms of the Non-Disclosure Agreement executed by {Vendor Name} and {Company Name}.

By agreeing to respond to this RFP, {Vendor Name} acknowledges that {Company Name} business procedures, ideas, inventions, plans, financial data, contents of the RFP, and other {Company Name} information are the sole and exclusive property of {Company Name}. {Vendor Name} also agrees that it will safeguard such information to the same extent as it safeguards its own confidential material or data relating to its own business information that is of confidential or proprietary nature. {Vendor Name} will not furnish the name of {Company Name} as a reference or use the name of {Company Name} in any advertising or promotional materials without the prior written consent of {Company Name}.

Supplementary

{Vendor Name} must identify the generally available product version information that was used to answer the RFP questions. If any answers are based on other product versions not currently available (futures), then those versions need to be identified.

{Company Name} is under no obligation to disclose the reasoning behind its decisions. {Vendor Name} should understand that all needs and requirements are outlined in this proposal and should not base their proposal on previous business or discussions prior to this RFP.

In the event that {Company Name} determines that any condition of the RFP has changed after the RFP has been issued, all vendors will be notified. Vendors who have already submitted a proposal will be allowed to amend it. If necessary, {Company Name} may specify a new proposal submission due date.

{Company Name}'s decision will be based upon the individual merits of the submitted proposals. Price is not the sole determinant, nor does {Company Name} have any obligation to select the lowest bidding response.

Selections are completely at {Company Name}'s discretion.

{Vendor Name} must understand that {Company Name} may require the assistance of internal departments, third parties, or external advisors in reviewing proposals, therefore requiring unrestricted rights to copy and distribute as needed, within the conditions of signed confidentiality agreements.

{Company Name} reserves the following rights:

- To proceed or not proceed with acquiring the goods and / or services requested in this RFP;

- To modify or amend any terms of this RFP;

- To reject any and all submissions received as a response to this RFP;

- To award the business to more than one vendor.

- No award of business will be final until the parties have executed a formal written contract.

All proposals, information, and RFP responses submitted by {Vendor Name} may be included in the final contract. No information or other material should be submitted that could not be included in the contract.

Unconditional Requirements

This section defines functional and technical requirements that {Company Name} considers to be absolutely necessary for us to consider your solution. If your solution is unable to meet these requirements, you should elect not to participate in the RFP process and notify the appropriate contact listed in this RFP.

Functional Requirements

The following functional requirements will be required for any vendor selection:

- The product must provide a full vulnerability management lifecycle solution.

- The product must report vulnerabilities using a risk-based model that incorporates multiple factors such as server criticality, data sensitivity, vulnerability severity, and existing compensating controls.

- The product must provide a mechanism to integrate with {Insert vendor if required}.

Technical Requirements

The following technical requirements will be required for any vendor selection:

- All aspects of your proposed solution, including products and services, must be generally available to us for purchase as of the date of your response.

- The product must provide role-based access controls to support the Principle of Least Privilege for administrators, users, and authenticated scan credentials.

- The product must integrate with our directory services.

Supplementary Requirements

The following supplementary requirements will be required for any vendor selection:

- Your company must be able to demonstrate strong financial health as stated in a current reputable financial report service such as Dun & Bradstreet.

- Your company must be able to demonstrate:

  - {insert any other business requirements such as common criteria, GDPR, FedRamp, or NIST compliance}.

319

Vendor Technology and Experience

Please respond to the following questions so that we may obtain a better understanding of your company and solution history. If your company provides several diverse product lines, focus the answers primarily at the Vulnerability Management product line where appropriate.

Company History

1. Please describe the history of your company and your Vulnerability Management solution including:

    - Names of the key founders and developers who have been significant to the development of this solution and whether those individuals are still with the firm.

    - History of any of corporate mergers and product acquisitions.

    - Your firm's founding product set and how you evolved into the product you offer today.

    - Any acquisitions/mergers that are in process or publicly announced.

    - Whether your company is looking to be acquired or you anticipate any acquisition attempts.

2. Please provide current organization charts that show Name, Title, Location, Email, and phone numbers for the sales/marketing, support, and finance/legal team.

Financial Information

3. Financial status is of significance during our evaluation and selection process. Therefore, we assess financial viability. Please provide the following data for your company's parent firm:

    - If public, 10K or similar reports for the current quarter and last two years of filings.

    - If private, independently audited financials package including auditor's certification.

    - Key financial ownership/stakeholder declarations.

    - Any subsidiary reporting of your company that is ultimately rolled into your parent company.

4. State your capital and operating IT expenses for the past three years. For the current year, provide your capital and operating budgets. Please include R&D investments.

5. State the number of IT workers you employ, broken down by management, consultants/analysts, sales, development, implementation/professional services, customer support, etc.

Customer Installations and References

6. Please provide at least three company references, preferably in the {specify vertical}, where solutions similar to those you are proposing have been fully installed and are in commercial production use. Please explain the scope of implementation at the customer site. The customer's requirements should align with the requirements expressed by {Company Name}.

Solution Functionality

This section contains questions regarding the use of your solution and how your solutions satisfy {Company Name}'s needs. Responses should be directed toward the *use* of the product, including its functionality and business processes that would impact its use or be impacted by its use.

7. Please provide a high-level description of the solution you propose in response to this RFP. How long has this solution been offered?

Assessments

8. Does your product include scanning functionality, or do you build upon another vendor's scanning technology? Does your company develop its own scanning technology, or license another vendor's technology? If you license another technology, please indicate whose technology.

9. Please describe the different kinds of scans that may be run, such as discovery scans, vulnerability scans, remediation validation scans, configuration scans, patch scans, etc. Can the product scan determine if a system meets configuration standards in addition to scanning for vulnerabilities? Can this be done through the network or agent technologies?

10. Please describe how scans may be scheduled. Be sure to carefully describe the various ways scans may be scheduled, including different types of single scans, repeated scans, validation scans, network and agent scans, etc.

11. Please explicitly define all systems and operating systems that your system is designed to scan. At a very minimum, please address to what level of detail your system can scan the following operating system and devices:

    • {Insert solution platforms for your company like Microsoft Windows, Apple MacOS, and/or Red Hat Linux, etc.}.

12. Please explicitly define specific applications and databases that your system is designed to scan.

13. Provide detailed information around the processes your tool supports for validation scanning (scans performed to validate a specific vulnerability was fixed). Describe how your tool focuses those scans to the systems and/or vulnerabilities identified.

14. Please describe how your tool implements the concept of scanning windows (allowed scanning time frames).

   - What sorts of scans follow scanning windows?

   - What sorts of scans take place outside of scanning windows?

   - How are scanning windows defined and organized?

   - Who has the ability to define and assign scanning windows?

   - Who has the ability to schedule or initiate a scan outside a window?

15. Please describe in detail how systems, scans, and reports may be organized and what functionality the organization applies to. For example, scanning or reporting based on IP range, scanning or reporting based on system criticality (or other metadata), scanning or reporting based on system functionality, scanning or reporting based on system age (e.g., all servers deployed within the past month), scanning or reporting based on operating system, etc.

16. Describe the relationships between different systems, scans, and reports. How does the tool support hierarchical relationships? (For example, all "Windows Servers" might be members of the "Servers" group due to a hierarchy). How does the tool support non-hierarchical relationships? (For example, a specific Windows Server might be a member of the "File Servers" group in addition to being a member of the "Windows Servers" group.)

17. Describe to what degree of accuracy your product can identify a particular OS or application, such as version level, patch level, or build level. How are the accuracies impacted by options (such as scanning parameters, use of an agent or a credentialed scan)?

18. Describe in detail how your tool performs credentialed (authenticated) scans:

   • What level of authentication is required?

   • How are results impacted if we use a user with fewer authorizations?

   • How are credentials stored?

   • How does your tool mitigate the risks posed by credentialed scans?

   • How does your tool address configurations that may block root or domain administrators from logging in remotely?

   • What processes do you recommend we implement to further mitigate the risks?

19. Describe your tool's reliance on agents installed on a system:

   • Are they required?

   • Are they an option?

   • When do you recommend using them, and when do you recommend avoiding them?

   • What operating systems do your agents support?

   • How do you support deploying and patching the agents?

20. How does your solution support scanning remote locations? Please address the specific challenges offered by locations with slow connections but significant infrastructure (e.g., a foreign office with one or more server rooms), locations with slow connections and minimal infrastructure, and time zone differences.

21. How does your solution support scanning devices such as laptops, which may or may not be on the corporate network at any given time?

22. How does your solution support assessing mobile devices?

23. Please describe any standard compliance scanning templates your tool may offer, such as PCI, HIPAA, etc. If you have a PCI template, please provide a complete explanation of what the template offers, whether it is intended to be used as is out of the box or as a starting point, and if you are PCI ASV certified.

24. What level of detail does your tool provide about the tests it performs when scanning?

25. Please describe the process for creating our own custom tests to be performed during a scan.

26. Please describe the process one should follow with respect to your toolset when a new system is put into production. Be sure to identify the specific steps performed by the vulnerability management tool administrator, and the steps performed by the system owner to onboard or decommission an asset.

27. If the tool negatively impacts a system during a scan (such as causing performance issues, causing an application to halt, or crashing or rebooting a system), how does the tool detect the impact and respond?

28. Describe what scanning parameters may be adjusted, how you recommend performing such adjustments, and at what level (system level, group level, scan level) those parameters are configured.

29. How does the tool handle a newly discovered device?

    • What does information about the system report?

    • What processes do you recommend for addressing such devices?

    • Do you recommend adding the asset to the tool before a discovery scan is performed, or do you recommend relying on discovery scans to discover new devices?

False Positive Mitigation

30. Describe how your product avoids false positives. What are our responsibilities as the tool administrators in helping the product avoid false positives?

31. Describe how your product uses knowledge of the operating system, applications, versions, patch levels, compensating controls, etc., to report vulnerabilities appropriately.

32. Describe how your product allows us to identify, handle, and document false positives. How does the person resolving a vulnerability know if the vulnerability was previously considered a false positive?

33. Describe how your product addresses the fact that a current false positive could become a true positive in the future.

34. Describe the roles and authorizations involved in identifying a false positive. How does the tool ensure a vulnerability that has been marked as a false positive has been validated and approved by the appropriate party?

Risk Prioritization

35. Describe how your tool allows us to categorize assets in terms of system criticality, data sensitivity, and any other parameters you may support.

36. Describe how your tool assigns default severities for vulnerabilities. Who determines if the default severity for a specific vulnerability is low, medium, or high?

37. Describe how your product allows us to change the severity of a specific vulnerability. What is the process? What authorizations are required? What opportunities are provided for documenting the change?

38. Describe the algorithm your product uses to calculate the risk for each vulnerability identified on a specific system. Please provide the complete mathematical equation and fully define all constants and variables.

39. How does your tool address compensating controls and other mitigation factors that may be present in the determination of risk? How does it allow us to document the presence of such controls?

40. How does your product allow us to manually define something as vulnerable?

41. How does your product allow us to manually override a vulnerability?

Reporting

Please describe your product's reporting functionality. Provide samples of standard reports that are available in the form of a report book.

42. What sort of dashboards does your product provide:

- How does the information on the dashboard change based on a user's role?

- What do the dashboards look like out of the box?

- Can the tool administrator customize the dashboard for everyone?

- Can users customize their own dashboards?

- What real-time status information do the dashboards display?

43. List the reports that are available out of the box. Identify the intended users and goals of each report.

44. What additional products, if any, do we need to purchase to create our own custom reports?

45. What scheduling and output options are available for reports, such as automatically saving to file systems, a webserver, SharePoint, etc. Describe the delivery mechanisms (e.g., PDF, Excel) available for distributed reports.

46. Describe how ad hoc queries and reports are generated. Identify how they interact with the data?

47. What industry standard vulnerability databases do your reports reference?

48. What references do your reports link to? Are hyperlinks to further information available from all reports or only some?

Third-Party Integrations

49. What methodologies do you support for integrating with other systems, such as via email, web services, message queues, RPC, etc?

50. Explain any known built-in or previously coded integrations with the following products:

    • {List required third-party integrations required}.

51. Please describe if you have any out-of-the-box integrations with third-party products, with no coding or special services required.

52. Describe your tool's logging functionality, and whether your logs may be forwarded to an external logging system via syslog, SNMP traps, or other mechanism.

53. Please describe any integration your tool may have with any vulnerability announcement/alerting systems or websites.

54. Please describe any integration your tool may have with any IDS/IPS systems.

55. Describe how data may be exported from competitive systems and imported into your system to ensure data continuity.

Data History

56. How much historical data can your system store? Do we have options to adjust how much historical data is available?

57. What data does your product store about systems?

58. How does it detect new systems?

59. How does it differentiate a new system from an existing system whose IP changed?

60. How does it detect new applications and changes to applications?

61. How does your system allow us to provide comments about assets?

Configuration Management

62. How does the tool allow us to provide comments about configuration changes?

63. What specific configuration changes can and cannot be documented?

64. How does the product keep track of the history of configuration changes?

65. How does the product support rolling back changes to a previous configuration?

66. How does the product allow us to compare current and previous configurations, or two former configurations?

67. How does the product allow us to determine the exact configuration on a specific date?

68. What level of detail about configuration changes are logged and can be forwarded to our central logging system?

Role-Based Access

69. Describe how your product uses role-based access controls to support the Principle of Least Privilege.

70. Are users assigned to roles, to groups which map to roles, or some other approach?

71. What roles and/or groups are available out of the box?

72. What is the process for us to add or change roles and/or groups?

73. How does the tool support the notion that certain roles may have different members for different assets? For example, John Titor may be a System Administrator, but only for IBM-based Windows servers, not for IBM-based Linux systems or any other vendor.

74. How does the tool support the need for users in the same group or team to be able to access each other's functionality in order to fill in for each other? For example, John may have started to remediate vulnerability on System X, but he goes on vacation, and Larry needs to be able to work with the tool in order to finish the remediation. Or, Richard schedules a scan, but Arthur needs to follow up in Richards's absence to ensure the scan completed properly and address any problems that arose.

75. What permissions does a server administrator who is responsible for addressing vulnerabilities in specific systems have within your product? What is the process for changing these permissions?

76. Describe how your product integrates with Active Directory or LDAPS for authentication and authorization.

Training and Professional Services

77. Provide a detailed description of the training your company or third parties offer for the nontechnical administrator of this product. What is the format (off-site, on-site, prerecorded web-based, interactive web-based, etc.)? How long is it?

78. What is the schedule for training in the next twelve months?

79. Provide a detailed description of the training your company or third parties offer for the technical security analysts who will help configure this product. What is the format (off-site, on-site, prerecorded web-based, interactive web-based, etc.)? How long is it? What is the schedule for training in the next twelve months?

80. Provide a detailed description of the professional services your company or third parties offer for the product implementation, particularly around setting up the scanning configurations for many different types of devices.

Technical Considerations

The questions in this section address your solution's and {Company Name}'s technical requirements. Responses should be directed toward the Information Technology professionals who will design, install, and support your solution. Some questions may not be pertinent to your particular solution depending on whether it is on premise, cloud-based (SaaS), or hybrid. Please answer all of the appropriate questions and flag any that are not relevant to your solution as not applicable.

Product Licensing and Component Model

81. Many software solutions consist of a core module plus additional modules or components. Many hardware solutions consist of hardware plus software or multiple hardware components. Please list each software and/or hardware module or component using your price list official name.

82. List any additional hardware, software licenses, or services needed beyond your core product that {Company Name} would have to acquire in order to use your product.

83. List any third-party products, commercial or open source, that optionally can integrate with your product that you believe are relevant to this RFP.

84. Describe your solution's licensing approach (e.g., site license, per-user, floating, per-machine, per-processor, etc.) and its enforcement mechanism (if any).

85. Describe the complete technical architecture of your product, including a description of the technologies used to implement the solution. Please include a diagram that shows your product in relation to a typical customer's infrastructure, data and services, and third-party components or tools.

86. What physical infrastructure will {Company Name} require to implement your proposed solution? If your solution uses a browser, what specific browsers and versions are supported?

87. Provide an architectural diagram of your solution that includes hardware, software, network, redundancy, hosting locations, etc. Where relevant, include third-party elements, including contracted services, off-site backup, reporting tools, etc.

Required Hardware and Operating Systems

88. Identify the hardware and operating system platforms on which your product operates:

- Include both client and server platforms;

- Indicate versions for your product, operating systems, and virtual environments;

- Indicate how many customers are using your solution on each platform you support;

- Indicate your tier-1 preference for platform and architecture.

89. Can the product be deployed across multiple hardware/OS platforms simultaneously?

90. What virtual and cloud environments are supported?

91. How does implementation in a virtualized environment differ from implementation on dedicated hardware?

92. Specify the number of personnel and skills required for administering the solution. List any special skills the Administrator may require.

93. Discuss the solution's support for multiple administrators and distributed administration. Are there limits on the number of users with administrative rights? Are there restrictions on where they may be geographically located?

94. Explain how version patches and upgrades are handled.

    - How would {Company Name} learn about patches and upgrades?

    - How would we obtain patches and upgrades?

    - What processes would we follow to implement them?

95. Does your solution expose any public APIs? If so, what functionality does each provide, and what languages can use the APIs?

96. Describe the role of database technologies in your product. What components use/access the database and for what purposes?

97. How is the data secured within the database?

98. How does one archive or purge old data within your solution?

99. Are database licenses included in your proposal's price?

Data Integration

This section focuses on what data your proposed solution needs from other systems and data it exports to other resources.

100. Describe the solution's ability to support *importing* data from various sources and formats. What formats and protocols are supported out of the box? How are other formats handled?

101. Describe the solution's ability to support *exporting* data to various sources and formats. What formats and protocols are supported out of the box? How are other formats handled?

Network Impact

102. Does your solution require any networking protocols other than IP? If so, please explain.

103. What are your expectations for our network infrastructure? Please describe both LAN and WAN expected characteristics. Do you have a mechanism to gate or limit consumption your network traffic to prevent your solution from completely consuming the network?

104. How does your solution work behind a firewall or with multiple levels of firewalls? What specific ports do you need to be open on firewalls? Is this configurable?

105. How should the solution be implemented in a globally distributed environment? Discuss the solution's tolerance to network-related issues such as latency, momentary unavailability, extended unavailability, etc.

106. Is multicast addressing required for any component of the solution?

107. Do you recommend deploying (or avoiding deployments) on wireless networks?

108. Discuss the load balancing capabilities of the solution and the impacts load balancers may have on the solution?

109. Discuss the scalability and failover characteristics of the solution?

Reliability, Implementation, and Scalability

110. What type of system monitoring capability is in place to measure data processing success specific to your product?

111. Describe the scalability of your solution and how it is developed to handle the increase in the volume of transactions, data, or users.

112. Discuss any known maximum volume or throughput levels and associated response times under minimal and optimal technical environments.

113. Describe how the solution can be monitored for uptime and transaction response time in order to demonstrate that the solution is operating in accordance with your published service level agreements.

114. Describe performance tuning procedures common in most installations.

Security

The software solution must be able to secure the exchange of corporate data across the enterprise and with {Company Name}'s extended business community without compromising security policies. To this end, the solution must incorporate appropriate security measures that ensure effective user authentication, access controls, and data encryption. Access to development, administration, and any other configurable tool or environment should be limited by user authentication, user authorization, and associated permission level.

115. Describe the security architecture for the solution.

116. Are there multiple levels of administrative access permissions?

117. Does your solution provide auditing, reporting, and alerting for security-related events and information?

118. How do you, the vendor, support any security patches that are published for the operating system, dependent databases, or other dependent third-party software?

119. What is your policy for the amount of time that passes between the release of an operating system security patch and your support for that patch?

120. How is the transmission of data secured across the network?

121. What is the level and type of encryption used for this purpose?

122. Does the solution require any downloaded components to execute (e.g., browser plug-in)? If yes, please describe their function.

123. Does your solution maintain a private copy of the authentication/authorization data structure, or do you dynamically obtain authentication/authorizations as needed?

124. Will you, the vendor, need to remotely log on to the system for administration or maintenance?

125. If any aspects of this solution need to interact with components, services, or users that reside outside of the business network, please describe those interactions in detail, including formats and protocols used.

Implementation Considerations

These questions address your solution's implementation at {Company Name}. Responses should include information that describes your typical implementation approach, reference implementations (logical, physical and business continuity), and the steps involved in implementing the solution.

126.   Please describe how {Company Name} may test or preview the product as a part of this evaluation.

127.   Please present, at a high level, the methodology you recommend for implementation. This should include how time and resource requirements are estimated, what planning and design stages are required, what the typical path to production is, and what role your organization would expect to play during implementation.

128.   In support of your methodology, do you provide or recommend any third-party tools that would help to support and accelerate the deployment of your solution?

129.   What are the recommended personnel and staffing requirements during implementation of the proposed solution?

130.   What are the recommended personnel and staffing *requirements after implementation*?

131.   What type of staff is required to maintain the production operations for the proposed solution?

System Maintenance and Modification

{Company Name} expects vendors to provide new releases, updates, and enhancements on a periodic basis. This expectation applies to both hardware and software vendors.

132.   How do you distinguish between major and minor releases?

133.   What types of upgrades are included in the license fee?

134. What types of upgrades are included as a part of an annual maintenance cost?

135. What types of upgrades require completely new licensing?

136. How often, on average, do you ship major and minor releases?

137. Explain your company's policy regarding supporting older releases of your product. How many previous releases are supported? How long is any given release supported?

User Support

138. What user conferences, cross-company user groups, or listservers do you provide or support?

139. Describe the administration documentation that is available within the application and/or online.

140. Describe your online, helpdesk support, and resource availability.

141. How would {Company Name} ask a question about how to use the product? Who would {Company Name} contact?

142. How would {Company Name} report bugs?

143. How would {Company Name} request new features?

144. Are support contacts limited to certain named {Company Name} individuals?

145. Discuss your support for users located outside the
      United States.

146. Will {Company Name} be willing to provide
      roadmap sessions to our organization?

Hardware Costs

Please provide a quote for all hardware that your company would provide
to us as a part of this proposal. This includes dedicated servers, scanners,
and/or appliances required.

Software License(s)

Please provide a quote on licensing options available to {Company Name}.
State any restrictions that are incorporated into the licensing scheme.
Please include any software licenses that may be required for operating
systems and databases not included in the solution.

Please explain the licensing models available to {Company Name}
and provide detailed pricing for each model. Explain how the licensing
is managed for each model that you offer. Explain the meaning and
implications of any terms used such as per CPU, per-user/seat, named
user, per-site/location, enterprise-wide, revenue based, etc. Please
address the impact of each model for multiple users who share the same
computer and users who may use multiple computers. Consider the needs
of telecommuting users, users who work across multiple campuses, job-
sharing (two individuals work part time to create one full-time equivalent),
users who use terminal services or remote desktop, development and test
lab machines, and other "special cases" of which you may be aware.

{Company Name} may opt to implement only certain components of the overall proposed solution and may implement to a subset of internal and/or external users. Please take this into consideration when proposing a pricing model.

Support and Maintenance Costs

Please provide detailed pricing on available support and maintenance offerings, beyond what is included with the base system. Support services include technical support, software maintenance, and version updates. Detail any "silver," "gold," or "platinum" level support offerings, phone support, business hours support, 24/7/365 support, new version support, incremental version, or maintenance version support costs.

Training Costs

Please provide detailed pricing on available training costs beyond what is included with the base system. For training pricing, please include a recommendation on the number and type of classes recommended for suggested development and support organizations, as well as a separate schedule of pricing for training on both a per-user per-class basis and on a per-on-site class basis.

Professional Service Costs

Please provide pricing on the availability of implementation and consulting service professionals to be provided by your company to assist in architectural design and implementation. Provide the pricing and rates on your various levels of professional services.

APPENDIX B

Request for Proposal Spreadsheet

Every vulnerability management vendor is capable of performing a network vulnerability scan. However, each vendor will vary in their capabilities to apply coverage across all of your resources from mobile to cloud. To simplify all of the vulnerability management variations, the proposed capabilities (Table B-1 – Sample RFP (or RFI) Questions) should be considered for your proposal and whether these operational requirements are needed for your environment.

Table B-1. *Sample RFP Vulnerability Management Requirements*

Solution Requirements	Weighting of Requirement	Vendor Success Level	Final Weighted Score
{Company Name and Confidentiality Statement}			
Vulnerability Scanning			
Built-in Automated Credentialed Scans (automate authenticated scans with continuously rotating credentials)			

(continued)

© Morey J. Haber, Brad Hibbert 2018
M.J. Haber and B. Hibbert, *Asset Attack Vectors*,
https://doi.org/10.1007/978-1-4842-3627-7

Table B-1. (*continued*)

Solution Requirements	Weighting of Requirement	Vendor Success Level	Final Weighted Score
Automatic Vulnerability Updates			
Built-in Reporting Templates			
Vulnerability alerting			
Network vulnerabilities			
Operating system vulnerabilities			
Application vulnerabilities			
Virtualization vulnerabilities			
Virtualized Applications (VMware Thinapp)			
Configuration Scanning			
Web Application Scanning			
Built-in Scan templates			
SCAP (OVAL) Scanning (Microsoft, UNIX, Linux, VMware, Cisco…)			
Custom Audit Groups			
Exploit intelligence (Mapping known exploits to vulnerabilities)			
PCI Scanning			

(*continued*)

Table B-1. (*continued*)

Solution Requirements	Weighting of Requirement	Vendor Success Level	Final Weighted Score
Cloud Assessment: Amazon			
Cloud Assessment: Azure			
Cloud Assessment: vCenter			
Cloud Assessment: RackSpace			
Cloud Assessment: GoGrid			
Cloud Assessment: IBM SmartCloud			
Offline VMware Scanning			
Database Scanning			
Scan scheduling			
Microsoft Patch Tuesday 24 hour SLA			
STIG Scanning Template			
Host-based scanning option			
Network-based scanning option			
Cloud-based scanning option			
IPv6 Support			

(*continued*)

Table B-1. (*continued*)

Solution Requirements	Weighting of Requirement	Vendor Success Level	Final Weighted Score
Reporting			
Threat analytics			
Threat analytics correlated with privileged user data			
Consolidated Reports (Patch Supersedence)			
Built-in Reporting Templates			
Executive Reporting Templates			
Remediation Reporting Templates			
Vulnerability Export Reports			
Export Formats (PDF, CSV, XLS, XML, HTML, Word, Text, etc.)			
CAG (SANS 20) Report Template			
PCI Scan and Report Templates			
Malware Reporting			
Delta Reporting			
Automated Reporting			
Attack Reporting			

(*continued*)

Table B-1. (*continued*)

Solution Requirements	Weighting of Requirement	Vendor Success Level	Final Weighted Score
Custom Reporting			
Integrated Data Warehouse			
Enterprise Report Management			
Scheduling			
Real-Time Alerting			
Email distribution			
Publication & Subscription			
STIG Scan and Report Templates			
Integration			
Restrict applications from execution based on vulnerability (vulnerability-based application mgmt.)			
Real-time alerting based on third-party connectors (Palo Alto)			
API			
PowerShell			
Asset Management Solution			
SIEM Solution			
Ticketing System			

(*continued*)

Table B-1. (*continued*)

Solution Requirements	Weighting of Requirement	Vendor Success Level	Final Weighted Score
Enterprise Scalability Features			
n-Tier architecture			
Role-based access			
Scan load balancing			
Unlimited scanners			
Unlimited Users/Consoles			
Single Sign-on Support			
Advanced Features			
Cross Platform Browser Support: Internet Explorer, Chrome, Firefox, Safari, etc.			
Interactive Dashboard with Drilldowns			
Rich Internet Application			
Exception Based Operational Status			
User-Based Security			
Database Storage of Scan Data			
Flexible scan data purging options			
Asset Scoring by Risk			

(*continued*)

Table B-1. (*continued*)

Solution Requirements	Weighting of Requirement	Vendor Success Level	Final Weighted Score
Enterprise Scanning Options including:			
Mobile device scanning			
CVSS Temporal Score Support			
CVSS Environmental Metrics Support			
CVSS Base Support			
Scanner Pooling			
Scanner Locking			
Advanced/Flexible Grouping			
Advanced/Flexible Asset Targeting			
Advanced/Flexible Asset Filtering			
Advanced/Flexible Rules Engine			
Integrated Data warehouse			
Trending Reports			
Business Scorecards			
Compliance Scorecards			
Executive and Summary Reports			

(*continued*)

Table B-1. (*continued*)

Solution Requirements	Weighting of Requirement	Vendor Success Level	Final Weighted Score
Interactive Analytical views (Built-in and Custom)			
Asset and Vulnerability Heat Maps (including third-party exploit intelligence)			
Report Snapshots			
True Ad Hoc Reporting (Pivot Grid)			
Advanced/Flexible Active Directory Integration			
Automated Audit Grouping based on Custom Rules			
Smart credentials grouping			
Regulatory Compliance			
Vulnerabilities mapped to control objectives of specific mandates			
Auto-update of new compliance reports			
Compliance Library Support			
PCI			
SOX			
HIPPA			

(*continued*)

Table B-1. (*continued*)

Solution Requirements	Weighting of Requirement	Vendor Success Level	Final Weighted Score
GLBA			
FISMA / NIST			
ISO			
CobiT			
HITRUST			
MASS 201			
Monthly compliance dashboards			
Daily compliance dashboards			
Detailed compliance reports			
Compliance scorecards			
Compliance delta reports			
Configuration Compliance (Benchmarking)			
Central Configuration of benchmark policy management			
Centralized benchmark (pass/fail) reporting			
Ability to consume industry of custom OVAL content			

(*continued*)

Table B-1. (*continued*)

Solution Requirements	Weighting of Requirement	Vendor Success Level	Final Weighted Score
Robust Built-in benchmark library			
CIS			
DISA			
DoD			
Microsoft Security Compliance			
NIST			
Integrated Patch Management			
Support for Multiple Patch Servers			
Windows patch management			
Third-Party Application Patch management			
Vulnerability to patch integration views			
Patch prioritization			
Targeted patch deployment			
Integrated patch reporting			

(*continued*)

Table B-1. (*continued*)

Solution Requirements	Weighting of Requirement	Vendor Success Level	Final Weighted Score
Deployment			
Software Installation			
Hardware Appliance Options			
Virtual Appliance Options (VMware)			
Virtual Appliance Options (Hyper-v)			
Virtual Appliance Options (Amazon)			
Virtual Appliance Options (Azure)			
Managed Service			
Agent Based Scanning			
External Scans			
Hybrid deployment options			
Implementation, Training, and Support			
Online Portal			
Phone Support			
SLA Response			
Training			
Consulting Services			

Index

A

Active vulnerabilities, 82, 84
Active vulnerability scanning, 50
Adobe, 107, 259
Advanced persistent threats
(APTs), 260
Adversarial Tactics, Techniques,
and Common Knowledge
(ATT&CK™), 239
Agent technology, 187–188
Amazon AWS assets, 264
Apple Security Updates, 101–102
Asset Reporting Format (ARF), 8
Assets, 256–257
Australian Signals Directorate
(ASD), 233
Authentication
administrative and root
credentials, 181
capabilities, 181
credentials, 183–184
null session, 182
privileged
integration, 185, 187
privileges, 181
resources, 182
Automate credentialed scans,
252–253, 310

B

Bandwidth, 202
Benchmarks, 59
Bring your own technology
(BYOT), 254
Bugtraq, 91
Business management, 264

C

Carrier vulnerabilities, 83, 85
Center for Internet Security (CIS), 243
Cisco, 103–104
Class B network, 287–288
Client applications, 128–129
COBIT, 242, 247
Common Configuration
Enumeration (CCE), 7
Common Configuration Scoring
System (CCSS), 8
Common Platform Enumeration
(CPE), 8
Common Vulnerabilities and
Exposures (CVE), 7, 73
Common Vulnerability Scoring
System (CVSS), 7, 81
base calculation, 75
components, 74

© Morey J. Haber, Brad Hibbert 2018
M.J. Haber and B. Hibbert, *Asset Attack Vectors*,
https://doi.org/10.1007/978-1-4842-3627-7

Printed in the United States
By Bookmasters